oR *The Future of Faith*

"Cox is the most important liberal theologian of the last half century because he could see around corners. . . . *The Future of Faith* is, quite simply, a beautiful book and a Cox classic."

—E. J. Dionne Jr., author of *Souled Out*

"*The Future of Faith* is a tour de force. As passionate and challenging as his classic, *The Secular City,* Cox's new book invites the faithful, the skeptical, and the fearful into a spirit-filled vision of Christianity that can renew a hurting world."

—Diana Butler Bass, author of *A People's History of Christianity*

"*The Future of Faith* is insightful, provocative, and inspiring—I even found myself uttering a hearty evangelical 'Amen' at many points!"

— Richard Mouw, president of Fuller Theological Seminary and author of *Calvinism in the Las Vegas Airport*

"Cox has been a voice of both reason and faith in our cynical times. Now, he offers a fresh vision for the resurrection of a new global Christianity that will restore our faith both in ourselves and the divine."

—Deepak Chopra, author of *Jesus: A Story of Enlightenment*

"Cox brings the eye of an historian and the heart of a theologian to explain where we've come from where we're going. *The Future of Faith* is an essential guide to that future."

—Jim Wallis, president of Sojourners and author of *The Great Awakening*

"This important book has not only helped me understand the past, present, and future of this amazing phenomenon called Christianity . . . it has also motivated me to keep working to help make actual the possible future Cox envisions."

—Brian McLaren, author of *A New Kind of Christian*

"For the last four decades, Cox has been the leading trend spotter in American religion."

—Stephen Prothero, author of *God Is Not One*

The FUTURE of FAITH

Harvey Cox

HarperOne
An Imprint of HarperCollinsPublishers

HarperOne

HarperCollins books may be purchased for educational, business, or sales promotional use. For information please write: Special Markets Department, HarperCollins Publishers, 10 East 53rd Street, New York, NY 10022.

HarperCollins Web site: http://www.harpercollins.com

HarperCollins®, 📖®, and HarperOne™ are trademarks of HarperCollins Publishers.

FIRST HARPERCOLLINS PAPERBACK EDITION PUBLISHED IN 2010

Designed by Janet M. Evans

Library of Congress Cataloging-in-Publication Data is available upon request.

ISBN 978–0–06–175553–8

11 12 13 14 RRD(H) 10 9 8 7 6 5 4 3 2

THIS BOOK IS DEDICATED TO MY GRANDCHILDREN:

Maximilian Davis Marshall
b. December 8, 1993

Sara Cox Kelemen
b. January 21, 1994

Josephine Maria Marshall
b. June 23, 1996

Lucille Boushall Kelemen
b. December 2, 1997

Miles Bennett Marshall
b. July 9, 1999

Logan Cazier Cox
b. October 6, 2002

Ethan Cutler Cox
b. September 11, 2004

Miranda Jasmine Cox
b. May 11, 2007

THEY EMBODY MY FAITH IN THE FUTURE

History may be servitude,
History may be freedom. See, now they vanish,
The faces and places, with the self which,
as it could, loved them,
To become renewed, transfigured, in another pattern.

T.S. Eliot,
Little Gidding

Contents

CHAPTER 1   An Age of the Spirit: The Sacred in the Secular?   *1*

CHAPTER 2   Einstein's Snuffed-Out Candles:
Awe, Wonder, and Faith   *21*

CHAPTER 3   Ships Already Launched:
The Voyage from Mystery to Faith   *37*

CHAPTER 4   The Road Runner and the *Gospel of Thomas*:
What Happens When It Wasn't Really That Way?   *55*

CHAPTER 5   The People of the Way:
The Devolution from Faith to Belief   *73*

CHAPTER 6   "The Bishop Is Your High Priest and Mighty King":
The Rise of the Clerical Caste   *85*

CHAPTER 7   Constantine's Last Supper:
The Invention of Heresy   *99*

CHAPTER 8   No Lunch with the Prefect: How to Fix the Papacy   *113*

CHAPTER 9   Living in Haunted Houses:
Beyond the Interfaith Dialogue   *127*

CHAPTER 10   Get Them into the Lifeboat:
The Pathos of Fundamentalism   *141*

CHAPTER 11   Meet Rocky, Maggie, and Barry:
Which Bible Do the Bible Believers Believe?   *155*

CHAPTER 12   Sant'Egidio and St. Praxedis:
              Where the Past Meets the Future   *171*

CHAPTER 13   Blood on the Altar of Divine Providence:
              Liberation Theology and the Rebirth of Faith   *187*

CHAPTER 14   The Last Vomit of Satan and the Persistent List Makers:
              Pentecostals and the Age of the Spirit   *199*

CHAPTER 15   The Future of Faith   *213*

              Acknowledgments   225

              Notes   227

              For Further Reading   233

              Index   235

CHAPTER 1

An Age of the Spirit

The Sacred in the Secular?

What does the future hold for religion, and for Christianity in particular? At the beginning of the new millennium three qualities mark the world's spiritual profile, all tracing trajectories that will reach into the coming decades. The first is the unanticipated resurgence of religion in both public and private life around the globe. The second is that fundamentalism, the bane of the twentieth century, is dying. But the third and most important, though often unnoticed, is a profound change in the elemental nature of religiousness.

The resurgence of religion was not foreseen. On the contrary, not many decades ago thoughtful writers were confidently predicting its imminent demise. Science, literacy, and more education would soon dispel the miasma of superstition and obscurantism. Religion would either disappear completely or survive in family rituals, quaint folk festivals, and exotic references in literature, art, and music. Religion, we were assured, would certainly never again sway politics or shape culture. But the soothsayers were wrong. Instead of disappearing, religion—for good or ill—is now exhibiting new vitality all around the world and making its weight widely felt in the corridors of power.

Many observers mistakenly confuse this resurgence of religion with "fundamentalism," but the two are not the same. Fundamentalism is dying. Arguments still rage about whether the Christian Right in America is fatally divided or sullenly quiescent. Debates boil about whether the dwindling support for radical movements in Islam is temporary or permanent. But as the twenty-first century unfolds, the larger picture is clear. Fundamentalisms, with their insistence on obligatory belief systems, their nostalgia for a mythical uncorrupted past, their claims to an exclusive grasp on truth, and—sometimes—their propensity for violence, are turning out to be rearguard attempts to stem a more sweeping tidal change.

However, the third quality, the equally unforeseen mutation in the nature of religiousness, is the most important in the long run. Not only has religion reemerged as an influential dimension of twenty-first-century life; what it means to be "religious" is shifting significantly from what it meant as little as a half century ago. Since religions interact with each other in a global culture, this tremor is shaking virtually all of them, but it is especially evident in Christianity, which in the past fifty years has entered into its most momentous transformation since its transition in the fourth century CE from what had begun as a tiny Jewish sect into the religious ideology of the Roman Empire.

Scholars of religion refer to the current metamorphosis in religiousness with phrases like the "move to horizontal transcendence" or the "turn to the immanent." But it would be more accurate to think of it as the rediscovery of the sacred *in* the immanent, the spiritual *within* the secular. More people seem to recognize that it is our everyday world, not some other one, that, in the words of the poet Gerard Manley Hopkins, "is charged with the grandeur of God." The advance of science has increased the sense of awe we feel at the immense scale of the universe or the complexity of the human eye. People turn to religion more for support in their efforts to live in this world and make it better, and less to prepare for the next. The pragmatic and experiential elements of faith as a way of life are displacing the previous emphasis on institutions and beliefs.[1]

It is true that for many people "faith" and "belief" are just two words for the same thing. But they are not the same, and in order to grasp the magnitude of the religious upheaval now under way, it is important to clarify the difference. Faith is about deep-seated confidence. In everyday speech we usually apply it to people we trust or the values we treasure. It is what theologian Paul Tillich (1886–1965) called "ultimate concern," a matter of what the Hebrews spoke of as the "heart."

Belief, on the other hand, is more like opinion. We often use the term in everyday speech to express a degree of uncertainty. "I don't really know about that," we say, "but I believe it may be so." Beliefs can be held lightly or with emotional intensity, but they are more propositional than existential. We can *believe* something to be true without it making much difference to us, but we place our *faith* only in something that is vital for the way we live. Of course people sometimes confuse faith with beliefs, but it will be hard to comprehend the tectonic shift in Christianity today unless we understand the distinction between the two.

The Spanish writer Miguel Unamuno (1864–1936) dramatizes the radical dissimilarity of faith and belief in his short story "Saint Manuel Bueno, Martyr," in which a young man returns from the city to his native village in Spain because his mother is dying. In the presence of the local priest she clutches his hand and asks him to pray for her. The son does not answer, but as they leave the room, he tells the priest that, much as he would like to, he cannot pray for his mother because he does not believe in God. "That's nonsense," the priest replies. "You don't have to believe in God to pray."

The priest in Unamuno's story recognized the distinction between faith and belief. He knew that prayer, like faith, is more primordial than belief. He might have engaged the son who wanted to pray but did not believe in God in a theological squabble. He could have hauled out the frayed old "proofs" for the existence of God, whereupon the young man might have quoted the equally jaded arguments against the proofs. Both probably knew that such arguments go nowhere. The French writer Simone Weil (1909–43) also knew. In her *Notebooks,* she once scribbled a gnomic sentence: "If we love God, even though we think he doesn't exist, he will make his existence manifest." Weil's words sound paradoxical, but in the course of her short and painful life—she died at thirty-four—she learned that love and faith are both more primal than beliefs.[2]

Debates about the existence of God or the gods were raging in Plato's time, twenty-five hundred years ago. Remarkably, they still rage on today, as a recent spate of books rehearsing the routine arguments for and against the existence of God demonstrates. By their nature these quarrels are about beliefs and can never be finally settled. But *faith,* which is more closely related to awe, love, and wonder, arose long before Plato, among our most primitive *Homo sapiens* forebears. Plato engaged in disputes about beliefs, not about faith.

Creeds are clusters of beliefs. But the history of Christianity is not a history of creeds. It is the story of a people of faith who sometimes cobbled together creeds out of beliefs. It is also the history of equally faithful people who questioned, altered, and discarded those same creeds. As with church buildings, from clapboard chapels to Gothic cathedrals, creeds are symbols by which Christians have at times sought to represent their faith. But both the doctrinal canons and the architectural constructions are means to an end. Making either the defining element warps the underlying reality of faith.

The nearly two thousand years of Christian history can be divided into three uneven periods. The *first* might be called the "Age of Faith." It began with Jesus and his immediate disciples when a buoyant faith propelled the movement he initiated. During this first period of both explosive growth and brutal persecution, their sharing in the living Spirit of Christ united Christians with each other, and "faith" meant hope and assurance in the dawning of a new era of freedom, healing, and compassion that Jesus had demonstrated. To be a Christian meant to live in his Spirit, embrace his hope, and to follow him in the work that he had begun.

The *second* period in Christian history can be called the "Age of Belief." Its seeds appeared within a few short decades of the birth of Christianity when church leaders began formulating orientation programs for new recruits who had not known Jesus or his disciples personally. Emphasis on belief began to grow when these primitive instruction kits thickened into catechisms, replacing faith *in* Jesus with tenets *about* him. Thus, even during that early Age of Faith the tension between faith and belief was already foreshadowed.

Then, during the closing years of the third century, something more ominous occurred. An elite class—soon to become a clerical caste—began to take shape, and ecclesial specialists distilled the various teaching manuals into lists of beliefs. Still, however, these varied widely from place to place, and as the fourth century began there was still no single creed. The scattered congregations were united by a common Spirit. A wide range of different theologies thrived. The turning point came when Emperor Constantine the Great (d. 387 CE) made his adroit decision to commandeer Christianity to bolster his ambitions for the empire. He decreed that the formerly outlawed new religion of the Galilean should now be legal, but he continued to reverence the sun god Helios alongside Jesus.

Constantine also imposed a muscular leadership over the churches, appointing and dismissing bishops, paying salaries, funding buildings, and distributing largesse. He and not the pope was the real head of the church. Whatever his motives, Constantine's policies and those of his successors, especially Emperor Theodosius (347–95 CE), crowned Christianity as the official religion of the Roman Empire. The emperors undoubtedly hoped this strategy would shore up their crumbling dominion, from which the old gods seemed to have fled. The tactic, however, did not save the empire from collapse. But for Christianity it proved to be a disaster: its enthronement actually degraded it. From an energetic movement of faith it coagulated into a phalanx of required beliefs, thereby laying the foundation for every succeeding Christian fundamentalism for centuries to come.

The ancient corporate merger triggered a titanic makeover. The empire became "Christian," and Christianity became imperial. Thousands of people scurried to join a church they had previously despised, but now bore the emperor's seal of approval. Bishops assumed quasi-imperial powers and began living like imperial elites. During the ensuing "Constantinian era," Christianity, at least in its official version, froze into a system of mandatory precepts that were codified into creeds and strictly monitored by a powerful hierarchy and imperial decrees. Heresy became treason, and treason became heresy.

The year 385 CE marked a particularly grim turning point. A synod of bishops condemned a man named Priscillian of Avila for heresy, and by order of the emperor Maximus he and six of his followers were beheaded in Treves. Christian fundamentalism had claimed its first victim. Today Priscillian's alleged theological errors hardly seem to warrant the death penalty. He urged his followers to avoid meat and wine, advocated the careful study of scripture, and allowed for what we would now recognize as "charismatic" praise. He believed that various writings that had been excluded from the biblical canon, although not "inspired," could nevertheless serve as useful guides to life. Still, Priscillian holds an important distinction. He was the first Christian to be executed by his fellow Christians for his religious views. But he was by no means the last. One historian estimates that in the two and a half centuries after Constantine, Christian imperial authorities put twenty-five thousand to death for their lack of creedal correctness.

The Constantinian era had begun in earnest. It was the epoch in which imperial Christianity came to dominate the cultural and political domains of Europe, and it endured throughout the medieval centuries, a time of both bane and blessing. It gave birth to both Chartres Cathedral and the Spanish Inquisition, both St. Francis of Assisi and Torquemada, both Dante's *Divine Comedy* and Boniface VIII's papal bull *Unam Sanctam*, which asserted the pope's authority over the temporal as well as the spiritual realm. Neither the Renaissance nor the Reformation did much to alter the underlying foundations of the Age of Belief, and the European expansion around the planet extended its sway over palm and pine. This middle era, the Age of Belief, was the one that prompted writer and historian Hilaire Belloc (1870–1953) to coin the phrase, "The faith is Europe, and Europe is the faith."

The Age of Belief lasted roughly fifteen hundred years, ebbing in fits and starts with the Enlightenment, the French Revolution, the secularization of Europe, and the anticolonial upheavals of the twentieth century. It was already comatose when the European Union chiseled the epitaph on its tombstone in 2005 by declining to mention the word "Christian" in its constitution.

Still, to think of this long middle era as nothing but a dark age is misleading. As we have seen, throughout those fifteen centuries Christian movements and personalities continued to live by faith and according to the Spirit. The vast majority of people were illiterate and, even if they heard the priests intoning creeds in the churches, did not understand the Latin. Confidence in Christ was their primary orientation, and hope for his Kingdom their motivating drive. Most people accepted the official belief codes of the church, albeit without much thought. Many simply ignored them while they thrived on the pageantry, the festivals, and the stories of the saints. Lollards, Hussites, and later thinkers like Italian philosopher Giordano Bruno (1548–1600) and many others explicitly rejected some of the church's dogmas. The medieval period, after all, was rife with what the officials called heresy and schism. The Age of Belief was also, for significant numbers of people, a spiritually vital "age of faith" as well.

Now we stand on the threshold of a new chapter in the Christian story. Despite dire forecasts of its decline, Christianity is growing faster than it ever has before, but mainly outside the West and in movements that accent spiritual experience, discipleship, and hope; pay scant attention to creeds; and flourish without hierarchies. We are now witnessing the beginning of a "post-Constantinian era." Christians on five continents are shaking off the residues of the second phase (the Age of Belief) and negotiating a bumpy transition into a fresh era for which a name has not yet been coined.

I would like to suggest we call it the "Age of the Spirit." The term is not without its problems. It was first coined in the thirteenth century when a Calabrian monk and mystic named Joachim of Fiore (ca. 1132–1202) began propounding an inventive doctrine of the Trinity. He taught that history, having passed through the ages of the Father (the Old Testament) and the Son (the Church), was about to enter an Age of the Spirit. In this new dispensation, Joachim declared, people would live in direct contact with God, so there would be little need for religious hierarchies. Universal love would reign, and infidels would unite with Christians.

Joachim died a pious Catholic, but some of his followers pressed his arguments farther, declaring that the new age had already dawned and there was no further need for priests or sacraments. They also contended that this would be the last age and that the world would soon end. They even began setting dates. But the hierarchy did not look with favor on the prospect of a church without hierarchies. And the world continued to exist. Finally, some sixty years after Joachim's death, the church under Pope Alexander IV pronounced his ideas heretical.

Joachim of Fiore, and especially his followers, obviously got carried away, and scheduling the end of the world is always a risky proposition. Nonetheless, his idea of an Age of the Spirit, or something like it, has always fascinated people. There is an irrepressible visionary or utopian streak in almost everyone. In any case, I hope the new stage of Christianity we now seem to be entering is not the final one (there may be many, many more), but I still prefer to think of it as an "Age of the Spirit" for a number of reasons.

First, for centuries Christians have claimed that the Holy Spirit is just as divine as the other members of the Trinity. But, in reality, the Spirit has most often been ignored or else feared as too unpredictable. It "blows where it will," as the Gospel of John (3:8) says, and is therefore too mercurial to contain. But some of the liveliest Christian movements in the world today are precisely ones that celebrate this volatile expression of the divine. The Spirit's inherent resistance to ecclesial fetters still vexes the prelates. But it also inspires Christians in what used to be called the "third world," but is now termed the "global South" by those living there, to discern the presence of God in other religions. As women come into leadership positions in Christianity, many prefer "Spirit" as their preferred way of speaking of the divine. By far the fastest growth in Christianity, especially among the deprived and destitute, is occurring among people like Pentecostals, who stress a direct experience of the Spirit. It is almost as though the Spirit, muted and muffled for centuries, is breaking its silence and staging a delayed "return of the repressed."

Second, increasing numbers of people who might once have described themselves as "religious," but who want to distance themselves from the institutional or doctrinal demarcations of conventional religion, now refer to themselves as "spiritual." They often say, "I am a spiritual person, but I am not religious." But what does this mean? Often church leaders and theologians wince at the vagueness of the term "spirituality," which is burdened with a long history of ambiguity and controversy. Within the early Christian orbit people spoke of Jesus and then of themselves as being "filled with the Spirit." As decades passed, "spirituality" came to mean the subjective aspect of faith in distinction to the objective teachings. It described a way of life rather than a doctrinal structure. Later, in the Roman Catholic sphere, "spirituality" characterized the different manners in which those in religious orders practiced their faith. One could speak, for example, of a distinctly "Ignatian spirituality," as followed by the Jesuits, or of a "Carmelite" or "Franciscan" spirituality.

But the term "spiritual" also turned controversial at times, especially during the medieval period, when movements like those inspired by Joachim arose that accentuated the immediate experience of God or the Spirit without the necessity of the sacraments or the hierarchy. Some of them even vented explicit protests against the institutional church. Many, like the Beguines, were inspired by women. Some were led by clergy. Meister Eckhart (1260–1327), a Dominican priest, for example, taught that the soul is a spark of God that is to be nourished until the person attains full communion with the divine and is filled with love. He did not condemn churchly observances, but thought they were only of limited value. Shortly after his death Pope John XXII, who was pontiff from 1316 to 1334, declared his ideas heretical.

That did not, however, kill the ideas. Eckhart's student John Tauler (ca. 1300–1361), also a Dominican, took the next step and openly denounced reliance on external ceremonies. The "Spiritual Franciscans," who appeared shortly after the death of St. Francis, taught, as he did, that the Spirit could be found in nature, in "brother sun" and "sister moon," but they also preached against the wealth and power of the institutional church. Most were excommunicated, and some were burned at the stake. Centuries later Simone Weil found the institutional church more of an obstacle than a help in her spiritual quest. Pierre Teilhard de Chardin (1881–1955), the most farsighted Catholic theologian of the twentieth century, envisioned the entire sweep of cosmic history as a process of "spiritualization." And the German pastor Dietrich Bonhoeffer (1906–45) wrote wistfully from a Gestapo cell of what he called a future "religionless Christianity," liberated from its dogmatic tethers. All of these figures were, in different ways, forerunners of today's dawning Age of the Spirit.[3]

As in the past, today "spirituality" can mean a range of different things. At a minimum, it evokes an ambiguous self-reflection devoid of content. For some it can become mere navel gazing, a retreat from responsibility in a needy world. Sleek ads in glossy magazines promise a weekend of "spiritual renewal" in a luxurious spa where, for a price, one can reap the benefits of a sauna, a pedicure, and a guru who will help you cope with the stress of your demanding job. For others, however, "spirituality" can mean a disciplined practice of meditation, prayer, or yoga that can lead to deepened engagement in society. A researcher named Seth Wax recently gathered 105 interviews of self-described "spiritual" people in eight different professional fields. He found that what most of them thought of as their "spirituality" actually enhanced their sense of responsibility in their work and in society by giving them a larger goal or by helping them to concentrate on doing a good job.[4] It is evident that different forms of "spirituality" can lead to either self-indulgence or a deepened social engagement, but so can institutional religion.

Recent studies have shown that the conflict between the religious and the spiritual, even between the spiritual and the secular, are not as sharp as some have supposed. People today can move back and forth from one to the other with little sense of contradiction. They carry "spiritual" attitudes and practices into the congregations and religious values into the secular world. They develop what researchers call "repertoires" that include elements from all of these overlapping spheres and are able to negotiate continuously among them. Clerical leaders often object to what seems like the blurring of important distinctions, but the process is making the borders between the religious, the spiritual, and the secular more permeable.

How does the spectacular growth of megachurches like Saddleback and Willow Creek figure into this new picture? Entering Saddleback church, with its large TV screens, piped music, coffee bars, and choice of different music "tents," is more like strolling into a mall than stepping into a cathedral. Its architectural logic is horizontal, not vertical. The line between inside and outside is almost erased. There are now more than four hundred of these churches, with congregations of ten thousand or more. They are *not* fundamentalist. Their real secret is that they are honeycombs of small groups, hundreds of them, for study, prayer, and action. Sociologist Robert Wuthnow estimates that 40 percent of all adult Americans belong to one or another of a variety of small groups both in and out of churches, and that many join them because they are searching for community and are "interested in deepening their spirituality." He adds that these small groups are "redefining the sacred . . . by replacing explicit creeds and doctrines with *implicit* norms devised by the group." Although he expresses some hesitation about this soft-peddling of theology, he nonetheless concludes that many people who grew up in a religious tradition now "feel the need for a group with whom they can discuss their religious values. As a result . . . they feel closer to God, better able to pray . . . and more confident that they are acting according to spiritual principles that emphasize love, forgiveness, humility and self-acceptance."[5]

The recent rapid growth of charismatic congregations and the appeal of Asian spiritual practices demonstrate that, as in the past once again today, large numbers of people are drawn more to the experiential than to the doctrinal elements of religion. Once again, this often worries religious leaders who have always fretted about mysticism. Echoing age-old suspicions, for example, the Vatican has warned Catholics against the dangers of attending classes on yoga. Still, it is important to notice that virtually all current "spiritual" movements and practices are derived, either loosely or directly, from one of the historic religious traditions. In addition, just as in the past offshoots that the church condemned were eventually welcomed back into the mother's household, the same is happening today. In India and Japan Catholic monks sit cross-legged practicing Asian spiritual disciplines. In America, people file into church basements for tai-chi classes. Challenged by the lure of Asian practices, Benedictine monks have begun teaching laypeople "centering prayer," a contemplative discipline that not so long ago church authorities viewed with distrust.

"Spirituality" can mean a host of things, but there are three reasons why the term is in such wide use. First, it is still a form of tacit protest. It reflects a widespread discontent with the preshrinking of "religion," Christianity in particular, into a package of theological propositions by the religious corporations that box and distribute such packages. Second, it represents an attempt to voice the awe and wonder before the intricacy of nature that many feel is essential to human life without stuffing them into ready-to-wear ecclesiastical patterns. Third, it recognizes the increasingly porous borders between the different traditions and, like the early Christian movement, it looks more to the future than to the past. The question remains whether emerging new forms of spirituality will develop sufficient ardor for justice and enough cohesiveness to work for it effectively. Nonetheless, the use of the term "spirituality" constitutes a sign of the jarring transition through which we are now passing, from an expiring Age of Belief into a new but not yet fully realized Age of the Spirit.

This three-stage profile of Christianity helps us understand the often confusing religious turmoil going on around us today. It suggests that what some people dismiss as deviations or unwarranted innovations are often retrievals of elements that were once accepted features of Christianity, but were discarded somewhere along the way. It frees people who shape their faith in a wide spectrum of ways to understand themselves as authentically Christian, and it exposes fundamentalism for the distortion it is.

There is little to lament about the present decline of fundamentalism. The word itself was coined in the first decade of the twentieth century by Protestant Christians who compiled a list of theological beliefs on which there could be no compromise. Then they adamantly announced that they would defend these "fundamentals" against new patterns that were already emerging in Christianity. The conflict often became intense. In 1922 Reverend Harry Emerson Fosdick (1878–1969) preached a famous sermon entitled "Shall the Fundamentalists Win?" It seemed for a few decades that, indeed, they might. But now they are on the defensive. The old struggle continues, and their reduction of faith to beliefs persists. But since the emerging Age of the Spirit is more similar to the first Age of Faith than it is to the Age of Belief, the contest today goes on under different conditions. The atmosphere today is more like that of early Christianity than like what obtained during the intervening millennium and a half of the Christian empire.

The three-period way of envisioning Christian history holds a special resonance for me. Biologists say, "Ontogeny recapitulates phylogeny"; that is, the development of an individual repeats the evolution of the species as a whole. My own spiritual evolution traces the same profile. The first, my "age of faith," began in early childhood. Like many children reared in a Protestant Christian home, I first learned that being a Christian meant to be a "follower of Jesus." Admittedly, he was a tough act to follow, but at least the goal was clear. Since Baptists did not have creeds, I never heard about them until years later. At fourteen I was baptized and joined the church. As I had been coached, I told the congregation, while standing up to my waist in the baptismal pool, that I accepted Jesus as Lord and that I would endeavor to be his disciple. Then the minister gently plunged me under and pulled me up sputtering. Along with the other young people who had just "passed through Jordan," after being dried off by the deacons, I changed out of my sodden clothes in a Sunday school room and then rejoined the congregation to be welcomed as a full member. I did not know the phrase "rite of passage" at the time, but, as I look back, this was a memorable one. After that I thought of myself as someone who was trying, never all that successfully, to be a follower of Jesus, and this phase continued into my first semester in college.

Then things changed. A couple months into my freshman year at Penn I found myself involved in long conversations in the dorms. Some were with agnostics or skeptics. Others were with Catholics, Presbyterians, and Episcopalians, who, I found, had something called creeds. I also met conservative Protestant evangelicals and fundamentalists. When one of them asked me directly if I was a Christian, I told him yes, that I tried to follow Jesus. But he fixed me with a direct stare and asked, "But do you believe in the substitutionary atonement?" I was not sure what that was, and for awhile I passed through a difficult period, worried that my faith might be fatally deficient. I began to think that maybe a "real Christian" had to believe a certain set of ideas about God, Jesus, and the Bible. This was my quasi-fundamentalist stage, which I will return to in a later chapter. For me it corresponds to Christianity's Age of Belief, which began in the third or fourth century, and, like the church with its historical period, I learned a lot from it and do not regret that it remains part of my life story. But eventually it had to be left behind.

Unlike the church's Age of Belief, mine did not go on for fifteen hundred years. It only lasted about two. In history classes I began reading about the endless debates over creeds and confessions that had roiled Christianity for so long, and I took a course in world religions, which made me see my own faith as one among many. I also became friends with several students who seemed to me to exemplify the Christian life better than some of the taut fundamentalists, although they were not particularly concerned with being doctrinally correct. By my senior year I had embarked on what was to become a lengthy transition into my third phase. But for a long while I remained confused over the vexed relationship between faith and belief.

Then, several years ago an acquaintance of mine described himself to me in a casual conversation as "a practicing Christian, not always a believing one." His remark puzzled me, but it also began to clarify some of the enigmas that had swirled within both my personal faith and my thinking about religion and theology. His remark suggested that the belief/nonbelief axis is a misleading way of describing Christianity. It misses the whole point of not only Christianity, but other religions as well. I have never heard this insight expressed more eloquently than I did one evening in Milan, Italy, where in 1995 Cardinal Carlo Maria Martini had invited me to give a talk at what he called his annual "Lectureship for Nonbelievers."

I had not known what to expect, but it turned out to be quite a glittering occasion. A large crowd draped in Armani and Prada had assembled in an ornate public hall, and I was already seated, when Martini, who stands well over six feet tall, entered in a scarlet cassock and black biretta, the full regalia of a prince of the church. He welcomed the audience and then went on to say that by calling this an event for "nonbelievers," he did not intend to imply anything about the people present. "The line between belief and unbelief," he said, "runs through the middle of each one of us, including myself, a bishop of the church."

To call oneself a practicing Christian, but not necessarily a believing one acknowledges the variable admixture of certainties and uncertainties that mark the life of any religious person. In August of 2007 the *New York Times* reported that in her collection of letters, *Come Be My Light*, Mother Teresa (1910–97) confessed that for years she had harbored troubling doubts about the existence of God, even as she worked ceaselessly to relieve the anguish of the sick and dying in Calcutta.[6] Her confession evoked a wave of criticism. Was she a hypocrite? Had she been faking it all along? But in the tumble of public comments that followed, a student named Krista E. Hughes made the most telling comment in a letter to the editor. "Mother Teresa's life," she wrote, "exemplifies the living aspect of faith, something sorely needed in a society where Christian identity is most often defined in terms of what a person believes rather than how he or she lives. Shouldn't it be the other way around?"[7]

Eliminating the spurious use of "belief" to define Christianity has another advantage. It recognizes that often people who call themselves "unbelievers" have episodic doubts about their unbelief. "Believers" go through similar swings. Beliefs come and go, change, fade, and mature. The pattern of beliefs one holds at ten are not identical with the ones one holds at fifty or seventy-five. To focus the Christian life on belief rather than on faith is simply a mistake. We have been misled for many centuries by the theologians who taught that "faith" consisted in dutifully believing the articles listed in one of the countless creeds they have spun out. But it does not.

When I first realized this, it came as a welcome liberation. Starting when I was quite young, I often had serious doubts about whether I "believed" some church teaching or something I found in the Bible. Did God really stop the sun so that Joshua could continue the battle? Did Jesus really turn water into wine or walk on the sea? Was Mary really a virgin? But I know now that even when I struggled with these childhood doubts, I never "lost my faith." Somehow I sensed instinctively that faith was something deeper than belief. Without knowing it, I was beginning to tiptoe, almost unconsciously, toward my personal "age of the spirit." Like any major change in one's life, this one did not take place suddenly. It took a while, and it was only much later that I began to apply this insight to my thinking about religious studies and theology.

During my adult life various experiences continued to nudge me along the path. My many encounters with the followers of other religions, especially Buddhists and Hindus, taught me that "beliefs," in the way we use the word, were not part of their vocabularies. In fact none of the other major world religions has a "creed." Even Islam, a close cousin of Christianity, only expects its followers to affirm, "There is no god but God, and Muhammad is his messenger" (the Shahada). In all these traditions, religion means something quite different from attaching credence to doctrines. My marriage to a Jewish woman, and with it an unusual opportunity to participate as a "fellow traveler" in the liturgies and holidays (and food) of her tradition, taught me things I had never known about her faith, and things I had never realized about my own (Jesus, after all, was a rabbi). Jews always say their religion is best understood not as a creed, but as a way of life. Slowly it dawned on me that the same is true of my religion. The earliest term used to describe it in the New Testament is "The Way."[8]

Once I realized that Christianity is not a creed and that faith is more a matter of embodiment than of axioms, things changed. I began to look at people I met in a new way. Some of the ones I admired most were "believers" in the conventional sense, but others were not. For example, the individuals with whom I marched and demonstrated and even went to jail, during the civil rights movement and the Vietnam protests, included both "believers" and "nonbelievers." But we found ourselves looking out from behind the iron bars in the same jail cells. This suggested to me just how mistaken conventional belief-oriented Christianity is in the way it separates the sheep from the goats. But then according to the Gospel of Matthew (25:31–46) Jesus also rejects this predictable schema. What he said then no doubt shocked his listeners. He insisted that those who are welcomed into the Kingdom of God— those who were clothing the naked, feeding the hungry, and visiting the prisoners—were not "believers" and were not even aware that they had been practicing the faith he was teaching and exemplifying.

As Christianity moves awkwardly but irreversibly into a new phase in its history, those who are pushing into this frontier often look to the earliest period, the Age of Faith, rather than the intervening one, the Age of Belief, for inspiration and guidance. This should not be surprising. There are striking similarities between the first and the emerging third age. Creeds did not exist then; they are fading in importance now. Hierarchies had not yet appeared then; they are wobbling today. Faith as a way of life or a guiding compass has once again begun, as it did then, to identify what it means to be Christian. The experience *of* the divine is displacing theories *about* it. No wonder the atmosphere in the burgeoning Christian congregations of Asia and Africa feels more like that of first-century Corinth or Ephesus than it does like that of the Rome or Paris of a thousand years later. Early Christianity and today's emergent Christianity appear closely akin. We now turn to how and why this dramatic change is occurring and what it means for the contour of Christianity and the other religions in the twenty-first century.

CHAPTER 2

Einstein's Snuffed-Out Candles

Awe, Wonder, and Faith

In 1930 Rabbi Herbert S. Goldstein, a prominent leader in the American Jewish community of New York, fired off a telegram to Albert Einstein. The rabbi did not waste words: "Do you believe in God? Stop. Answer paid. 50 words."

The telegram was prompted by a public altercation that had arisen when Einstein published a statement that, to the consternation of some of his fellow scientists, he always referred to himself as "religious." He had written:

> The most beautiful emotion we can experience is the mysterious. It is the fundamental emotion that stands at the cradle of all true art and science. He to whom this emotion is a stranger, who can no longer wonder and stand rapt in awe, is as good as dead, a snuffed out candle. To sense that behind anything that can be experienced there is something that our minds cannot grasp, whose beauty and sublimity reaches us only indirectly: this is religiousness. In this sense, and in this sense only, I am a devoutly religious man.[1]

As some recent writers busily exhume the worn-out "scientific" arguments against religion that were marshaled so energetically in the nineteenth century, it is useful to note that the greatest physicist of the twentieth century had quite different ideas on the subject. Einstein, it seems, considered himself to be a "devoutly religious man." He recognized both the strengths and the limitations of science. And he also recognized the place of mystery in human life. Still, it is also important not to consign the discoverer of $E = mc^2$ to the conventional religious camp either. I doubt that Einstein's answer satisfied Rabbi Goldstein. Using even fewer than the fifty words allotted him, he told the rabbi that he leaned toward the kind of God Spinoza describes, "who reveals himself in the harmony of all that exists." He did not, however, believe in a God "who concerns himself with the fate and the doings of mankind."[2]

Faith starts with awe. It begins with the mixture of wonder and fear all human beings feel toward the mystery that envelops us. But awe becomes faith only as it ascribes some meaning to that mystery. Since we are creatures who use language and symbols that vary from age to age and culture to culture, the meanings we ascribe inevitably differ. All religions and cultures are responses to the same fundamental mystery, but each perceives and responds in its own way.

Novelist Flannery O'Connor (1925–64) once wrote that mystery is a great embarrassment to the modern mind. It may well be, but it was an eminently "modern" man, a scientist and not a theologian, who brought the term "mystery" back into circulation. Today, Einstein might place himself among those people described in the previous chapter who say, "I am spiritual, but not religious."

Einstein's cryptic telegram is a harbinger of the rising Age of the Spirit for another reason. It reminds us of how much our feelings of awe before the beauty and complexity of nature have been eroded by both a cool, objective science and a religion too wedded to a human-centered view of the universe. One of the most fascinating features of the new spirituality, often introduced by women, is its retrieval of seasonal rituals and its recognition that human beings exist as an integral part of natural processes. Einstein's perspective also helps sort out the complex interaction between awe, faith, and spirituality. Awe is a basic and nearly *universal* human emotion. Not to feel it was, for Einstein, to be less than human. Faith, on the other hand, is a *particular* human *response* to what awakens awe. It differs from person to person and culture to culture. Spirituality, as we have seen, is an ambiguous term, but often implies an element of dissent against belief-bound religion. The sage of Princeton's refusal to bite on the rabbi's bait ("Do you *believe* in God?") recognizes once again the folly of reducing either awe or faith to "belief," and it helps explain why "spirituality" has returned as a rejection of this distortion.

Einstein's message also provides a promising link to a fruitful school of religious thought that has not received sufficient attention in recent years. In 1917 a German scholar named Rudolf Otto published a book entitled *Das Heilige*. It was a masterful examination of the mystery Einstein later described, the same experience that psychologist William James (1842–1910) had once called the "oceanic feeling." Due to an obtuse mistranslation, Otto's book appeared in English as *The Idea of the Holy*. It was *not*, however, about the "idea" of anything. It was about the primal *experience* of awe or wonder, not any ideas about them. Otto coined the phrase *mysterium tremendum et fascinans*, which incorporates both the object of awe (the mystery) and the responses it induces: a kind of terror (hence the trembling) and fascination. Admittedly there are people who claim never to have sensed anything like this. But Einstein describes such individuals as snuffed-out candles and as good as dead. Still, maybe his judgment is a bit too harsh. My own reaction to such people is similar to the one I might feel about someone who is color-blind or tone-deaf. It is even possible that one day brain researchers may uncover the portion of the brain that activates awe, and then find that there are certain people in whom it is underdeveloped. Might the capacity for awe be enhanced by a drug similar to the ones that enhance memory or alertness?

In the meantime, however, we need to find a way, however inadequate, to speak not just about awe, which is subjective, but about what calls forth awe. Many different words have been used to characterize this awe-evoking "other," but they all turn out to be feeble and ineffectual. Still, since we are language-using creatures, we have to try, realizing that any word will fall short. This is why Einstein's use of the word "mystery" is so helpful. A mystery is different from a problem. A problem is something that someone might eventually solve, but the mystery Einstein refers to is not the kind we find in the books of Agatha Christie or P. D. James, in which the perpetrator of the foul deed is always found out in the end. A mystery is not something anyone solves. It is something we live with, and people find that this mystery touches them in different ways. Albert Einstein's primary experience of mystery came from his encounter with the intricacy of the natural world. But people discover the mystery in other places as well. Many find it in more than one. Like Einstein, they marvel at the awesome scope and complexity of the universe. But they also find the mystery he spoke of in their encounters with other people and in reflecting on themselves.

The mystery of the universe often first confronts us when we feel overwhelmed by its utter vastness. Does it have an edge or stop anywhere? And what is beyond that? Many also feel baffled by the conundrum of time. When did it start, and what was there before? Will it ever end? Then what? Even when they learn about a space-time continuum that is "finite but unbounded," this hardly answers the dilemma. Then there is the inevitable question our prehistoric ancestors began asking soon after they stood upright. Is the universe friendly, hostile, or just indifferent to human life?

At some point in evolution our forebears came to the realization that one day they would die, and this deepened the mystery. However advanced other animals might be—chimpanzees use tools, and dolphins exhibit the rudiments of speech and empathy—only humans marked the spots where they placed the remains of their dead, at first only with a small pile of stones. Already they were trying to wrench meaning from mystery, and this is what set them apart from the other creatures. The awareness of one's own mortality raises the question of the meaning of life, and this eventually spawned philosophy, religion, and culture. But the enigma remains and eventually leads any thoughtful person to face the terrifying issues it inevitably poses: What am I? What are we in all this?

Einstein was right that the mystery of the universe begins with awe. But it hits home when I realize that I am an inextricable part of this whole big picture and then begin to ask what, if anything, that means. Such musings may begin in childhood, but they provide our first introduction to the unavoidable "mystery" of the universe and of the human place within it. Struggling with these questions has generated our greatest art, music, poetry, and literature from the cave paintings at Lascaux to Mozart's *Requiem*. To repress such thoughts would not be to "grow up," but to regress to a prehumanoid state. We would wilt into snuffed-out candles.

Again, there are thoughtful people who suggest that since these questions are essentially unanswerable, we should just stop asking them. But what does it mean that we never do stop asking? The sheer persistence of such questions tells us something about what it means to be *Homo sapiens,* and their intractability demonstrates what science can do, and also what scientists agree it cannot and should not be expected to do. They remind us, as Einstein put it, that "behind anything that can be experienced there is something that our minds cannot grasp, whose beauty and sublimity reaches us only indirectly."

Despite the efforts of well-intentioned people who shrug them off as "meaningless," we *do* go on wondering and asking, even though we recognize there will never be "answers" to these questions as there are answers, if always provisional, to scientific ones. That is why "mystery" and not "problem" is the appropriate designation. If in some distant future generation people do stop asking them, they will begin to look more like the humanoid robots of science-fiction novels. We are human not just because we sense that we are a part, albeit a minuscule one, of a space-time continuum and ask, "What does it mean?" but also because we puzzle about why we cannot stop asking. Human beings might be defined as *Homo quaerens,* the stubborn creatures who cannot stop asking why and then asking why they ask why.

Here religion emerges in the evolution of humanity. Creation myths such as the Gilgamesh epic, the Aztec creation stories, and the first chapters of Genesis were not primarily composed to answer the "how" or "when" questions. They are not scientific accounts, even though their poetical language, when read literally (which is always a mistake), may sound that way. Rather, they grapple, at one and the same time, with the linked mysteries of both *why* there is a universe and *what* our place in it is. Human beings have continued to fashion such narratives for thousands of years. They are not to be compared with evolution or string theory. They are more like lyrical cantatas, symphonies of symbols through which humans have tried to make sense of their place in the world. But what is to be done with these archaic narratives today?

This is where the distinction between faith and belief is vital. These stories are—literally—"not to be believed." They are, rather, artifacts human beings have crafted to try to wring some meaning from the mystery. They are not themselves the mystery. They seek to find a place for humankind in the face of it. Faith does not mean "belief in" this or that myth of creation. These narratives are the vehicles through which human beings symbolize their orientation toward the mystery that evoked their search.

We are sometimes warned that we should simply rid ourselves of these gnarled old myths and that we would be better off without them. But I disagree. Instead, we should recognize and appreciate them for what they are, an invaluable reminder that, although we differ in many respects from the thousands of generations that have preceded us, we are really not all that unique. True, we benefit, as they did not, from the Hubble telescope, mood-altering drugs, CAT scans, laser surgery, and the Internet. But we still wrestle with the same fundamental ambiguity as did our fur-clad ancestors who scrawled those pictures on the cave walls and their successors who composed the *Lotus Sutra* and painted the *Last Judgment*. We are still trying to find our way through a *terra* that will always remain *incognita*.

But there is a dilemma. Today this luxuriant legacy of the myths through which we have striven for meaning and the rituals that dramatize them has become morally and intellectually confusing. Much of the misunderstanding is due to the way religious leaders, especially in Christianity, have cheapened them into doctrines, propositions, and pseudoscientific theories, which people are exhorted to "believe." But the result of this "literalization of the symbolic" is that something essential has been lost in translation. The ill-advised transmuting of symbols into a curious kind of "facts" has created an immense obstacle to faith for many thoughtful people. Instead of helping them confront the great mystery, it has effectively prevented them from doing so. This was the case with Unamuno's earnest young man from the city. But the priest knew

the truth. The young man's genuine doubts about religious doctrines, even about God, do not render him ineligible for prayer or
incapable of faith. So what do we do with the plethora of beliefs and
practices we have inherited from our various religious traditions?

Some well-meaning theologians think Christians are indeed
asked to believe too many things. They suggest, therefore, that the
best way to cope with this overload is to pare down the number of
items, to discard some and keep others, though they often disagree
on which ones to keep and which ones to consign to the wastebasket. This has been called the "modernist approach," but it
might better be called the "subtraction solution." Popular among
some liberal Christians, unfortunately it is exactly the wrong strategy. However well-intentioned and however trimmed the list of
"must-believes" becomes, it simply reinforces the belief/nonbelief
axis. It implies that there are still some things—albeit fewer—that
we really "must believe."

This is no solution. Rather, we should stop asking whether we
"believe" them or not. Instead, we can appreciate this dazzling
array of myths, rituals, and stories as an invaluable legacy of the
human race. Like scientists, we can build on the past, not dispense
with it. When we recognize that in many respects we denizens of
the twenty-first century are really not all that exceptional, this ap-
preciation of the past teaches us a little humility, an essential quality in good scientists, a vital attribute in religious people, and a
desirable trait in mature human beings. Then we can learn from
the partial successes and many failures of our meaning-making
forebears. Like them, we find ourselves in a long human saga,
reaching out for what is never fully attainable and trying to name
what is essentially unnameable. It is that effort, with all its frustra-
tions and rewards, that has made our ancestors and ourselves
human, and if we ever give up on it, we could become sputtering
wicks of once burning tapers.

The mystery of the universe is not only "out there" where Einstein found it. It is also unavoidably "in here." We know that we are a part of it. But what kind of part are we? As *Homo quaerens,* we not only wonder about ourselves, but wonder why we are wondering. Just as part of the mystery of the universe is that we find it a mystery, so part of the mystery of the self is why we find it a mystery. Who am I to reflect on myself and on myself reflecting?

Theologian Reinhold Niebuhr (1892–1971) confronts this on the first page of his classic *The Nature and Destiny of Man:*

> Man has always been his most vexing problem. How shall he think of himself? . . . If (he) insists that he is a child of nature and that he ought not to pretend to be more than the animal, which he obviously is, he tacitly admits that he is, at any rate, a curious kind of animal who has both the inclination and the capacity to make such pretensions. If on the other hand he insists on his unique and distinctive place in nature, and points to his rational faculties as proof of his special eminence, there is an anxious note in his avowals of uniqueness which betrays his unconscious sense of kinship with the brutes. . . . Furthermore the very effort to estimate the significance of his rational faculties implies a degree of transcendence over himself which is not fully defined or explained by what is usually connoted by "reason."[3]

Niebuhr is describing what some call "myself as mystery." Not only can we watch ourselves thinking; we can watch ourselves watching our thinking. The next step, watching the watcher watching, opens onto endless and baffling horizons, like mirrors reflecting mirrors. However freighted with infinite regression our thoughts about time and space are, our experience of ourselves seems even more perplexing. Modern psychology has approached this dilemma with the concept of "identity," and it seems clear that identity is inextricably tied up with ethics. "What should I do?" is always linked to "Who am I?"

Once when I was teaching a class on ethics, a student proudly announced that his only rule for living a moral life came from his being a "Polonian."

"Don't you mean an Apollonian?" another student asked.

"No," the first insisted. "A Polonian, like Polonius in Hamlet. You know, 'To thine own self be true, and it must follow as night the day, thou canst not be false to any man.'"

"Yes, but that's just the problem," the other student immediately retorted. "Just who is this 'myself' I am supposed to be true to?"

This student's reply not only exposed the fatuousness of Polonius's advice to Laertes (which Shakespeare wanted to sound inane); it also pointedly illustrated what is meant by a "mystery." That student, like all of us, will continue to ask the "Who am I?" question and may come to more or less satisfactory answers. But then circumstances will change, and the "identity" that seemed in place last year will no longer serve. This is why the "I" is not a problem that can be solved, but a mystery that remains with us as long as we live. The apostle Paul came closer to the truth than the bard's loquacious Polonius when he complained that the very thing he wanted to avoid doing was what he always seemed to do, and what he wanted to do he did not (Rom. 7:15, 19).

The self is not a static entity. It is a battle site. Sometimes there are truces in the conflict, even fairly long ones, but inevitably the melee begins again. There is never a final settlement as long as we live. Further, the significance of this continuing conflict itself poses its own dilemmas. The "universe within" is just as mysterious as the universe out there. Some whole cultures, like that of

Tibet, have devoted immense energies to its exploration. Some Western mystics, like Teresa of Avila (1515–82), and writers, like Marcel Proust (1871–1922), have done so as well. So did Sigmund Freud (1856–1939), the inventor of psychoanalysis, and his disciples. The testimonies of these intrepid voyagers to the inner reaches of the self can be both puzzling and inspiring to those of us who live in a culture determined to travel outward. But we still find ways to undertake this inward pilgrimage, even if it is coded as an outward one. The long time TV favorite *Star Trek*, though cast as a series of journeys into space, was in actual fact an inspired exploration of the multiple dimensions of the human. This was the real source of its appeal. It found an audience because the self remains a mystery, one that we cannot stop probing.

Inevitably, however, looking inward, like looking outward, generates anxiety and frustration. Creation myths are often quickly followed by narratives of self-destruction. The Garden of Eden is followed by the story of Adam's attempt to become a god and Cain's murder of Abel. In the archaic Greek myth, Narcissus became so entranced by his own reflection in the pool and then so furious at it that he killed himself. Both the universe and the self can stir up *tremendum* as well as *fascinans*. Faith involves our response to both.

But mystery has still another locus, namely, the "other." Not only do the universe and the self open onto mystery; so do the other people we meet and live with. Existentialist philosopher and writer Jean-Paul Sartre (1905–80) once described the scene of a man seated alone in the waiting room of a dentist's office. Bored and a bit ill at ease, he glances at the cheap prints on the wall, the frayed magazines on the table, and the spotted old rug. Then the situation changes. The door swings open and in walks another patient, who sits down across from him. For a moment they try to ignore each other. Then they glance at each other furtively, but finally their eyes meet. Now, in Sartre's gloomy view, a deadly duel begins. They stare for a moment, but then one eventually looks away. Sartre's moral is that either I am an object in your world, or you are an object in mine. For this joyless French thinker, there was no other possibility.

But is this the only possible ending? No wonder the same Sartre wrote a play entitled *No Exit*, in which the most famous line is, "Hell is other people." Still, Sartre had an insight. Encountering another person can ignite the same fascination and terror, the same hope and longing that the vastness of the universe and my place in it generate. They all seem part of the same unfathomable mystery.

The Jewish philosopher Emmanuel Levinas (1906–95) who spent his long life probing the other-as-mystery, had a more hopeful view, at least up to a point. Levinas was born in Lithuania, where a particularly strict school of text-oriented Orthodox Judaism held sway, and he received a traditional Jewish education. In 1924 he began studies at the University of Strasbourg and went on to become one of France's most prominent philosophers. Throughout his life Levinas pursued a dual career. He was both a highly respected philosopher, who introduced German thinkers like Heidegger and Husserl to France, and a consummate scholar of the Talmud, on which he wrote several interpretive essays. Although members of his family died in the Holocaust, the Germans captured Levinas in his French army uniform, so he survived in a prisoner-of-war camp. He taught at the Sorbonne from 1973 until his retirement in 1979.

Levinas nourished a lifelong fascination with how human beings encounter each other. The keystone of his approach is his reversal of the traditional definition of philosophy as the "love of wisdom." Levinas prefers the "wisdom of love." Without citing Sartre's dentist-office scenario, he nonetheless sees every encounter with another person as a kind of distillation of human life as such, and he agrees that, at least at first, we want to either dominate or withdraw. Like an animal, we feel the impulse to flee or fight. But, Levinas reminds us, we do not experience just one such encounter. All of life, day in and day out, is made up of such meetings. Some are casual, with shopkeepers and waiters, people we may never see again. Some are with people we see now and then. But other encounters bring us together with people with whom we interact on a regular basis. This is why Levinas felt so intensely interested in family life. His fascination is also something that differentiates him from Sartre, who seems to have tried, not always successfully, to dodge long-term commitments, most noticeably in his famously wobbly nonmarriage to Simone de Beauvoir.

For Levinas, as we experience longer-term encounters with the "other" repeatedly, we notice something focal. Our compulsion to dominate or to withdraw is limited by two qualities. First, the "face" of the other carries with it a message to me that is almost like a plea. If I am torn between dominance and withdrawal, but unable to find a third way, then so is the other, and paradoxically this failure on both our parts makes that third way possible. Second, I begin to notice that my encounter with the "other" opens a dimension of reality I do not find anywhere else. Since ultimately I cannot be simply an object to the other and the other cannot just be an object to me, clearly the possibility of "objective" knowledge in this crucial realm of existence is not possible.

Levinas's reflection on the interpersonal and Einstein's awareness of mystery led them both to a similiar conclusion: the objective knowledge science rightly insists on is not the only kind of knowledge human beings need. This recognition is not a "religious" event in Levinas's thought, but it is something analogous. It is, as he says, "nonfinite," because it pushes me beyond myself toward a sense of responsibility, one that repeats itself and deepens with each encounter. It is, Levinas believes, "a signal of transcendence," an undeniable indication, drawn from the "secular" world, of a kind of knowledge that is radically different from the way we know other things. It demonstrates a way of knowing that is not only possible, but imperative.

Levinas's thinking helps but up to a point. Interpersonal encounters do reveal a kind of knowing that is different from the objective, scientific kind. And he is right that permanent or completely satisfying harmony or reciprocity is not fully possible in human encounters. But Levinas was markedly unwilling to extend his thinking into the realm of society. He stopped short of asking: Why do some people, those of a certain color, gender, or social class, often think they *do* have the right to view other people as objects? And, sadly, why do those who are treated as objects often begin to think of themselves as objects? Why do so many people who live with each other a long time treat each other so badly, even abuse and kill each other? Why did seemingly ordinary peasants in Poland, just across the border from Levinas's native Lithuania, grab scythes and hatchets and brutally murder the Jewish neighbors they had lived with for years? How do power and money distort the self-other encounter? Our meeting with the "other" carries with it horror as well as promise.[4]

There is another question. The self-other split seems to mirror a split *within* oneself. It echoes the peculiar duality between "I" as subject and "me" as object. The anxiety generated by my discovery of my own finitude and mortality drives me toward futile efforts to control a self and a world that constantly elude my attempts. The failure can prompt a violent reaction. The myth of Narcissus's self-absorption and the story of Cain's murder of Abel belong together. These are divisions that cry out for some resolution, but appear insurmountable. True, the mystics of the different religions seem to transcend the internal dichotomy, and the social reformers constantly strive to reshape the human community so that more equality and mutuality are possible. But is there any real basis for their efforts?

This is the point at which the encounter with mystery meets the possibility of faith. The three ways we encounter the great mystery—the universe, the self, the other—all leave us with a sense of uneasiness, incompleteness, and dissatisfaction. Do we have any clues, even provisional ones, to the question of why there is something and not nothing? Is time going anywhere? Or is it cyclical or maybe just illusory? What about the fracture I find in myself as both the subject and the object of my reflection, ad infinitum? Is that a permanent feature of being human? Is my hope that my encounter with the other need not always be a conquest, a capitulation, or a stand-off a futile one? Faith, although it is *evoked* by the mystery that surrounds us, is not the mystery itself. It is a basic posture *toward* the mystery, and it comes in an infinite variety of forms.

CHAPTER 3

Ships Already Launched

The Voyage from Mystery to Faith

Faith begins with awe in the face of mystery. But awe becomes faith only when it takes the next step. The Danish philosopher Søren Kierkegaard (1813–55) once remarked that as soon as we are old enough to look around, we find ourselves on a ship that has already been launched. As we become aware of the mysteries of world, self, and other, they always arrive suffused with the specific languages, emotions, and thought patterns of a particular cultural tradition. And these supply the theories, myths, and metaphors with which we respond. Living *with* the mystery is something we all have in common. But *how* we live with it differs. To extend Kierkegaard's metaphor, we sail on one launched ship among many, large and small, that often seem to be crisscrossing, colliding, and heading in different directions.

This metaphor has its limits. There are similarities and overlapping between and among these traditions. Scholars of comparative religion often point them out, as Huston Smith has done in his many books. Psychologist Carl Jung (1875–1961) believed he could discern what he called "archetypes" common to all of them. But there are also elements of irreducible particularity in our distinct religious and cultural worldviews. Hindu and Buddhist perspectives on time and history differ markedly from those of Christianity and Judaism. Nirvana is different from the Kingdom of God. There are radical dissimilarities in views of the human self and its relations to others.

I frequently meet people who, when they discover that I teach religion, assure me that "underneath, all religions are really the same." I used to respond that, during a lifetime of studying them, it appeared to me that they are not. But since that usually ended the conversation on a disagreeable note, I have recently just let their opinion pass. It is true that we are all responding to the same mystery, the one that confronts us all not just as mortal beings, but as beings aware of our mortality. Still, we sense it and cope with the mystery in quite disparate ways. The various world religions constitute complex codifications of these responses, and they differ from each other in significant respects. This is what makes the study of comparative religion so absorbing. If all religions really *were* essentially the same, it would soon become unbearably boring.

The ship I found myself on—the narrative through which I came to awareness of the different facets of the mystery—is the Judeo-Christian one. Of course this is largely a matter of the circumstances of my birth and upbringing. Had I been born in Bombay or Baghdad or Beijing, I would have found myself on a different ship and would undoubtedly have absorbed different customs and narratives. Not only are we traveling on different vessels; the tradition that first formed our consciousness gets under our skin. Even if we reject it, we reject it within its own frames of reference. A Christian atheist is different from a Buddhist atheist, in part because they are each rejecting radically different concepts of the divine. This is important for the study of religions, since what we eventually come to see is that there is no neutral platform, no place where anyone can stand outside of all of them and make comparisons and judgments.

Of course one can always try to understand other religions, to be sympathetic, or to "get the feel" of them. I have spent much of my career in this effort. But when I recite a verse from the Qur'an, sit in Buddhist meditation, or chant a Hindu mantra, I do so as one steeped in a tradition different from those. I do not agree with those who claim that only people with no attachment to their own religion can possibly understand another. On the contrary, my *participation* in my own, my experiencing one faith tradition "from the inside," deepens my understanding of the others. Most practicing Hindu, Buddhist, and Muslim scholars who also study comparative religion agree on this point. The allegedly neutral observer is really operating from some basic posture, some faith stance, even if it is unacknowledged. In trying to understand religions, no space platforms or skyhooks are available.

The "launched ship" of the Judeo-Christian tradition within which I meet the mystery has three main foci. Like other people in a host of different traditions, I was first exposed to the tradition in which I find myself through stories and rituals. I call them the Hebrew cycle, the Christmas cycle, and the Easter cycle.

The Hebrew Cycle: Most people describe the Baptist denomination, in which I grew up, as not having any rituals. Even Baptists often make this claim. But it is not true. Rituals are *enactments*— in song, story, visual representation, and gesture—of the narratives that inform a people's identity. In our church we heard sermons galore about Old Testament episodes, and we sang hymns about its key figures. The Sunday school walls were plastered with pictures of Noah, surrounded by giraffes and zebras, in his storm-tossed ark; Abraham trudging up the mountain with Isaac and the donkey loaded with kindling wood; Joseph sporting his flashy coat in front of his scowling brothers; and spunky little David slinging his pebble at the hapless Goliath. There were several depictions of Moses—staring at the burning bush, confronting the pharaoh, or lifting his staff over the receding waters of the Red Sea. One picture that made me uneasy was of Absalom, David's rebellious son, hanging by his hair from a tree limb. As I neared pubescence, my favorite showed a shapely Delilah seducing a strapping but naïve Samson into getting a haircut. Of course there were also pictures of Jesus, from the nativity scene to the events of Passion Week.

Not only did these pictures cover the walls. As tiny children we crayoned them in coloring books and stuck their cutouts on flannel boards. If I close my eyes now, I can still see them. We chirped little songs about them, some of which I still remember. As we got older, we sang cantatas, choir anthems, and spirituals about them, and we pulled on worn bathrobes and acted out their escapades in church plays. By the time we were ready to leave Sunday school, these sagas had become permanent features in the topography of our imaginations. They did exactly what rituals are supposed to do.

As I grew older and learned more about the religion of the Israelites, I discovered that the God these people served, although he could lose his temper and change his mind, in the end was just and powerful. I also noticed that this God was a God of *promise*, always pointing people toward the future. He told Abraham to leave the place where he lived and to go to one that he would show him. Later, when Moses asked him who he should tell the Israelite slaves had dispatched him to lead them out of captivity, the voice from the burning bush said something that is usually translated, "I am who I am," but that some Hebrew scholars claim should be, "I will do what I will do." Later the prophet Isaiah declared that God would deliver them from their captivity in Babylon. The latest books of the Old Testament look forward to a time when God will transform the whole world into a place of concord and justice. As the German philosopher Ernst Bloch (1885–1977) once wrote, the biblical God is one "whose essence is futurity."

From the Hebrew cycle I also learned that the God of the Bible favors the little guy. He makes his most dramatic appearance in the book of Exodus by liberating a ragged band of ungrateful peons from bondage in Egypt. He fingers younger sons for special assignments and demonstrates a distinctive bias for widows and orphans. He promises to vindicate the poor and to restore captives and refugees. His prophets inveigh against the indolent rich who "lie on beds of ivory, and lounge on their couches, . . . who drink wine from bowls, and anoint themselves with the finest oils" (Amos 6:4–5). Years later, when I read the liberation theologians who wrote about God's "preferential option for the poor," they did not seem to be inventing anything new.

The Old Testament cycle begins with creation and ends with the renovation of the world into a commonwealth of *shalom,* a place of justice and peace. This is a very large promise for which the promised land of Canaan is mere foreshadowing, a sort of down payment. This enlarged promise is not just to Jews, but to everyone. Also, according to some of the most lyrical passages in the Hebrew scriptures, it includes the whole creation, the plants and animals, the seas and the stars. This means that one way to see the mystery of space-time is to view it as an unfinished epic, a work in progress. It can be seen as a process in which the new, the surprising, and the unexpected constantly emerge. It means we live in a world whose potential is yet to be fulfilled.

This biblical perspective is *one* way to perceive the mystery of the universe, not the only one. It is the view one gets from the deck of the ship I happen to be on. But there are other vessels in this flotilla and other narratives. The biblical story portrays a universe that is "going somewhere," but the Buddhist one, for example, has no account of creation and denies any beginning or end of space or time: what is now always has been and always will be. The Hindu saga consists of endless cycles of time and innumerable universes.

The biblical story is neither static nor cyclical. It depicts a reality that is moving in a certain direction, even though that direction is hard to discern. The Bible opens poetically with a world rising out of chaos ("the earth was a formless void and darkness covered the face of the deep," Gen. 1:2) and ends, also poetically, with a world in which "there are no more tears" (Rev. 21:4). This view of the world as a creative process, not the changeless substance the ancient Greeks favored, explains why *hope* is such an important component of the way of life it shapes. Hope is that virtue that sees the past and the present in light of a future horizon. Later, in the New Testament, the apostle Paul places hope along with faith and love as the three principal virtues (1 Cor. 13:13). In this way he was very much the Hebrew. The heartbeat of Israelite faith was the expectation of a messianic era in which all would sit under their own fig trees, the lion would lie down with the lamb, and swords would be beaten into plowshares (Mic. 4:3–4; Isa. 11:1–9). This would take place not in some transcendental realm, but here on earth. I cannot imagine how the more specifically Christian cycles would have made any sense to me, had I not been grounded in these Old Testament chronicles.

The Christmas Cycle: The Christmas stories distill the themes of the Old Testament in the life purpose of one man. Like the ancient Israelites, Jesus and his family were themselves refugees. Mary and Joseph were not married (something our Sunday school teachers skipped over rather lightly). The tyrannical king tried to kill the baby, so he butchered all the boys in the neighborhood, and the family became displaced persons. Later, Jesus's teachings and his activities demonstrated his habitual favoritism toward the poor, the sick, and the socially ostracized—tax collectors, Samaritans, and lepers. But, like the Old Testament prophets, the constant leitmotif of Jesus's life was his reiteration of God's promise of a new day, an age of peace and goodwill, the "Reigning of God," which he said was already coming to pass in a preliminary way.

I remember wondering as a small child why King Herod wanted to kill this baby so badly that he was willing to slay all the children. We did not have any *pictures* of the "slaughter of the innocents" in Sunday school, but somewhere I ran across a print of Brueghel's painting of the scene and felt devastated by his depiction of pleading mothers, infants impaled on soldiers' spears, and blood spattered on the snow. No wonder there was no picture of it in Sunday school. Later, in seminary, I learned that our Christmas accounts were written many years after Jesus's death as an overture to the main events of his life. The portrait of a family without shelter, penniless shepherds, and relentless opposition from the rulers foreshadowed what was to occur as this baby grew to manhood.

Even later, when I read the historians who place Jesus within the context of Roman imperial rule, my childhood question received a more complete answer. Ancient inscriptions show that officials of the empire celebrated the life of Augustus Caesar as "good news" (gospel) and declared him a "savior" and a "god" who had brought peace to earth. But the angels sang exactly the same praises of the baby Jesus. This is why Matthew and Luke, who wrote the nativity narratives, but who also knew how the story had turned out, represented the powers that be, personified by King Herod, as wanting this baby dead.

Almost as if to justify the frantic fears of Herod and his imperial cohorts, the moment Jesus reached adulthood, he began to tell people that a new regime—the "Kingdom of God"—was about to replace the existing one, that the insiders would be out and those at the bottom would be on top. Naturally the ruling elites heard this promise of a "regime change" as a threat. But the phrase "Kingdom of God" is one of the most misused and misunderstood in the entire Bible. It is too often thought of as where you may go after you die, or something that begins after this world's history is over, or something that is entirely inward. However, the Hebrew prophets, Jesus himself, and the last pages of Revelation, the final book of the Bible, all teach that the Kingdom of God is something that happens in and to *this* world. The glimpse the prophets convey about a reign of God's *shalom* is doggedly earthy. For example, Isaiah, using the New Jerusalem as a synonym for the whole creation, describes it this way:

> The sound of weeping, the cry of distress
> will be heard in her no more.
> No child there will ever again die in infancy,
> No old man shall fail to live out his span of life. . . .
> My people shall build houses and live in them,
> Plant vineyards and eat their fruit;
> They will not build for others to live in
> Or plant for others to eat. (Isa. 65:19–22)

This is, of course, poetry. But it is earthy and this-worldly. It evokes a picture that is far different from the ones we see in magazine cartoons featuring bored angels in ill-fitting white robes, perched on clouds and strumming harps.

The biblical idea of the Kingdom of God also includes an essential inward element. As the prophet Ezekiel puts it, "A new heart also will I give you" (36:26). In his Sermon on the Mount, Jesus says that only the "pure in heart" shall see God (Matt. 5:8). It also includes the expectation that death, either of the planet or of an individual, is not their ultimate destiny, and it points to a cosmic fulfillment that transcends human history, encompassing the celestial bodies. This in no way undercuts the fact that the Kingdom of God, as envisioned by Jesus and the prophets, contains an undeniably utopian element, but since this is what Christians have often neglected, this futuristic dimension has frequently migrated into secular movements. It has sometimes been said that while Christians have tried to have God without the Kingdom, secularists have tried to build the Kingdom without God. But this is an oversimplification. It is true that embracing Jesus while ignoring the Kingdom's requirement for justice inevitably results in an individualistic pietism, and that Lenin's mausoleum is not the only monument to the disasters that result when human beings make themselves into the gods of the future. But the yearning for a different world, is thoroughly human. As the Latin American theologian Jon Sobrino writes, "the utopian impulse provides the possibility of a universal, human ecumenism of all those who hope and work for a kingdom."[1]

Still, the word "kingdom" is problematical. It inevitably evokes the static idea of a spatial realm. The Hebrew word, *malkuth*, however, does not convey this inert feeling, but suggests something actively occurring. For this reason, in my own teaching I prefer to use the phrase "Reign*ing* of God." It implies something that is going on—not a place, but a "happening." This is the grammar Jesus used in speaking of it. To be a "follower" of Jesus means to discern and respond to the initial signs of this "happening" and to work to facilitate its coming in its fullness. To follow Jesus, however, does not mean to be a mimic. It means to continue in our times what he did in his.

Jesus was a man of faith. Recall how we defined "faith" in a previous chapter. Calling Jesus a man of faith does not suggest that we must somehow uncover Jesus's "beliefs" or his ideas *about* God. These would be, in any case, matters of speculation, since we cannot know much about his inner life. Rather, by seeing the way he lived his life, we learn what his primal orientation was and see what he trusted and placed his confidence in. These are the components of his faith. Clearly the object of Jesus's own hope and confidence—his faith—was the Kingdom of God.

Jesus inherited the traditional Jewish faith of his family and his people, but just as the gospels say that he "grew in wisdom and in stature" (Luke 2:52), his life story demonstrates that he also grew in faith. Some paintings of the Holy Family show Jesus as a wise little old man while he was still in swaddling clothes. But if Jesus was fully human, as Christianity has always insisted, then his childhood faith matured as he grew, faced disappointments, and felt the pain of betrayal, rejection, and misunderstanding. He struggled with crises and passed through stages of reframing and deepening his faith. It is important to notice, however, that the assaults on his faith did not come from intellectual doubts about the existence of God. They had nothing to do with "unbelief." They arose from the conflicts he faced in his effort to demonstrate and announce the coming of God's just and peaceful order.

So much Christian theology and preaching has fastened on to the need for faith *in* Jesus that the faith *of* Jesus has often been ignored. Thomas Aquinas (1225–74), still the most influential Catholic theologian, even insisted that, since Jesus was divine, he could not have had faith. But the reason Aquinas gives for this assertion is worth noting. He says faith is directed toward that "which is hidden from sight." But since he believed Jesus had the full vision of God from his conception on, he did not need faith, and so had none.[2] Here Aquinas is relying on the intellectualized reduction of "faith" that confuses it with affirming something we don't know for sure to be true, the idea that dominated Christian theology in what I have called the Age of Belief. He also implies that we "believe" something to be true largely because it is what the church's hierarchy teaches. Fortunately, some more recent Catholic theologians, among them Hans Urs von Balthasar (1905–88), who was Pope John Paul II's favorite, have pointedly disagreed with Aquinas on this matter, another sign that a different understanding of faith is emerging from its belief-dominated constriction.

Jesus cannot be understood, let alone followed, without reference to his own faith. The biblical book of Hebrews refers to him as "the author and pioneer of our faith" (12:2). But the faith *of* Jesus cannot be understood without recognizing that its focus was the "Reigning of God." His message was not about himself, and not even about God. It was about the imminent coming of a new era of *shalom*. This is clear from the opening verses of the Gospel of Mark (oldest of the four canonical gospels) in which this Kingdom is equated with the "good news of God" (1:14). The most explicit expression occurs when, early in his ministry, Jesus returns to his home town of Nazareth and is invited to speak in the synagogue. Clearly wishing to align himself with the prophets before him, he reads from the prophet Isaiah:

> The Spirit of the Lord is upon me, because he has anointed me
> To bring good news to the poor
> He has sent me to proclaim release to the captives
> And recovery of sight to the blind, to let the oppressed go free,
> To proclaim the year of the Lord's favor. (Luke 4:18–19)

Virtually all Jesus's parables are about the dawning of this Kingdom and the change of heart people would need to notice it and live in it, even though its coming had only just begun. When we try to figure out again today how to describe the relationship between Jesus and God, as the bishops tried to do at Nicaea, we ought to stay away from the mistake they made in completely leaving out any reference to the Kingdom. We should also avoid the archaic language they used about the two being of the "same substance" (*homoousios*), which means little to anyone today. Rather, we could say that Jesus in his life trajectory completely embodied the purpose and "project" of God.

Moving the focus from Jesus as an individual to his life purpose greatly widens his relevance in a religiously pluralistic world. When the Harvard faculty asked me to teach a course on Jesus to undergraduates in the Moral Reasoning division of the curriculum, I was apprehensive at first about what the Hindu, Buddhist, Muslim, and Jewish students who might sign up would make of it. But I quickly learned that Christianity has no monopoly on Jesus. Hindus understood him as an avatar, Buddhists as a bodhisattva, and both Muslims and Jews as a prophet of God. Even agnostics found something fascinating and admirable in him. They were not all that attracted to Christianity, but they were all drawn to Jesus for his exemplary courage, his compassion for the disinherited, and his willingness to stand up to corrupt political and religious authorities. But what attracted them more than anything else was his emphasis on the possibility of another kind of world where gentleness and equality prevail.

As we have already mentioned, Jesus called this other possible world the "Kingdom of God." It was the heartbeat of his life, his constant concern and preoccupation. The possibility of "another world" is always the reason many non-Christians give when they ask Christians to "go back to Jesus." This utopian hope, even when modestly expressed, links Jesus and the prophets to a much wider history of human longing. It is the antidote to fatalism and the corrosive fear that there are no alternatives to any status quo. The slogan of the Social Forum, an international coalition of social change organizations is, "Another world *is* possible.

Jesus's constant emphasis on a coming new order obviously sounded like a threat to those in charge of the old one. A new order meant the existing one would have to go, and with it their cozy perches in the alcoves of power and privilege. Consequently, Jesus found himself in serious trouble with the elites of his time. He probably could have avoided a confrontation. But he did not. Moving from Galilee, where the threat he posed was somewhat remote, to Jerusalem, where it was immediate, he faced down the occupation authorities and their local quisling supporters. Although he did it nonviolently, he paid a high price for living out the hope he taught. The story of Jesus is a logical extension of the Old Testament cycle, but in no way a displacement of it.

When it comes to understanding the mystery of the self, this Christian story builds on the Jewish one, but also introduces an important refinement. Jesus repeats again and again that we do not have to wait to begin living the kind of life the Kingdom of God makes possible: we can start now. He often used the analogy of seeds to suggest that, although the new era of human reciprocity and peace has not yet come, it is "at hand." Its hints and signs are already present. In this respect, Jesus's message found an echo in the idea dissident Vaclav Havel stressed during the Communist rule over Czechoslovakia. Havel told people to try to live *as though they were free* even under a freedom-denying regime.

In theological idiom, Jesus is the manifestation of true human personhood under depersonalizing conditions. Viewed in the light of his life story, the "mystery of myself" that I described in the previous chapter receives at least a provisional response. Simply stated, Jesus was not preoccupied with himself. The age of *shalom* that God had promised continued to be his ultimate concern throughout his life. It was the object of his faith.

It is important that, the biblical book of Hebrews calls Jesus the "pioneer" of faith. He is an exemplar, especially since, like all faithful people, he wrestled constantly with tests of that faith. These were not, however, the intellectual doubts that sometimes trouble people today. His hope and confidence—his faith—was constantly focused on the new world God had promised "on earth as it is in heaven." Jesus's struggles were, rather, setbacks and losses that seemed at times to defeat the coming of the Kingdom. These reversals culminated in his own arrest and execution, which appeared to mark the ignominious failure of his life's work. This, however, moves us toward the Easter cycle.

The Easter Cycle: The Easter stories begin with Jesus leaving the relative safety and remoteness of Galilee and traveling to Jerusalem, the hub of Roman imperial power in the eastern Mediterranean and its elite Judean collaborators. It is true that he had already contended with fierce opposition and had even fled his home town of Nazareth once and moved to Capernaum to avoid arrest. But he knew that by entering Jerusalem he would be making it impossible for his enemies to avoid a decisive showdown. How could the imperial forces and their local clients disregard someone riding into town while crowds hailed him as king? How could they ignore someone storming into the Temple and chasing out the racketeers? They had to act, and they did. They arrested him, subjected him to a bogus trial, flogged him, and then killed him by slow torture as a public example.

Many churches mark the final days and weeks of Jesus's life by observing the forty days of Lent, a season of fasting and preparation. The word itself has a curious background. In most languages the forty days are referred to by a term deriving from the Latin word for "fortieth," *quadragesima.* Thus in Spanish it is *cuaresma* and in French *carême.* The English word "Lent" comes from the Anglo-Saxon word for March (*lenct*), the month in which it often falls, a valuable reminder of how many pre-Christian seasonal observances found their way into Christianity and why it is not entirely bizarre that Easter, despite constant warnings by preachers, continues in many people's minds to fuse a celebration of both the Resurrection and the return of spring.

In any case, as Baptists, we did not "do Lent," which caused our Catholic playmates considerable shock and consternation. I was never urged to "give something up for Lent" and have only done so sporadically as an adult. I have never taken to fasting for either dietary or spiritual purposes. But even as a child I was stirred by the descriptions I heard of Jesus's final days and even more so by the music that recalled them, like "The Seven Last Words on the Cross," which our church choir always performed. I also looked forward to the annual Easter sunrise service. Held in a park, it was the one occasion in which all the Protestant churches of our little town participated, and all the choirs sang together. It was followed by a breakfast of steaming hot pancakes topped with melting butter and ladles of maple syrup, served in one of the church basements. Years later, when I learned that the word "Easter" is derived from "Eostre," the Anglo-Saxon goddess of the dawn, it reminded me again, as with Lent, of the many ways Christianity has blended "pagan" elements into its worship. We should not fret unduly that the same blending continues in African and Asian churches today.

There are shelves of treatises about "what actually happened" on the first Easter Sunday, and the gospel accounts are not consistent. What is clear, however, is that, although the disciples had lost hope and fled in panic after the crucifixion, *something* happened to convince them that Jesus and the coming peaceable kingdom he embodied had not been defeated by death. The disciples soon came to believe that, in some sense that is hard to define, he still lived.

In thinking about this difficult issue, some find it helpful to make a distinction between the historical, or "pre-Easter," Jesus and the post-Easter "Christ." In this reading, "Christ" (which means one who is anointed or designated for a purpose) signifies the Spirit that had empowered Jesus during his earthly lifetime and now empowered a previously dispirited band of followers. But, although the distinction between the historical Jesus and "Christ" can be useful, it is also important not to lose sight of the continuity between the two. For the early Christians, the reality of "Christ" *included,* but was *not exhausted by* the historical Jesus. The cause Jesus espoused, his confrontation with the power wielders, his vision of the coming era of *shalom*—all these elements constituted his life. They made him who he was.

The stories of the Resurrection, as hard as they are for modern ears to comprehend, mean that the life Jesus lived and the project he pursued (the Kingdom of God) did not perish at the crucifixion, but continued in the lives of those who carried on what he had begun. This is what the theological language about Christians as the "Body of Christ" or the "extension of the Incarnation" attempt—with only limited success—to articulate. When Jesus referred to himself as the "vine" and his friends as the "branches" (John 15:5), this is what he had in mind.[3]

"Christ" means more than Jesus. It also refers to the new skein of relationships that arose around him during and after his life. Several biblical references support this interpretation. Paul frequently speaks of the Christ who dwells within him and within the other followers. When, for example, he writes that among those who share the Spirit of Christ, "There is neither Jew nor Greek, there is neither slave nor free, there is neither male nor female, for you are all one in Christ Jesus," he means something more extensive than the historical Jesus (Gal. 3:28). The Easter cycle, with all its harshness, joy, and impenetrability, tells of this enlargement of the historical Jesus story into the Christ story. It says that who Jesus was, as the embodiment of a "different possible world," was not ultimately defeated by the crucifixion, but continues.

It is also important to note that according to the Easter cycle the "Christ Spirit" is not restricted to the Christian community alone, but is present, albeit often unrecognized, throughout the entire created order. The story of Pentecost (Acts 2:1–13), which continues the Easter narrative, tells of the gift of the same Spirit that had animated Jesus to the disciples, and from them to those they met as they spread his message abroad. The account states that the Spirit—dramatized by tongues of flame—was "poured out on *all* flesh" (2:17). The symbolic significance of the disciples understanding each other even though they spoke in different languages signals a universal community. But the fact that they spoke in many different languages, not just in Greek or Hebrew, shows that the new and inclusive community preserves the cultural particularity embodied in languages.

One of the most devastating blunders made by the church, especially as the Age of Belief began, was to insist that the Spirit is present only in believers. St. Cyprian of Carthage, a third-century bishop, first phrased it in elegant Latin: *Extra Ecclesiam nulla salus,* which means "Outside the Church there is no salvation." Since then the Catholic Church has largely retracted this claim to exclusivity, and rightly so. In a famous passage Jesus says that the Spirit "blows where it will," and that no one knows "where it comes from and where it goes" (John 3:8). In other words the Spirit cannot be restricted by doctrinal or ecclesial boundaries. In a similar vein, Christianity has always insisted that the image of God, the *imago dei,* is present in all human beings. The Quakers speak of "that of God that is in every man."

The truth of the Easter cycle is that the life work of Jesus was not annihilated by his execution. It continues, among both those who follow him explicitly and those who contribute to the realization of the "possible world" that he demonstrated, whether they acknowledge him or not. This possible world, which Jesus exemplified, introduces a type of relationship among human beings that is radically different from Sartre's grim choice between submission or domination described in a previous chapter. It suggests that communities of love and reciprocity, forgiveness and compassion are within our grasp, even if they cannot be fully realized.

The faith of the earliest Christians combined that of the Old Testament with the Christmas story, the other accounts of Jesus's life, and the Passion and Easter stories. Their faith took the form of a loyalty to Jesus rather than Caesar and a hope that the new world of *shalom* Jesus personified would one day appear in its fullness.

They lived their faith in fellowships that, even amid fierce persecution, needed neither creeds nor clergy. But by the time Constantine became emperor, much of that original lifestyle had already begun to corrode. Hierarchy had begun to replace fellowship, and belief to replace faith. How this distressing story unfolded takes us to our next chapters.

CHAPTER 4

The Road Runner and the *Gospel of Thomas*

What Happens When It Wasn't Really That Way?

Recent discoveries about the first three centuries after the crucifixion of Jesus shed a bright new light on a series of old enigmas. They help clarify how Christianity deteriorated from a movement generated by faith and hope into a religious empire demarcated by prescribed doctrines and ruled by a priestly elite. They trace how a loose network of local congregations, with varied forms of leadership, congealed into a rigid class structure with a privileged clerical caste at the top ruling over an increasingly disenfranchised laity on the bottom. They help explain why women, who played such a vital leadership role in the earliest days, were pushed to the underside and the edges. These discoveries suggest that Christianity was not fated to develop as it did, that what happened was not simply a natural process like a tiny acorn growing into a mighty oak. A different historical trajectory was possible, and this has significant implications for the future:

In short, Christianity now has a second chance. A combination of circumstances makes possible a new outlook that might be more like the first three centuries and less like the last fifteen hundred years. Not only do we know more about the actual origins of the Jesus movement than any generation since the first century itself, but—even more important—Christianity is no longer a "Western" religion; it has recently exploded into a global one. Its vital centers now lie in Asia, Africa, and Latin America, and this affords unprecedented new opportunities.

There is a clear link between origin and future. But it does not consist of trying to return to a lost golden age. Some Pentecostals believe they are reviving the church described in Acts of the Apostles, complete with healing, miracles, and speaking in tongues. "New Age" groups often assert they are drawing on secret or suppressed esoteric lore. Catholics appeal to "apostolic succession," a straight line of authority from Jesus to Peter and down through all the popes to the present one. Baptists, Congregationalists, and Presbyterians claim their forms of church administration are identical with those of the New Testament. But there is no road back to the primitive church some Protestants long for, or to the splendid medieval synthesis many Catholics dream of, or to the "old-time religion" American revivalists sing about. Much of this attempt to revert to the "way it was" is based on fanciful reconstructions of some previous period. Still, its advocates have a point.

Despite the imaginary pasts they sometimes contrive, all these denominations agree on one thing. What Christianity should be doing today and tomorrow must continue what Jesus and those who immediately followed him were doing; otherwise it has become something different. Looking backward in order to move forward can be confusing and contradictory. But it is not frivolous. Unlike Hinduism, whose beginnings merge into the mists of primeval legend, there was a real historical time when there was no Christianity; then suddenly there it was. It is understandable, therefore, that Christians periodically revisit Jesus and the first few Christian generations to remind themselves what the original movement was about at its onset. Knowing about the past is vital not to *return to* it, but to *learn from* it, from both its mistakes and its successes.

The past, as someone has said, is not forgotten; it isn't even past. Our past shackles us, especially when we don't realize it. But it can also liberate us. Understanding our past can reopen roads that might have been taken, but were not. This is why it is so imperative that we have both the most accurate picture of the origins of Christianity possible and the clearest grasp of the sweep and dynamism of the new global Christianity. The next chapters are devoted to the first issue, drawing on current research to sketch a historically trustworthy picture of early Christianity. We then turn to the widened horizons brought about by an internationally expanded Christianity and what they portend for the future.

The biggest hurdle we face in thinking about Jesus and early Christianity is the skewed image we carry in our heads of that period. The picture is littered with debris, and much cleanup work is required before reconstruction can begin. My generation grew up with the flawed depiction of that important era embedded in our consciousness. But in recent years hardworking scholars have scraped away some of the clutter and have greatly corrected and clarified the portrayal.[1]

My initial understanding of Christian beginnings was defective in three important respects. First, when I attended seminary, most historians conveyed the impression that once upon a time there was a single entity called "early Christianity," but that gradually certain heresies and schisms arose on the margins and disrupted the initial harmony. Second, they also assumed that what they called "apostolic authority" took shape right away, as did the creeds and hierarchies that seemed necessary to combat these assaults from the edges. Third, they taught that although the Roman Empire formed the political and cultural locale in which the early

Christians lived, it was mainly just the "background" and, except for the persecutions and the martyrs, had little to do with how early Christian leaders shaped their own ideas and actions.

In the last few decades, however, all these assumptions have proven erroneous. The following are now evident. First, there never was a single "early Christianity"; there were many, and the idea of "heresy" was unknown. Second, it was not the apostles themselves, but subsequent generations who invented "apostolic authority," and both creeds and hierarchies emerged much later than had been thought. Third, an essential key to comprehending the earliest Christians, including those who wrote the New Testament, is to see their movement as a self-conscious *alternative* to the empire that tyrannized them. And the best way to understand the succeeding generation of Christian leaders is to notice how they reversed course and gradually came to admire and emulate that empire.

History, as the old dictum puts it, is always written by the winners. Not only did the winning contenders among the many first "Christianities" write the history; they also tried to destroy any counterevidence. This is why the so-called heretics hid their texts in caves, only to be discovered many centuries later. Then the winners used their rewritten history to bolster their own claims to authority. In the meantime, they softened their attitude toward the Roman Empire from passive resistance to docile subservience; then they tried to suggest that the Christian movement had been made up of loyal subjects of the divine emperor from the beginning. This primitive revisionism produced a clumsy effort to shift the blame for Jesus's death from the Romans to the "Jews," with what turned out to be disastrous long-term consequences. Today, however, it is evident that this whole winners' version is not only wildly inaccurate, but demonstrably dangerous.

The process that has brought a clearer picture of early Christianity into focus is almost as exciting as the picture itself. A combination of a more precise and scientific archaeology, the un-expected discovery of ancient Christian documents hidden in caves for millennia, and the refinement of historical research methods all render the acorn-to-oak-tree assumption untenable. A better metaphor for early Christianity might be of seeds widely sown and sprouting in varied soils and climates. But it is also important to see that these new insights have an important meaning for Christianity in the twenty-first century. They free us from the narrow picture that reigned for so long, and they enable us to reexamine both the roads not taken and the paths that were closed down by those who eventually came into power. How is that distant past relevant to the immediate future?

The *first* thing recent research on early Christianity reveals is how multifaceted it was. Among the various congregations scattered throughout the Roman Empire from Antioch to Gaul, there was no standardized theology, no single pattern of governance, no uniform liturgy, and no commonly accepted scripture. In faith all focused on Jesus, but there were decisive differences in interpretation. Some, especially around Jerusalem, emphasized the historical Jesus; others, the universal Christ; and still others, a mystical inner Christ. In organization, of course the older and more experienced members tended to guide the younger ones, but there was no clerical caste. In liturgy, all shared a common meal of bread and wine, prayers, and readings, but the patterns differed from place to place. All Christians were baptized, but the modes varied. All read what we now call the Old Testament, usually in its Greek version (the Septuagint), and other documents and letters that circulated among them, some of which eventually became part of the New Testament and some of which did not.

Yet, despite their dissimilarities, these widely dispersed congregations plainly felt a strong sense of unity. What bound them together, however, was not an organization or a hierarchy, and it was not a creed. Rather, it was a powerful confidence that they shared the same Spirit and were all engaged in the common enterprise of following Jesus and making his message about the coming of God's Reign of *shalom* known to the world. Thus, it is now clear that the "official Christianity" that eventually emerged was only one among a range of "Christianities" that thrived during the earliest years. The distinction we still make today between "orthodox" and "heretical" movements did not exist. There was nothing inevitable or preordained about which version, if any, would predominate. This, in turn, suggests there is nothing fated about how Christianity could develop in the third millennium. The most disturbing question is how the degeneration into hierarchy, imposed uniformity, imperial organization, and a standardized creed happened. We take that up in the next chapter.

The *second* key discovery about early Christianity critical for today is that what came to be called "apostolic authority" is a fiction invented considerably later. In the years immediately following Jesus's crucifixion, as more and more people joined the movement he had initiated, usually those who had known and followed him during his short career were respected as the leaders in the first congregations. But that was not always true. The most dramatic exception is Paul, who admitted he had never known Jesus "in the flesh." Rather, he had met the Risen Christ in a blinding mystical encounter on the road to Damascus. As a Jew and a Pharisee, trained to be a scholar of his people's tradition, Paul knew that a sure sign of the arrival of the long awaited messianic era would be that Gentiles would begin to enter the commonwealth of Israel, previously restricted to the "seed of Abraham." Paul also knew, even before his encounter on the Damascus road, that this ingathering was already beginning to occur. All over the empire, Gentiles—some no longer inspired by the pantheon, some repelled by the moral decay around them—had begun attending synagogues, attracted by the monotheism and the strict morality of the Jews. Paul taught that the mission of Jesus had been to break down the Jewish-Gentile barrier once and for all and that his own mission as the "Apostle to the Gentiles" was to make this message known to everyone.

Paul referred to himself as an "apostle," which means "messenger." Most important, as we look for the appearance of hierarchies and the claims to "apostolic authority" on which they were based, Paul never claimed that his authority derived from previous apostles. In fact, he often denied it. It came from his personal encounter with Christ. Further, he warned the congregations in his letters against granting such authority to any other apostle. He did not believe that the apostles should hold some unique kind of higher sway, but taught that the Spirit distributes among its members all the varied "gifts" a congregation needs. And he underscored time and time again that the greatest of these gifts was love. Again, we will return to this issue in a later chapter.[2]

But why, until recent years, has "apostolic authority" remained such an unexamined fixture? When I arrived at seminary, the teachers who taught about these formative decades, even though all were Protestants, emphasized both how early and how important it was. But they were wrong. What came to be called "apostolic authority" was not early. What happened, instead, was that, later on, the concept was read back into the earlier history. It was read back by those who, after the original apostles were dead, wanted to claim authority for themselves. The winners, or those who would eventually become the winners, were already at work rewriting the history very early on. When we realize that the idea of apostolic authority did not originate with the apostles, who themselves placed their confidence in the authority of the Spirit's presence among the people, this has major implications today for the future of global Christianity.

The *third* insight illuminated by the recent research on early Christianity has to do with the Roman Empire. It is now apparent that it was never merely the "background." In one way or another it preoccupied Christian thinking. The first Christians understood themselves as an essentially *anti-imperial movement,* one whose vocabulary, organization, and rituals created an *alternative* to those of the Roman Empire, whose imminent collapse they expected. This expectation is signaled in the book of Revelation:

> *Fallen, fallen is Babylon the great!*
> *It has become a dwelling place of demons,*
> *a haunt for every foul spirit, a haunt for every foul bird, . . .*
> *Alas, alas the great city, clothed in fine linen,*
> *in purple and scarlet,*
> *Adorned with gold, with jewels, and with pearls!*
> *For in one hour all this wealth has been laid waste!*
> *(18:2, 16–17)*

This is an invective against Roman rule, written probably around 120 CE by a man named John, living as a political exile on the craggy island of Patmos. "Babylon" here is a code word for the city of Rome, capital of the empire, where the emperors decked themselves out in purple and scarlet.

During the past century fundamentalists have made the imminent "end of the world" a central feature in their preaching. They insist we are living in the "last days" before the battle of Armageddon occurs and the universe itself dissolves in flames. The *Left Behind* series of novels spells out this scenario in grisly detail. But their plotline is a gross distortion of the biblical texts. For the early Christians, including John of the book of Revelation, what was about to end was the *imperial world* of Rome, not God's physical creation. Jesus had taught that God's Kingdom would come *on earth.*

Early Christianity was a fiercely anti-imperial movement, and for good reasons. Representatives of the Roman Empire had crucified Jesus, hounded his disciples, and sent the next generation of his followers into the arena with the wild beasts. But this anti-imperial attitude did not last very long. Gradually the empire came not only to surround the Christians; it got inside them. Christians from the more privileged classes first became enamored of the empire, and then became its fawning imitators. This often happens in situations of oppression. The victims first fear, then admire, and then sometimes emulate their persecutors. Some of the prisoners in Nazi concentration camps began to wear bits of their captors' uniforms and imitated their swaggering abuse of the inmates when they were accorded the shameful privilege of assisting guards.

Something like this seems to have seized certain leaders among the Christians, and it produced one of the most ironic reversals in history. Roman legionnaires had executed Jesus as a threat to the *imperium* when the pro-Roman crowds in Pilate's courtyard shouted, "We have no king but Caesar." The Palestinian rabbi had sparked a movement that threatened both the Roman rulers and their collaborators, the priestly elite in Jerusalem. Paul raced from city to city in the doomed empire establishing "assemblies" (the Greek word is *ekklesiai,* a political term meaning gatherings of citizens) that would be ready when "Babylon" collapsed and the Reign of God began. Christians called Jesus "Lord" (*kyrios*) and "peacemaker," both titles claimed by the Caesars.

By the late third century, however, some Christian leaders were casting envious eyes on the power and efficiency of the imperial bureaucracy and the authority of its military. In the fourth century, as the empire became nominally Christianized, the church also became imperialized, blurring the essence of Christianity almost beyond recognition. Not only did some Christians reverse their opposition to the empire; they allowed their religion to be used as an ideology to shore it up as it staggered toward decline. In short, all the alleged main features in the profile of early Christianity that I first learned—its unity, its apostolic authority, and its relationship to the empire—have proven to be far wide of the mark. In retrospect, all this now seems obvious. How could my own teachers have missed it?

Those teachers did their best by the lights they had, but they nonetheless succeeded in painting a highly distorted portrait. They were not aware of the diversity among the early Christians, the lateness of the invention of inherited apostolic authority, or the centrality of the empire. But it would be ungrateful of me to blame them for not teaching me what they could not possibly have known. They were simply passing on an old set of ideas for which there was little counterevidence at the time. Now, however, in the decades since I was a seminarian, that has changed. Four developments in historical research have radically altered our understanding of the first centuries of Christianity, producing the more accurate portrayal I have just described.

The *first* was triggered in 1946 when a young boy looking for some stray sheep chanced upon a whole library of ancient texts stashed in a cave near Nag Hammadi in Egypt. For some years these invaluable codices meandered through the hands of a series of shady middlemen and greedy antiquities dealers. The best known of the documents by far is the *Gospel of Thomas*, first published in 1959. When a consensus among scholars agreed that it was just as old as any of the gospels in the New Testament, maybe even older, it exploded a bombshell in early Christian studies. It undermined notions about a unified or uniform early Christianity. It meant the belief, which had lasted for centuries, that one could make a distinction between authentic and inauthentic, "orthodox" or "heretical" versions of early Christianity now had to be jettisoned. These distinctions had all been invented considerably later.

Some scholars contend that *Thomas* and the other texts need not be taken seriously, since they are all infected by "Gnosticism." But Karen King, in her book *What Is Gnosticism?* demonstrates that this term is so imprecise and contradictory that it is simply too vague to be of any use. There are similarities and differences between the various documents used by different early congregations. Many of these ancient works contain both passages that were later classified as "orthodox" and others later dismissed as "Gnostic." Of the Nag Hammadi texts she writes, "Whereas we might have expected these works to solidify the ancient distinction between orthodoxy and heresy, instead [they show] that distinct varieties of Christianity developed in different geographical areas, at a time when the boundaries of orthodoxy and heresy were not yet fixed."[3] King does not stop with these historical observations. She rightly points out how often the language of "orthodoxy" and "heresy" has been wielded by those in power (or seeking power) against those they wish to dominate or exclude and warns against using such language in "the increasingly pluralistic and multicultural globe we inhabit."[4]

The *second* new development, the one that exposed the myth of apostolic authority, was more the result of connecting dots than of the discovery of new sources. Until only a couple decades ago historians and New Testament scholars belonged to different circles and did not talk with each other enough. This was due in part to the traditional separation between ministers preparing for pastoral work in seminaries and faculties engaged in the historical study of religious antiquity. The assumptions on which the scholars in these fields proceeded differed from each other. After all, the books of the New Testament studied in seminaries were thought to be "inspired" or at least canonical, but the sources the historians worked with were not. The biblical scholars knew that neither Paul nor the other apostles had passed on any "apostolic authority," that they had in fact warned against it. But many historians understandably relied on ancient writers they still somehow thought of as "historians," even though they wrote on papyrus in the first few centuries. Twentieth-century scholars sometimes innocently accepted the portrayal of the "earliest Christianity" as it was framed by writers who lived immediately afterward, as though they were the somewhat roughhewn forerunners of modern historical scholars. After all, they must have known, since they lived close to the events they recorded.

But this is where the problem arose. As we have seen, these early Christian "historians" were neither critical nor neutral. They were not even historians. They were churchmen who aspired to become the leaders of the next generation of Christians. They were anything but disinterested, and they had an agenda that was not particularly hidden. Looking for a potent way to establish their own authority, they seized upon a very compelling idea. They claimed to have inherited their right to rule from the first disciples, and that they themselves possessed "apostolic authority," because they formed a part of what they began to call the "apostolic succession." This was a self-justifying fiction. But fiction calcified into fact and lasted for a long time. It was still in circulation when I first studied the history of Christianity. The undoing of this long-established fable only began when, so to speak, the historians and the biblical scholars began to have coffee together and both had to cope with the new evidence from Nag Hammadi. Comparing notes, they concluded that authority based on an alleged "apostolic succession" should be understood as an invention of later arrivals, and that authority in early Christianity was actually far more protean and diffuse.

Fortunately, the current generation of biblical scholars and the historians of early Christianity now drink coffee together more often. In fact, many of them are now the same people. Increasingly, scholars study both canonical and noncanonical texts, and both scrutinize the shards and grave inscriptions constantly being turned up by the archaeologists. The picture of early Christianity students now learn is a far different one from the one I heard about. But how much difference has that made?

Unfortunately, once they are established, some myths—especially myths that give certain people power over others—often survive for a long time after convincing evidence against them is widely known. This is the case with apostolic authority and succession, which still provide the basis for governance particularly (but not only) in the Roman Catholic Church. Like Wile E. Coyote in the "Road Runner" cartoons, who continues to walk out onto the air after he has come to the edge of a cliff, rulers in many realms, not just the religious one, continue to wield their scepters long after the myths supporting their authority have been cut away. I saw this in action during a conversation I once had with Pope Benedict XVI when he was still Cardinal Joseph Ratzinger. I return to this informative chat in a later chapter.

The *third* development that came after my seminary days and that has made a crucial difference in our knowledge of the Christianity of the first few centuries, is the emergence of what is called "people's history." The thrust of this method is straightforward: most of what we have usually called "history" has actually concerned itself with the elites and the leaders, not the vast majority of ordinary people. This is especially true of most histories of the first two or three centuries of Christianity. They have focused on the theologians who wrote the treatises and the bishops who argued about questions of authority and have therefore presented a truncated, indeed mutilated, "history" that leaves out 95 percent of those who actually constituted the Christian movement.

To help correct this long-standing misrepresentation, "people's history" widens the scope of investigations to include not only documents, but games, toys, graffiti, inscriptions on coffins, what we can learn from dishes, house furnishings, and plates, and even the detritus from ancient garbage pits, where archaeologists now say some of the juiciest bits of evidence can be exhumed. When combined with what can be learned about the first Christian centuries from studies of tax law, prostitution (Jesus talked about both taxes and prostitution a lot), and the organization of the Roman military, a much fuller sketch appears.

For example, although the bishops of the early church may have become progressively more fawning toward the empire, there are serious questions about whether the common people shared their sycophancy. Just as the bishops were increasing their support, revolts were breaking out all over the realm. Maintaining a far-flung army required higher and higher taxes, and people found more and more clever ways to avoid paying them. Laws were difficult to enforce. Tribal peoples from the north, whom the Romans called "barbarians," streamed in. The emperors were overthrown and replaced. The paradox, of course, is that when the ship of state, like Melville's *Pequod,* eventually sank beneath the waves, the church, like Queequeg's coffin, bobbed to the surface. The papacy eventually became, as philosopher Thomas Hobbes (1588–1679) once wrote, "nothing other than the ghost of the deceased Roman Empire, sitting crowned upon the grave thereof." The result of this rediscovery of the church's complex relationship with the empire is, as we will see in a subsequent chapter, that Christians who constitute the new majority in the global South have become highly wary of their relationship to today's world empires.

In addition to missing the contribution now made by "people's history," there is another reason why my own teachers missed the centrality of empire in early Christian history. Their blind spot was the result of an old, if impossible, American axiom: "Do not mix religion with politics." They favored a Jesus who was a strictly "religious" figure, albeit badly misunderstood, they said, by some of his contemporaries as a dangerous subversive. They told us that the early Christians had utterly no interest in earthly politics, but lived in daily expectation of a "second coming" that would either lift them from this sordid world or bring heaven down to earth. They attributed the persecution and execution of Christians to attacks by rival "religions," such as the Jewish priests, pagan rulers, and the custodians of the emperor cult. The mostly unspoken implication was that, although Christianity in our day might indeed have social, even perhaps political, "implications," these were decidedly secondary to its primary spiritual mission

Actually, however, Jesus's enemies understood him all too well. He was, in truth, a real threat to the empire. What my teachers misunderstood is that the separation we make today between "religion" and "politics" is a modern conceit. It did not obtain in first-century Palestine. Religion was political, and politics were religious. When Jesus told his disciples to pray for the coming of God's Kingdom "on earth as it is in heaven," it was all too evident to the current rulers that, if this really were to happen, they would be displaced. The "world" that would end would be their Roman world. The imperial officials in Jerusalem and their local collaborators did not make a mistake when they executed Jesus as a subversive. He was one, and—from their perspective—they took the necessary measures.

We have already indicated how the biblical book of Revelation should be read as an anti-Roman diatribe. But as scholars today become more aware of this anti-imperial quality in early Christianity, it has helped explain some other puzzling parts of the New Testament. For example, generations of biblical teachers have overlooked the fact that, in the famous account in the Gospel of Mark of Jesus freeing a young man from demons, the collective name of those demons is "legion," which everyone who originally heard the story would have recognized as a squadron of occupying Roman troops. Both the boy and their homeland were occupied by foreign bodies from which they needed to be liberated. Earlier teachers had not noticed the symbolism in the fact that the exorcised demons invade a herd of pigs, who then hurl themselves over a cliff to destruction, but the Jewish peasants of Galilee did not eat pork, but raised swine only for sale to the troops. This is only one example of how the lens of empire studies is helping us to understand the Bible better.

The execution of Jesus did not end the threat. During the next decades his movement, now including both Jews and Gentiles and spreading rapidly throughout the known world, continued to pose a danger to the empire. The practice of "horizontal" and reciprocal sharing of financial resources among the nascent Christian assemblies undercut the top-down patronage pyramid through which the Romans cemented their influence. The Christian refusal to participate in the emperor cult was persecuted not because it was "religious," but because it was treasonous. Doing obeisance at the altar of the divine emperor, far from a merely symbolic gesture, was the key ritual of the ideology through which Rome ruled. It is undeniable that from the outset Christianity was both anti-imperial and counterimperial. Why, then, did so many thoughtful scholars allow the modern democratic concept of church-state separation to color their reading of ancient history?

This happened because the separation of religion from politics, which began in the late eighteenth century, not only became an integral element of the modern mind; it also became a lens through which modern scholars viewed other eras. A product of the Enlightenment and the modern revolutions, it sank in as a mainstay of the modern mentality. But our newly clarified understanding of the deeply antagonistic relationship of earliest Christianity to empire and then its subsequent embrace of that empire is important for Christianity today for two reasons.

First, the two eras bear a striking similarity. Again today, as in those first centuries, Christians live in a culturally polyphonic world in which their faith is spreading rapidly. Like then, some Christians now live at the center of a powerful empire (the American one); others, on its edges. The comparative study of empires allows us to comprehend better the convoluted process by which an anti-imperial movement degenerated into the religious ideology of the very empire it had opposed, and how, contrary to the equalitarian practice of Jesus, the church imposed an imperial structure on itself. Consequently the early history serves as a cautionary tale. It warns us to be aware of analogous tendencies today in which Christian rhetoric and American imperial interests can be so easily blended.

Second, the question of how empires shape the institutions within them is of special concern today. A recent book by Harvard historian Charles S. Maier, *Among Empires,* provides an excellent example. He observes that empires, whether Roman or Mogul, British or American, use similar methods to control their subjects. That method is a combination of military might, either used or threatened, and cultural domination, through education, religion, language, and– especially in the American case—popular culture. The most telling point in Maier's analysis, however, is that empires all tend to spread their pyramidal-hierarchical pattern into all the institutions within their orbit. People not only live within empires; the empires live within them. Maier carefully documents how empires by nature tend to transform grassroots institutions into their own top-down image. They "[extend] their gradients of privilege and participation outward through space and downward into society. . . . They replicate their hierarchical structures and their divisions at all spatial levels, macro and micro—at the level of community and the workplace as well as the continent. . . . All recapitulate the structure of the whole."[5] This tendency to replicate the structure of empire helps explain why so much of the Christian movement, which began as the persecuted victim of the Roman Empire and provided an alternative to it, then became an obsequious mimic of that empire and finally its compliant acolyte.[6]

These, then, are the three alterations that inform the way we now see Christian history—its polymorphic variety; its disparate patterns of authority; and the fact that its leaders, if not its ordinary people, first defied but then succumbed to the empire. These insights can widen the options Christianity has as it enters the twenty-first century, an era that in several ways bears a remarkable resemblance to its first centuries. The more accurate account of "how it was then" is a result not only of historical research, but of the biblical studies and theologies of those who have not been as shaped by the Western worldview. Liberation theologies and feminist biblical studies in particular have questioned the assumptions of modern scholarship and drawn a more reliable portrait of Christian origins. We return to this in a later chapter, but before we do, we need to take a more careful look at just *how* the descent from theological variety to inflexible orthodoxy, from spiritual fellowships to "apostolic" authoritarianism, and from an anti- to a pro-imperial stance took place.

CHAPTER 5

The People of the Way

The Devolution from Faith to Belief

Christianity erupted into history as a movement of the Spirit, animated by faith—by hope and confidence in the dawning of an era of *shalom* that Jesus had demonstrated and announced. This "Reign of God" would include both Jews and Gentiles. The poor would be vindicated, the outsiders brought within. For nearly three centuries the Age of Faith thrived. Then, however, in a relatively short time, faith in this inclusive new Reign faded, and what had begun as a vigorous popular movement curdled into a top-heavy edifice defined by obligatory beliefs enforced by a hierarchy.

Theologians from a range of different backgrounds have tried for years to explain how and why this degeneration set in and have suggested a number of different diagnoses. Protestant Reformer Martin Luther (1483–1546) thought that what he called the "fall of the church" coincided with the rise of the papacy. Other Reformers suspected it had set in much earlier. The sixteenth-century Anabaptists held that Christians had taken a fatal wrong turn when, under Constantine and his successors, they began to become soldiers. Some of the first Quakers thought that the misstep took place when the scriptures were written down, thus stifling the free flow of the Spirit. Greek and Russian Orthodox theologians date the deviation at about 1000 CE, when the Roman Catholic Church accelerated its dismissive attitude toward the Eastern Church, culminating in the pope's excommunication of the Orthodox patriarch of Constantinople in 1054. Catholics of course hold a more benign view of the Age of Belief. They contend that what troubles there were began with the early "heresies," which persisted throughout the medieval period and culminated in the Reformation. Nearly everyone, however, agrees that at some point something went quite wrong.

The current rediscovery of early Christianity sheds some light on these disputes. The picture that is now emerging indicates that a big change began in small ways within a few decades after the life of Jesus and congealed into a permanent pattern in the late third and early fourth centuries, when Christian leaders began erecting hierarchies and then fabricating creeds and requiring their people to accept them. After that, composing creeds quickly became a habit—some would say an addiction—and has continued ever since, laying the foundation for all later Christian fundamentalisms. Throughout the early medieval period creeds were churned out on a regular basis, as were the bitter feuds they engendered. During the Protestant Reformation of the sixteenth century, church leaders were still formulating conflicting confessions and contradictory statements of belief. As recently as 1950, Pope Pius XII enunciated a dogma, the Assumption of the Virgin Mary, which all Catholics were henceforth to hold. Today Protestant fundamentalists still clutch lists of beliefs they insist are nonnegotiable and without which one cannot be a true Christian. In the years of the Age of Belief, the net result of this compulsive creed creating was that the hope for a different world that had enlivened early Christianity faded. Catholic theologians identified the Kingdom of God with their church. Many Protestants pushed it into an afterlife. Meanwhile, mandatory belief systems nearly eclipsed faith and hope.

Some scholars excuse the craze for creed making as a necessary adjustment the expanding Christian movement had to make as it spread through the Roman world. It certainly was an adjustment, but was it a necessary one? Was something essential lost in the process? Without engaging in imaginative how-it-might-have-been-different historical fiction, it is nonetheless important to notice where certain choices were made, mainly to be able to think more clearly about future possibilities.

Creeds are products of their times. They are road markers of key points in Christian history. They provide invaluable indices of how some Christians, though not all, responded to largely internal disputes in the past. But to make "believing" them a permanent feature of Christianity today misunderstands the invaluable function they can serve. The numerous creeds theologians have devised over the centuries enable us to glimpse the historical challenges they faced. But their circumstances and ours are not the same. Only by seeing them for what they are, landmarks along the long path Christianity has trod and not walled barriers, can they help us face current difficulties and opportunities.

The other question about creeds is whether they should be taken literally or understood as poetry. Roman Catholic theologian Stephen C. Rowan in his book on the Nicene Creed holds that only when the creeds are appreciated as metaphor and poetry can they can serve a useful purpose today. Poetry, he says, is not a *less* exact, but a *more* exact form of language, and we have to learn to "read symbolic language symbolically." He admits this is hard to do in what he rightly calls a "prosaic world," a literalistic culture in which the voice of the poetic muse has almost been tuned out.[1] Sadly, Christianity itself has also been afflicted by the tone-deafness of literalism. The main feature of Protestant fundamentalism is its literalism. Thus when the creeds are understood as factual descriptions of God and Christ and people are still supposed to "believe" them, they become obstacles to faith rather than aids. Maybe the only way to preserve the real value of creeds today is to sing them, as was often done in the past, to dance them, or to print them in iambic pentameter. As the apostle Paul writes, "The letter kills, but the Spirit gives life" (2 Cor. 3:6).

Taken literally, creeds continue to constitute more of a hindrance than a help to Christian faith. They keep people stalled in the obsolete Age of Belief. But there are signs that they are becoming less important every day. Our "post-Christian" era is becoming more like the first century than like the many centuries of creed-making "Christian civilization" that followed. Rick Warren, the influential evangelical pastor of Saddleback Church in Orange County, California, says that what the church needs now is a "second Reformation," one based on "deeds, not creeds."[2] Poetry, drama, and dance are finding their way back into the sanctuary. This may be why an enlivened liturgy of Holy Communion is returning to many churches.

A few years ago, drawn by curiosity, a totally "unchurched" young woman named Sara Miles wandered into St. Gregory's Episcopal Church in San Francisco. She must have arrived late, because just as she stepped in, Communion was being served. She watched for a moment, then on sheer impulse decided to receive the bread and wine. Something she finds impossible to describe in prose happened. Despite the fact that she distinctly disliked the creeds and the "mumbling liturgy," she felt drawn to return again and again. Soon she began organizing a food pantry for homeless and hungry street people, gathering in the sanctuary and using the altar as the table. Within a short time two hundred fifty people crowded in each time and Sara enlisted first church members, then the street people, to help prepare and serve the meals. Without knowing much about early church history, she was in fact reestablishing a practice in early Christianity in which—as scholars now agree—the poor were also fed at the Lord's Supper.[3] Sara Miles's experience demonstrates that it is important to remember what the Christian movement was like in those first "precreedal" centuries, to notice how the devolution into what might be called "competitive creedalism" took place, and—most important—to recognize how the earlier precreedal practice is now returning.

During its first years people called the movement that had begun with Jesus and his disciples "the Way." Jesus himself was addressed as the one who taught "the way of God in truth" (Matt. 22:16). Those who followed him were described as walking the "way of peace" (Luke 1:79) and "the way of truth" (2 Pet. 2:2). When Paul started to Damascus to arrest the Christians there, he was equipped with warrants, "so that if he found any who belonged to the Way, men or women, he might bring them bound to Jerusalem" (Acts 9:2). This was the original usage, but it is significant, because we use the word "way" today when, for example, we speak of a "way of life." During the first two centuries, a period of unparalleled growth and vigor, the only "creed" Christians had was not an inventory of beliefs. It was a straightforward affirmation: "Jesus Christ is Lord," which was more like a pledge of allegiance. It meant, "I serve Jesus, not some other sovereign." This also meant Christians placed loyalty to Jesus above loyalty to Caesar, which eventually stirred up fateful trouble. But the dispute was not about a clash of creeds; it was about a clash of loyalties. It was about two different ways of life.

During the first two and a half centuries of its life, the nascent Christian movement ("the Way") flourished despite periodic persecutions and did so without relying on theological agreement. What we now call doctrines or dogmas, let alone creeds, were yet to appear. Historians of that period agree that what bound Christians together in their local congregations was their common participation in the life of the Spirit and a way of living that included the sharing of prayer, bread, and wine; a lively hope for the coming of God's *shalom* on earth; and putting the example of Jesus into concrete practice, especially his concern for outcasts. With regard to theological questions, opinions differed widely. In other words, in this most vibrant period in Christian history, it was *following* Jesus that counted; there were no dogmas to which one had to adhere, and a rich variety of theological views thrived. It was the era of a thousand flowers blooming, and the idea of "heresy" had not yet stepped onstage.

The time is ripe to retrieve the term "Way" for Christianity and "followers of the Way" for Christians. It is at once more accurate, more original, and more contemporary than "believers." It would reassure those people who are discouraged because they mistakenly assume that, whereas other religions are "ways of life," Christianity is about dogmas. This is a clear instance in which we can learn something vital from our first-century forebears. We need not assume that creedal Christianity is the only option. But how did the devolution from "the Way" to a system of beliefs take place?

It began during the explosive geographical expansion of the Jesus movement. Born in Palestine, it spread rapidly into the wider Mediterranean reaches of the Roman Empire and even beyond. It encountered a host of new challenges, and the first was a linguistic one. Jesus and his followers spoke in Aramaic and prayed in Hebrew, but now the movement found itself in a world in which Greek was the *lingua franca*. The message had to be translated. But translation is never simply a matter of making a more or less accurate rendering of what a word means. Different languages incorporate different views of the world, and the worldview of those in the Greek-speaking areas was different in important respects from that of those in Palestine. How soon this jarring change of linguistic gears had to take place becomes evident when we remember

that the entire New Testament, much of it written only a few decades after Jesus's life, is not in Jesus's native language, but in
Greek.

It was not, however, this new environment that lured some
Christians into fashioning creeds. There were other challenges the
young movement met in its widened scope. Among these was the
myriad of "new religions" that, along with Christianity, had swirled
into the empire from its eastern frontiers. Mithraism, for example,
which originated in Persia, centered its worship on the ritual
slaughter of a bull whose warm blood the priests spattered on
chanting adepts. It promised its followers an assurance of immortality and was especially popular among soldiers.

A few years ago I visited a Mithraeum (Mithraic worship center)
that had recently been discovered during some excavation under
the Church of San Clemente in Rome. Later I examined a fresco
from another Mithraeum in Marino on which Mithras is depicted
in a Phrygian cape, slaying the bull with his bare hands. A dog and
a serpent lick the bull's blood while a scorpion chews on its geni-
tals, evoking—even with its faded colors—a combination of fascination and repugnance two millennia later. The sheer rawness and
explicit violence of the picture at first seemed to explain why the
priests of Mithra and the military men who worshiped him refused to allow women to join. Of course, depictions of the crucifixion can be almost as grisly, but during these first centuries the
main Christian symbols were the fish and the "good shepherd."
Bloody renderings of the crucifixion appeared only after the conversion of Constantine, when Christians, who had refused military service until then, began to enlist as soldiers.

Some historians claim that Mithraism was Christianity's main
rival for over two hundred years. The emperor Julian, who sought
to restore the Roman pantheon and whom Christian historians
dubbed "the Apostate," was an initiate into the Mithraic mysteries.

But the cults of Isis and Osiris and of the Magna Mater (Great Mother) also flourished, as did other less widely known local shrines and household devotions. The empire was crawling with gods.

In this respect, the world Christians lived in during those first couple centuries, with different religions jostling each other, is noticeably similar to ours. Today, despite all predictions, God does not seem to be dead after all. Instead, we have witnessed, for good and ill, a global resurgence of the gods and goddesses. In America mosques and pagodas spring up next to churches and synagogues. All around the globe we see the revival of religions once considered moribund. Japanese prime ministers ostentatiously worship at Tokyo's Shinto Shrine. Kremlin rulers pray in restored gold-domed Orthodox churches. Islamic militants fight to replace regimes they detest in Egypt and Saudi Arabia with "Qur'anic" governments. In Myanmar, Buddhist monks in saffron robes lead street demonstrations against military rule. Some West Bank Jewish settlers demand that Israel become a Torah state. The world of the twenty-first century does not appear to be secular at all. In an uncanny way, it looks more like the one the first generations of Christians experienced than like the one ruled by a virtual Christian monopoly, at least in the West, during the intervening centuries.

There can be little doubt that many people who today feel a strong attachment to the life and message of Jesus become disenchanted, and sometimes even disgusted, with much of what historic Christianity became. Despite many glowing moments, it is often not a pretty picture. But the picture can be clarified when we notice both how much of that historic Christianity is a caricature of its essential core and that some of the liveliest and most promising Christian movements today are casting off this distorting crust.

Early Christianity, however, was not as concerned with the Mithra adepts and the Osiris devotees as it was with two other alternative religions. One was relatively new, the other one quite old. The new one was the recently devised cult of the emperor, in which Caesar was reverenced as a deity. This was what we might today call a "civil religion"; it had its holidays, processions, and holy sites throughout the empire. Adherence to it was required of all of the emperor's subjects, wherever they lived and whatever other deities they also worshiped. It was the religious and ideological mucilage that held the far-flung empire together.

The second alternative religion was classical "paganism," the worship of Zeus and Apollo, Juno and Dionysius, and their fellow Olympians, whose endless intrigues, lustful escapades, and blood rivalries so adroitly mirrored human foibles. By the time Christianity began to spread into their territory, many people had already recast the stories of these gods in a metaphorical manner. But the Olympian religion still continued to exert a powerful cultural and moral influence. Its advantage was that it could easily be melded with the emperor cult. If you already worshiped numerous gods, why not one more?

Christians developed two different strategies in their contest with these two rivals, the emperor cult and the pagan pantheon, but neither of them impelled Christianity toward formal doctrines and creeds. Regarding worship of the emperor, Christians responded with an unequivocal "no." They claimed that Jesus Christ was God's *kyrios* ("anointed one" in Greek), but since *kyrios* was one of the titles attributed to Caesar, they refused to participate in the imperial cult. They were willing to pray *for* the emperor and for his health, but they stubbornly refused to pray *to* him or offer ritual tribute. They recognized that one could not be a follower of Jesus while also honoring a rival to the loyalty their faith in him and his Kingdom required; therefore, "not even one pinch of incense on the imperial altar." This defiance of the political religion of the empire, which led their critics to brand them subversive, landed many of them in arenas with salivating lions. In our time, when fusing the cross with the flag has become so popular and religiously saturated nationalisms are on the rise around the world, the early Christian refusal to mix the two is a cautionary reminder.

Their enemies made a second accusation against the early Christians: They were cannibals who devoured human flesh. This charge obviously grew out of a misunderstanding of the words used in serving the Communion meal, which symbolizes the body and blood of Christ. But the words excited lascivious rumors especially among those who despised the Christians for other reasons. What is noteworthy, however, is that even though the Christians of course denied they were cannibals, they did not elaborate a doctrine of the "real presence" or the "transubstantiation," which they then expected other Christians to believe. These doctrines came much later and grew out of internal conflicts within the movement, not in response to canards from without.

The Christian response to classical Greek (by then also Roman) religion and the philosophies that emerged from it was much more nuanced. On the one hand, Christians claimed that Homer, Plato, and Aristotle had prepared the way for Christ. But they also insisted that since Christ had now come, although these great predecessors could still be appreciated, they had also been superseded. They also thought of other ways to include such classical ancestors in the new Christian story. Some taught that since Christ was the eternal *logos* (word or Spirit) of God, present in all ages, he had already spoken to the ancient sages, inspiring them as they wrote the *Symposium* or the *Nichomachean Ethics*. Others claimed that the Greek philosophers, and even Homer, must have been familiar with the Old Testament and that the good things they taught were

derived from Moses and the prophets. Christians often disagreed
with each other about the fine points of this ambitious ex post
facto adoption process. They argued, but they did not force their
views on each other. They coped with Greek philosophy, paganism, eastern cults and emperor worship, without resorting to
creeds.

Despite persecution, Christianity thrived. It continued to expand
geographically and soon comprised Visigoths, Greeks, Syrians,
Egyptians, and other people of widely disparate cultural and
ethnic backgrounds. Now some Christian notables saw a need for
creed making due not to threats from without, but to divisions
among the growing numbers of different kinds of people within.
This and the lure of money and power combined to transform
what was essentially a Spirit-guided movement of faith into a
"belief-demarcated" confederation.

In retrospect it is not hard to see how this happened. We have
noted that short summaries of basic Christian teachings began to
appear here and there in the third century, mainly to instruct new
members. But gradually Christian leaders began to stiffen them
into obligations. Today historians of the creeds often explain them
as fences, boundary markers delineating who was in and who was
out. However, a more appropriate metaphor would be "partitions."
A fence is constructed on the *outside* edges of the property. A par-
tition is something built *inside* a house, separating those who live
in it from each other. There is not a syllable in any of the early
creeds about Mithra or Zeus or Caesar. Without exception they
are worded not to proscribe outsiders, but to fence out fellow
Christians whose theological views were different. These Christians,
however, were now partitioned off, or more precisely, shown the
door. The era that welcomed what historians call "great differences
in theological speculation," what I have called the Age of Faith,
was ending. Further, not only were the creedal barriers directed

against brothers and sisters; they were, in retrospect, a painful example of overkill. They pushed out whole clusters of Christians, whole regions, and even eventually whole countries (like Armenia, the first Christian nation), because people differed on one or another point in one of the creeds.

Nearly everyone now agrees that much of this barricade building was mistaken. But there is a certain poignancy in watching the painful efforts of popes like John Paul II and a host of ecumenical organizations to build bridges to parts of the worldwide Christian family that should never have been fenced off in the first place. The seeds of hierarchy and of creeds as well as the temptation to power and the lure of money had undoubtedly begun to vitiate the Christian movement quite early. But these currents won the day when, in possibly the most fateful event in its entire history, the emperor Constantine embraced Christianity, and his successors later made it the official religion of the empire in the early fourth century. Now the "People of the Way" was becoming an ecclesial *imperium*, and beliefs were squeezing out faith. Before we can discuss how Constantine's corporate acquisition brought about this ruinous alternation, we must first step back and trace the tortuous pathway from the Roman cross on Calvary to the one the emperor ordered emblazoned on his soldiers' shields.

CHAPTER 6

"The Bishop Is Your High Priest and Mighty King"

The Rise of the Clerical Caste

When the World Council of Churches assembled in Canberra, Australia, in February 1991, few of the four thousand delegates expected the opening ceremony would ignite a tumult. But it did. When a young Korean female theologian entered accompanied by a procession of nineteen dancers with gongs, bells, and clap sticks, led by two Aboriginal dancers in body paint and loincloths, a gasp went up from the crowd. German bishops, American Methodists, and Orthodox prelates were learning, many for the first time, that the era of Euro-American churchly dominance was over. The Christianity of the future would be culturally, racially, and theologically heterogeneous.

Christianity in the first three centuries of its history faced a similar challenge. Like today, it was growing and spreading into a cacophonous range of cultures, each with its own customs, language, and religion. A plethora of different theologies and liturgies were budding, from Syria in the east to Spain in the west to the lands of the Gauls and the Goths in the north. This spectrum of variegation undoubtedly troubled those who prefer their religion tidier and more predictable. The *earliest* Christians did not handle the dissonance by trying to impose a uniform system of doctrines and rites. Instead, they welcomed a wide array of expressions and trusted that the Spirit, not a hierarchy or a creed, would maintain their unity in love.

In his authoritative book *Paul and His World*, New Testament scholar Helmut Koester shows in a chapter entitled "The Authority of the Spirit" that their life in the Spirit was the link that held the early congregations together. He demonstrates that Paul's letters should not be read as laying down theological formularies, but as ad hoc political and administrative advice to particular local churches. Paul had no interest in nurturing uniformity, but was mainly concerned that Jewish and Gentile followers realize they now all belonged to the same community, one that had come to birth with the descent of the Spirit at Pentecost, described in Acts of the Apostles: "And it shall come to pass, says God, that in the last days I shall pour out my Spirit on all flesh" (2:17).[1]

But within a few decades this effervescent diversity began to worry a new generation of Christian leaders. Eager for more standardized product, they began to argue that if this or that practice had not existed from the days of Matthew, Paul, and John, then it must be a deviation and therefore illegitimate. The same tactic is employed today by companies that insist you buy only the "original" brand-name commodity and "accept no substitutes." It is a time-tested technique. Even the Roman Catholic Church, which is accused by its Protestant and Orthodox critics of appending novelties over the centuries, takes pains to argue that at least the seeds of every innovation—from papal infallibility to the Assumption of the Virgin Mary—were already present in principle at the beginning. The same strategy is used by old-school Protestants, whose favorite epithet for those they disagree with is "modernists."

The logic seems straightforward: if it is not the original, if it was not there at the beginning, then it is spurious and illegitimate. But what happens when we discover that what those third- and fourth-century Christian purists labeled as innovations *were*, in fact, "there from the beginning"? James Robinson, one of the most respected scholars of early Christianity, says that in the period he studies the beliefs and practices were "variously understood and translated or transmitted." As he puts it, "There seems not yet to be a central body of orthodox doctrine distinguished from heretical doctrine. . . . To this extent the terms *heresy* and *orthodoxy* are anachronistic."[2] In short, both "apostolic authority," which was a self-reinforcing prejudice, and the true-because-original argument turn out to be without basis in actual history. But once established, such fictional inventions harden over time, until people come to believe they are true even when they are not.

The congealing does not take long. As early as the beginning of the third century, the Christian writer Tertullian (ca. 160–225) based his searing critique of those he called "heretics" (*De proscriptione hereticorum*) on the claim that what they taught *had not been present at the beginning*, and this allegation continued to serve as the proof positive others mounted against all "heretics," ancient or modern: they were "innovators." But now their case is no longer credible. What they condemned *had*, in fact, been there from the beginning. Chronologically the *Gospel of Thomas* is as "original" as Mark's gospel and may be even more "original" than the Gospel of John.[3] This realization is a troubling one for many. Some simply cannot accept the idea that there might be five, not four, "original" gospels. Some are troubled by the mystical theology of *Thomas*, which seems at odds with the other four. Still others are offended by the low view of women the text takes. Nevertheless, the discovery of *Thomas* opened the door to a refreshing new understanding of the first centuries of Christian life. What if today's Protestant fundamentalists and Catholic traditionalists are the real "modernists" and innovators?

I cannot blame my teachers either for the fact that I occasionally nodded off in a seminary class or that the undiscovered *Gospel of Thomas* still lay sleeping peacefully in a cool cave in the Egyptian desert. They could not have foreseen the dramatic discoveries that were soon to come. Today, however, we cannot avoid asking what the undercutting of the time-honored heresy/orthodoxy dichotomy means for a mottled and global Christianity and what the drastic transformation of all we know about the early Christians suggests for the future.

It is easy to see why a previous generation of teachers still talked so confidently about heresy and orthodoxy. But why, in addition to not connecting the dots to biblical studies, did they also so easily accept the now widely dismissed claims for early "apostolic authority"? Unfortunately, they put too much stock in what the ancient Christian writers had said, but that only raises another question. Why had those venerable figures, many of them bishops like Eusebius (275–339), painted this deceptive picture in the first place?

The reason has to do with the all too human obsession with acquiring and holding on to power. As Paul and Mark and the other original apostles began to die, their prestige and stature increased. Maybe this happened for the same reason that antique shops thrive or that a painter's canvasses command a higher price the moment after the artist dies. In any case, it did not take long for succeeding generations of those guiding in the Christian movement to devise the idea of an inherited "apostolic authority," even though the apostles themselves had never claimed to hand on any such authority. Nevertheless, these would-be leaders claimed that they themselves were the true successors of these first apostles and therefore should exercise the same authority they declared that those apostles had exercised.

Next, some of the new generation of leaders began to compose gospels and epistles and to guarantee their authority by attributing them to one of the now deceased apostles. These texts (some of them found in the same cave at Nag Hammadi) were not really written by Barnabas, Philip, Thomas, Mary Magdalene, and Judas, as their title pages claim, but they have become the favorite cover-story features of the drugstore magazines that are always on the lookout for breathtaking new religious gossip. Of course these "lost gospels" are, in a modern sense, forgeries. But forgery was not recognized in those days, and in any case they make fascinating reading. As New Testament scholar Elaine Pagels puts it, maybe they don't belong in the canon, but they don't belong in the wastebasket either. They are indispensable in helping us catch a glimpse of the Christian movement a hundred years or more after Christ, namely, when a spurious "apostolic authority" was already being invented and wielded, in some cases quite successfully.

One example illustrates this tactic well. It seems that across the Adriatic Sea from Rome, in the congregation in Corinth, the one to which Paul had written two of his letters, a youth rebellion had taken place. Some of the younger members had replaced the older ones and assumed leadership. The tiff may or may not have been a significant one in its own right. But when the congregation in Rome heard of it and then tried to do something about it, a letter was produced in about 96 CE, the *First Epistle of Clement,* that eventually became an important factor in the transition from the original, more egalitarian leadership style to the pattern of domination we have come to call a "hierarchy" (which means "rule by the holy").

First Clement urges the congregation in Corinth to reinstall the sacked elders, but the reasons it advances for this action are telling. It takes no position on whatever issue caused the rift. It has nothing to say about heresy, immorality, or false teachings. It never mentions a creed. It is solely concerned, rather, with who is to be in charge and why. Curiously, a mere seventy years after a detachment of Roman legionnaires had executed Jesus, it commends the example of the Roman army for its clear lines of authority and argues that only the displaced leaders in Corinth, who—it asserts—were the authentic successors of the apostles, had the right to rule. The subsequent deployment of this letter in other disagreements makes it a key marker in what was to happen later.

Naturally, ever since *First Clement* appeared, anyone who believes in a hierarchically governed church based on "apostolic authority" likes to exhibit it as evidence of how early these institutions began. And those who hold that the word of the bishop of Rome should carry a special kind of weight, even at some distance from the seven hills by the Tiber, like it even more.

But *First Clement* can be read in another way. If the Christians in Rome needed to persuade their Corinthian brothers and sisters about the prerogatives of those who considered themselves the successors of the apostles, clearly the Corinthians, at least the younger ones, did *not* adhere to this concept of authority at the time. As to the prerogatives of the bishop of Rome, the text itself does not indicate an author. It was only a later tradition that ascribed it to *a* bishop (there may have been more than one) named "Clement" in the Roman congregation. Later still, this same Clement was said to have been the fourth pope, the direct successor of Peter, whom Catholic teaching holds to have been the first bishop of Rome.

Still, *First Clement* made an impact, and some even wanted to include it in the New Testament. It eventually was not included, but Hans von Campenhausen, the leading expert on the history of ecclesiastical authority, summarizes its warnings to the Corinthians and its considerable influence as follows:

[The warnings] are not directed against heresy, nor do they have as their content religious or moral instruc-

> tions . . . which the elders are to uphold. Instead it is the
> system of elders as such which is created simply for the
> sake of order. . . . The protection of an express apostolic
> injunction . . . thus acquires a weight and significance
> which it has not hitherto possessed.[4]

Even though *First Clement* did not make it into the New Testament, it did mark a turning point, for it signals the emergence of
what would later become "canon law," and it contributes an essential element of what was later to be called the "apostolic succession." It is also important to underline, however, that what is on
the mind of the author(s) of *First Clement* is neither heresy nor
creeds, but simply *the question of who is on top*. The model of a
military command structure is coming to the fore. Already, at the
end of the first century, at least in some congregations, the early
Christian "fellowship of equals," which was never fully equal of
course, was beginning to evolve into a segmented pyramid. The
process was just beginning, but it foreshadowed events to come.
Establishing authority always entails establishing jurisdiction, and
eventually who is inside and who is outside would be determined
by a creed. With *First Clement* the train of Christianity had left the
station and was headed for Constantine's imperial church and the
Age of Belief that eventually produced Christian fundamentalism.

Still, as the Christian movement entered the second century, it
continued to thrive, sometimes in the face of severe persecution,
with a polyglot of theologies and numerous different styles of governance. In seminary, when we read the standard histories of that
turbulent period, I found many of the early church fathers fascinating, albeit a bit odd. I was intrigued, for example, by Ignatius
(d. 110), the bishop of Antioch, who declared that he looked forward eagerly to being a martyr and boasted that, if the wild beasts

were not hungry, he would urge them on. He was, in fact, eventually arrested and taken to Rome and martyred, but whether the lions were hungry is not part of the historical record.

Another intriguing theologian of the time, Irenaeus of Lyons (ca. 142–200), leaped into a currently feverish argument about how many gospels of the dozens then in circulation should be included in the New Testament canon. He advanced a creative line of reasoning. There must be four, he concluded, since there had been four faces in the vision of Ezekiel: a man, a lion, an ox, and an eagle (1:10). Although his logic may appear a little out of the ordinary today, he won his case. Not only are there only four gospels in the New Testament, but for centuries after him pilgrims and tourists have learned from their guidebooks to recognize these symbols as the ensigns of Matthew (an angel), Mark (a lion), Luke (an ox), and John (an eagle), usually without knowing their origin.

Ignatius and Irenaeus had definite ideas of how the young Christian congregations should be governed. Both authoritarians, they were hardly advocates of participatory democracy. Still, they respected the remarkable diversity of the churches and did not try to enforce any standardization. Despite their colorful lives and courageous deaths, however, their influence ultimately plunged Christianity farther down the slope toward creed and hierarchy. They were both complicated figures. The standard textbooks credit them for strengthening the early church to fight "heresy" by solidifying its hierarchical structure. But this is only part of the story.

Ignatius, himself a bishop, emphasized the sovereignty of the bishop's office. And Irenaeus took the next momentous step—combining the idea of the centrality of the bishop with apostolic succession. For my teachers, again, this seemed to have been a steady, indeed almost inevitable, development. But when one re-reads these venerated writers against the backdrop of the highly variegated Christianity we now know existed in the second century, they can be interpreted in a different way. There is no doubt that Ignatius embraced a strictly autocratic view of how a congregation should be governed. He would have little patience with today's congregational meetings or parish councils. But, despite all his emphasis on the bishop as the sole leader, he also insisted that the unity of the congregation in love was of uppermost importance. Further, he never suggested he wished to impose a uniformity of belief on all Christians everywhere. He was concerned only about how individual congregations should be led.

For his part, although Irenaeus was even less the democrat than Ignatius and argued for an even more exalted view of apostolic authority, he was firmly opposed to excluding anyone, even "false prophets," from the congregation. His writings also indicate that Ignatius noticed the beginnings of short statements of beliefs, proto-creeds, in congregations here and there, but he was not troubled by the differences among them. He saw no need for a universal binding creed. Still, by making apostolic succession the basis for the power of the bishops, he launched a practice that is still operative today, a fact driven home to me by my *tête-à-tête* with Cardinal Ratzinger (see Chapter 8).[5]

Clearly what most worried these leaders of local congregations was not "heresy." Rather, it was those members of their flocks who continued to have visions and dreams, who felt God or the Spirit was speaking directly to them. Today we call such people "charismatics." There are millions of them in Pentecostal churches and in other churches as well, all over the globe. At that time they were called "prophets," but they were hardly a new problem. They were evidently already among the people Paul wrote to, but, like Irenaeus, Paul did not want them to be shown the door. He just reminded them that he, Paul, had also had heavenly visions and could also "speak in tongues" with the best of them. He insisted, however, that all such gifts and prophecies had to be subsumed under the law of love.

Neither Paul, Ignatius, nor Irenaeus solved the "pentecostal" problem. The tensions between ecstasy and order, between spiritual freedom and group cohesion, between mystics and administrators have persisted for the full two thousand years of Christian history. They show no sign of abating. Mystics always make prelates nervous, but it seems they are always with us. They have appeared and reappeared both within the Catholic Church and around its edges every century, sometimes to be banished, sometimes to be burned at the stake, and other times (after they are safely dead) to be canonized. Today, Pentecostals, whom sociologist Margaret Poloma aptly calls "main street mystics," are by far the fastest-growing sector in world Christianity, and the ebullient worship of these "holy rollers" still upsets the more staid denominations.[6] They are a living example of a new Age of the Spirit. Their animated worship and concern for the downtrodden and left-out people of the world provide a portrait of the current period's transition out of the Age of Belief. We will return to them in subsequent chapters.

Also within today's Roman Catholic Church a vigorous Pentecostal-like "charismatic" movement is growing in many places in the world, while bishops and popes watch apprehensively. But the issue today, as it was in the early church, is not about creed or belief. It was, and is, about order, an appropriate chain of command. Pentecostals and charismatics claim that the Holy Spirit speaks to them directly, without intermediaries. Naturally this worries the supporters of hierarchies, and since the defenders of order are by definition better organized than those they are trying to bring into line, they usually, at least temporarily, come out—literally—on top. It is they who make the rules and write the books. This is clearly what was happening in the second and third centuries, so we have to read Ignatius and Irenaeus remembering that their

Christianity was only one variety among several that were abroad at the time. It was the one they were establishing and advocating. But there were others, and today's followers of Jesus do not have to be restricted only to theirs.

During the third century, the trends that propelled Christianity from a loose network of local fellowships with no uniform creed, polity, or ritual toward a clerically dominated multinational corporation gained speed. As in any such conglomerate today, the leaders at the time increasingly demanded what they thought of as quality control and brand recognition. These trends were largely the work of a new clerical aristocracy, made up of bishops who asserted that they held the authority of the original apostles and constantly enlarged their powers until ordinary laypeople were almost entirely excluded from responsibility.

One particularly ominous expression of this seizure of power is a document that appeared in Syria sometime in the third century called the *Didascalia Apostolorum*. I still remember puzzling over this rambling text in a seminar. It is alleged to have been written by the original apostles, which, as scholars without exception today agree, it surely was not. The document exalts the bishops to nearly absolute power over the laity and bestows on them something close to semidivine status. It instructs laity that the bishop is "your high priest, teacher, mediator and, next to God, your father, prince and governor. He is your mighty king. Let him who rules in God's place be given by you like honor. . . . [He] has received from God power over life and death."[7] This is a long way from Jesus washing his disciples' feet and assuring them that they should refer to each other and to him as "friends." It also seems a large step away from Paul's warning the members of a congregation that the head should not lord it over the feet.

The celebrated third-century theologian Origen of Alexandria (185–254) also added his considerable weight to the inflation of the power of bishops. When I read Origen in seminary, I found him an absorbing, but somewhat pathetic figure. He was said to be the first genuine "theologian" in Christian history, and since I nurtured ambitions about becoming a theologian, that impressed me. But Origen lived a terribly sad life. His Christian father was martyred in 202, so he had to provide for his mother and six younger brothers. He was so avid about remaining chaste that, at least according to the fourth-century historian Eusebius, he castrated himself. He too praised martyrdom, but when his turn came, in 250, he was not killed; he was imprisoned and tortured. He never fully recovered.

Origen thought of himself as a very orthodox, very "catholic" theologian, but even though he is still hugely respected today, his ideas would hardly pass muster now in the Vatican's Congregation for the Doctrine of the Faith. For example, he did not hold that the Son was in every way equal with the Father, so—had he been present at the Council of Nicaea, eighty years after his death—he would certainly have been deemed a heretic. He held a somewhat spiritualized view of the Resurrection, which prevents him from being what American fundamentalists consider a "real Christian." He thought, like present-day Mormons, that souls were preexistent and believed, like Nietzsche (and Hindus), that history moves in cycles. He also held that no one was ever eternally lost and that even Satan would one day be redeemed. Except for the fact that he lived eighteen hundred years ago, Origen might very well qualify as a "New Age" thinker.

Still, for all his intellectual creativity and the free-wheeling character of his reflections, Origen cemented another brick into the battlements of a creed-bound, hierarchical church. Although he rightly worried about the possibility of bishops abusing their divine authority, he nevertheless warned people that they were required to obey even unjust bishops. After all, their ordination had imbued them with an inviolable sacred quality that placed them on a higher plane.

Cyprian (d. 258), another third-century theologian, pushes the clericalization process a step farther. Born into a wealthy pagan family in Carthage, upon his conversion to Christianity he sold all his goods and gave the money to the poor. Eventually selected bishop of Carthage, he became an exemplary leader of his flock through trying times. During the persecution under the emperor Valerian he was beheaded in 258 CE. Sadly, however, Cyprian's view of the power of bishops widened the class cleavage in the church and further decimated the role of the laity. Recalling Paul's repeated calls for unity and concord within the congregations, Cyprian in his *De Catholicae Ecclesiae Unitate*, gave the idea a new twist that would have surprised Paul. He stated that what was essential for Christian unity was unity *among the bishops*. Hence it was no longer the men and women within the congregations or even those in all Christian congregations who should love one another. The implication is that they may not be capable of it. Rather, it is the bishops who should love one another, since they now represent the whole Christian community.

Cyprian's equation of the "church" with the clergy has lasted a long time. Until quite recently, when people spoke of "entering the church," it meant becoming a clergyman. Not until the Second Vatican Council (1962–65) did the Roman Catholic Church modify its language to refer to the *whole* church as the "People of God," but that message has yet to modify popular ideas about what the "church" is. In any case, by the end of the third century, the earlier more egalitarian fellowships were fading into a dim memory, and the imperial version of Christianity—with its princes and monarchs above and its common folk below—had won the day, at least among the elites.

The parody of Christianity that took shape in the fourth century was not only a radical subversion of the teaching of Jesus and the apostles, albeit carried out in their name. It also resulted in an equally radical subversion of the original meaning of the word "faith." Students of the history of language know that changing contexts alter the meaning of words, and this is what happened to the word "faith." Along with the "imperialization" of the church and the glorification of the bishops, now "faith" came to mean *obeying the bishop and assenting to what he taught.* Faith had been coarsened into belief, and this distortion has hobbled Christianity ever since.

But the worst was yet to come. The skid from faith to belief, from trusting *in* God to assenting to propositions *about* God, was now under way, at least among the bishops. The stage was set for the denouement, when under Constantine and with the bishops' fawning compliance the church and the empire would, in effect, amalgamate. The consequence of this ancient corporate merger would be the strenuous attempt of the emperor and the bishops to enforce a common creed: "This is what you *must* believe."

CHAPTER 7

Constantine's Last Supper

The Invention of Heresy

On February 17, sometime around the year 280 CE, a baby was born in the town of Naissus in Macedonia and given the name Flavius Valerius Constantinus. The circumstances of his birth and upbringing differed completely from those of another child born some two hundred and fifty years earlier in Bethlehem of Judea. Still (with the exception of the apostle Paul), Flavius—known to history as Constantine the Great—exerted an influence on Christianity second only to that of Jesus. The Macedonian child was the eldest son of Constantius I by his first wife, Helena. However, instead of fleeing to Egypt from a cruel king, as Jesus and his parents had to do, the youthful Constantine grew up in the palace. He had been placed in the royal court of the emperor Diocletian when his father attained the title of Caesar, and he probably witnessed the brutal persecution of Christians that took place in 303 CE.

As a young man he became a skilled military commander and led the Roman battalions in Gaul where, when his father died, his troops proclaimed him the new emperor. Back home in Rome, however, another claimant, one Maxentius, also craved the purple. To buy off Constantine, he offered him the chance to be emperor of Gaul. This was not enough for the ambitious young warrior, however, so he marched his troops back to Italy and defeated

Maxentius's armies in battle after battle. Eventually, with the culminating confrontation at the Milvian Bridge, Maxentius was killed,
and Constantine marched into Rome at the head of his victorious
legions to become the sole emperor.

Except for one incident, the battle at the Milvian Bridge would
have been relegated to a historical footnote, just one more in the
endless inventory of bloodlettings spattered across Roman history.
However, according to the Christian historian Eusebius, who was
also the emperor's fervent admirer, Constantine claimed many years
later that just before the battle he had seen a cross in the sky. It was
fashioned, he claimed, out of a long spear with a transverse bar
emblazoned with the words "In this sign conquer." Constantine,
the story goes, instructed his troops to stencil this emblem on their
weapons, and he won the battle. As emperor, he then decreed that
the cross, crowned with a triumphal laurel garland, should become
the imperial standard.

Constantine did not describe this episode until decades later,
and the account carries the overtones of campaign boiler plate.
The Romans had always believed that invoking the gods was the
only way to assure victory in war and that the most powerful deity
would win. Constantine obviously believed this. Hardly a mono-
theist, he continued to venerate both the god of chance, Tyche, and
the sun god, Helios, along with the Christian God, and he never
bothered to be baptized until he was on his deathbed. Not quite an
exemplary Christian, he was undoubtedly responsible for the
murder of both his son and his mother. What can we conclude
about his "conversion"? Was it cynical expediency? Was he merely
opportunistic, just a canny politician? Or did he experience a genuine personal epiphany? Perhaps he just came to think that the
God of the Christians was more potent than the other deities and
therefore a useful ally in his endless wars. No one will ever know.

By and large Christian historians have either eulogized Constantine for seeing the light and refashioning a pagan empire into a Christian one or reviled him for corrupting a pure religion. My own view is that both verdicts focus too heavily on the emperor. Whether it was a love marriage or a mutual seduction, plainly both parties entered into it freely. If the liaison between church and empire was some kind of unnatural act, at least it was consensual, but a large share of the fault lies with the hierarchs of the Christian community, who had become infected with what a psychoanalyst might term "empire envy." They coveted the potency imperial officials, especially in the army, wielded over those in their charge. They calculated that by allowing themselves to be merged into the empire, maybe they could benefit from that kind of clout as well.

As for Constantine himself, whatever the depth or shallowness of his piety, he acted for an understandable *raison d'etat*. For the Romans, the main purpose of religions (the word literally means "bonds") was to hold a people together. Religion provided social cement, and as the older religions declined, Constantine—always a realist—saw the need for something to take their place. He knew little about Christianity, but he knew—or thought he knew—what he, and his empire, needed.

Obviously we will never uncover exactly what went on in Constantine's mind, but the results of his actions are clear. Suddenly Christianity was no longer just one religion among many in the empire. True, the other religions remained legal during his lifetime and—some historians claim—never really disappeared. Now, however, the religion of the Galilean was the chosen favorite of the emperor, and soon of the empire. The opportunistic wave of "conversions" this stunning reversal in imperial policy produced is easy to imagine. The cross, which had once functioned as an instrument of torture on which a Roman brigade had executed a radical Jewish rabbi and was then one of the signatures of a harassed and persecuted minority (another was the fish), now festooned the shields of the successors of the same imperial troops who had carried out the execution on Calvary.

The cross symbol also soon attained popularity among the upper classes, which hastily aligned themselves with the emperor's new religion. Beginning in the middle of the fourth century crosses with laurel crowns began to appear on sarcophagi, often fixed to a cruciform imperial standard. Then, when Constantine's mother, Helena, made her famous pilgrimage to the Holy Land and returned with a chunk of wood she believed was a piece of the "true cross," what had once been one symbol among others of Christianity now became its principal emblem. It has remained so ever since.

In order to learn something from the fateful events of the fourth century, it will be necessary to move beyond either bashing Constantine or deriding submissive bishops. Constantine knew what he was doing. As for the Christian leaders, obviously they had their motives as well. It must have been a relief to have an emperor who—if only for his own reasons—colluded with them instead of feeding them to the lions. But there were other factors at work as well. Many today are unaware that Constantine not only pronounced himself to be a convert to Christianity; he also made himself its principal patron and chief administrator. Further, he let it be known that, according to his personal theology, God had given him a special place in history—he was not just to rule the empire, but to govern the church as well. At least one part of Constantine's logic is clear. Rulers, whether religious or secular, always want to find or concoct an ideology that will unite their realm. Constantine was no different, and many Christian bishops at the time were all too happy to cooperate. This was where the influence of money and power as principal factors in promoting creed making and in congealing faith into belief came in.

As patron-in-chief of Christianity, Constantine had vast sums of cash to disperse in order to sustain the church's charitable work, maintain its buildings, and—not incidentally—support its clergy. But to whom, exactly, should this money go, and in what amounts? Christians, who had formerly scratched for contributions from their members and an occasional wealthy patron, now found to their gratification that the trough was brimming over. The elbowing and shoving to belly up to it may have been unsightly, but it was understandable, and it was always tempting to push closer by casting aspersions on a rival bishop's credentials or character or the soundness of his views. The situation proved ripe for internal wrangles when another concern of Constantine, now the emperor-patron, soon caused these quarrels to break out in a particularly ugly fashion.

The second of the emperor's worries was this: his fond hope that Christianity as a religious ideology would unify the empire was just not working out. Pagans, who still constituted a great majority of his empire and were often his most loyal subjects, complained furiously against his policies. Furthermore, disputes among Christian bishops and theologians, often based on jealousy, pique, and ambition or sometimes on theological differences that might once have seemed less urgent, now popped up everywhere. One such squabble, about the exact nature of the relationship between Jesus and God, involved Arius (d. ca. 335), a brilliant parish priest in Alexandria. An admirer of the theology of Origen (see Chapter 6), Arius taught that, although Jesus was indeed the Son of God and the incarnation of the divine logos and God's agent in the creation of the world, he was not coeternal with God. "There was a time," he said, "when Christ was not."

The theological views of Arius found considerable support among bishops in some parts of the empire, but others harshly condemned them. Constantine, fearful that this sectional rivalry within the church might threaten the unity of the empire itself, desperately wanted to do something to end the bickering. But although a bold soldier and a skilled administrator, he did not understand the theological argument and probably did not care who was right. He just wanted it ended, and as quickly as possible. He wrote to the disputants that their disagreement was "small and very insignificant" and "too sublime and abstruse to be settled with any certainty." He also thought it was a matter that was over the heads of most people and, throwing in a lightly veiled warning, he suggested that perhaps the bishops and theologians were debating it because they had too much free time on their hands. He urged them, in short, to cool it, to lower their voices, and to treat each other with "an equal degree of forbearance."[1]

But Constantine's plea for restraint went unheeded, and the controversy continued to boil. Frustrated by what threatened to be the failure of his ambitious unity plan, the emperor acted. He summoned an "ecumenical council," the first assembly of all the bishops in the whole world. It should be noted that it was an emperor, not the bishops, the congregations, or the bishop of Rome, who convened this first council in 325 CE. Also, the 220 bishops were not to gather in a church building, but—in keeping with the emperor's self-designated new role as a kind of high priest–administrator—in his sumptuous palace in Nicaea, on the lovely western coast of what is now Turkey.

When I was in seminary we spent several class sessions on the Council of Nicaea. It was, we were assured, perhaps the most important gathering ever to take place in Christian history. We heard fascinating lectures about it, and we tried to trace the logic of the various views on the relationship between God and Jesus held by the different factions. One of my professors imaginatively divided the class into Arians, followers of Arius, and Athanasians, those who followed Athanasius (295–373), Arius's chief opponent, so we could get a feel for the debate. I was assigned to the Athanasian camp. The Arians in the class really had little chance of winning. Our lecturers had already suggested that the Council of Nicaea had succeeded in keeping the peace in the church by quashing the incipient heresy of "Arianism" (even though it persisted for centuries and has returned in one form or another ever since). Some of the more pious church historians even declared that the Holy Spirit had surely guided the bishops in their deliberations.

I have no idea whether the Holy Spirit hovered over the royal palace in Nicaea, but there is little doubt that Constantine hovered there, and that it was he who exerted the most formidable earthly influence on the proceedings. He hosted the entire affair, arranged elaborate ritual processions, and, although he was not a baptized Christian and had no training and little real interest in theology, presided over the sessions. His own theological adviser, Osiosus of Cordoba, had suggested that the Greek word *homoousios*, meaning "same substance," should be used to describe the relationship of God to Jesus, so this was the solution Constantine urged the bishops to adopt. A few balked. The word was not found in the Bible, and some were inclined not to pretend they could define this mysterious relationship so precisely. They would have preferred to live and let live and to settle for the emperor's earlier suggestion that the matter was small and insignificant. But by this time Constantine was firmly wedded to his own adviser's plan, and he deployed his considerable influence—power and money again—to prod the bishops into supporting it. He also wined and dined them in sumptuous imperial style. A well-known description of one of the lavish banquets the bishops enjoyed appears in Eusebius's *Life of Constantine:*

> Detachments of the body-guard and troops surrounded
> the entrance of the palace with drawn swords, and

through the midst of them the men of god proceeded with without fear into the innermost of the imperial apartments, in which some were the Emperor's companions at table, while others reclined on couches arranged on either side. One might have thought that a picture of Christ's kingdom was thus shadowed forth, and as dream rather than reality.[2]

It is unfortunate that Leonardo da Vinci never painted a portrait of this sybaritic scene. It would contrast nicely with his *The Last Supper*, in which a hunted Jesus and the disciples take cover in a rented second-floor room and serve each other a modest meal, while the imperial swords are already being drawn not to protect this trouble-making rabbi, but to arrest and crucify him.

Constantine, not Jesus, was the dominant figure at Nicaea, and it is hardly surprising that almost all the bishops, to the emperor's satisfaction, arrived at a nearly unanimous decision in his favor. Only Arius himself and three other stubbornly independent bishops withheld their approval. Constantine promptly exiled Arius to the remote province of Illyricum. Then, in a statement that suggests he had forgotten his previous view both that this was all a matter of small significance and that all the parties should show forbearance to one another, he decreed:

If any treatise composed by Arius be discovered, let it be consigned to the flames . . . and if anyone shall be caught concealing a book by Arius, and does not instantly bring it out and burn it, the penalty shall be death; the criminal shall suffer punishment immediately after conviction.[3]

But the emperor's draconian measures did not succeed. The historic Council of Nicaea, as an effort to unify the church and the empire by imposing a creed, proved a dismal failure. Within months arguments flared up again. One of the bishops who had attended the Nicaea council and had not supported the final decision, Hilary of Poitiers (d. ca. 367), found himself banished to Asia. No doubt his experience tinctured his opinion of councils and creeds, but a letter he wrote from his place of exile at the time pinpoints how little the Council of Nicaea had accomplished and what a debacle it had been. Hilary says:

> It is a thing equally deplorable and dangerous that there are as many creeds as opinions among men, as many doctrines because we make creeds arbitrarily and explain their inclinations ... arbitrarily ... every year, nay every moon we make a new creed and describe invisible mysteries. We repent what we have done. We defend those who repent. We anathematize those whom we defended. We condemn either the doctrine of others in ourselves, or our own in that of others; and reciprocally tearing one another to pieces, we have been the cause of each other's ruin.[4]

The history of Christianity during the decades after Constantine makes for dreary reading. The subversion of the church into a religious empire widened. The bishops continued to bicker among themselves and deployed the power of the state against their theological enemies. Corruption increased. One can almost become sympathetic with the emperor Julian, who ruled from 360 to 363. Schooled as a Christian in his youth in the midst of the conniving and argumentative church factions of the time, he soon became disgusted and decided that what Rome needed was a return to its classical values, including its traditional religion. Unlike what some of his detractors have claimed, Julian never tried to abolish

Christianity, only to remove the privileged status Constantine and his immediate successors had given it. He wanted to create a level playing field for all the gods. But he only reigned for a short time, died leading his troops against the Persians, and has borne the stigma of being labeled "Julian the Apostate" ever since.

Meanwhile the Christian bishops went on debating the fine points of theology. Now they argued over what *homoousios* really meant and the nature of Mary's relationship to God and Christ. They composed more creeds and excommunicated more people. After the fall of Rome in 476 CE, the ensuing centuries toll a dismal story of the repeated failure of using creeds and excommunications to achieve any result, except for further rancor. If, as some psychologists claim, at least one form of mental illness can be defined as doggedly repeating the same tactic over and over again even when it has always failed, creeds could be thought of as symptoms of a long psychological disorder.

History teems with movements that considered themselves Christian, but that some bishop or council found heretical. In seminary we learned the names of many of them, for example, the Sabellians, Socinians, Ebionates, Erastians, Anabaptists, and Antinomians. The list goes on. Sometimes we were supposed to remember what their teachings were and how they deviated from some alleged norm. Many have long since disappeared. Those that survived have often gradually been recognized as different, but legitimate variants of Christianity. The same is true for individuals. In 1431 Joan of Arc was burned as a heretic. In the twentieth century she became a saint.

Philosopher and poet Ralph Waldo Emerson (1803–82) once said, "The religions we call false were once true," but it could also be said that, within Christianity, movements once considered heretical are now often welcomed into the ecumenical household. All Protestant churches fall into this category, even though in 2007 the Vatican repeated its insistence that they cannot properly be called "churches." At the same time the Vatican affirmed that the Eastern Orthodox Church can properly be called a "church," although "a wounded one." This judgment comes even though the Roman Catholic pope and the Eastern Orthodox patriarch once excommunicated each other. It was the lifelong goal of Pope John Paul II, one at which he did not, however, succeed, to reunite what he called the "two lungs" of the church. Yesterday's heretics and schismatics become today's "separated brethren."

My own favorite example of a "heretical" group that survived centuries of excommunication, persecution, and exile to become a small but significant part of the Christian family is the Waldensi ans. First organized by Peter Waldo as the "Poor Men of Lyon" around 1176, they emphasized living with simplicity. Waldo himself, a rich merchant, gave all his money away and suggested that the church could more credibly preach the message of Jesus if it did the same. The Waldensians taught that the Bible should be the sole authority and therefore eventually questioned the authority of the papacy and rejected the idea of purgatory and the practice of granting indulgences. Like the Franciscans, who came to birth at about the same time, the Waldensians, although they were laypeople (as St. Francis was), preached in the streets and the markets. But unlike the Franciscans they allowed women to preach and did not try to seek approval from the pope. The papacy responded by branding them heretics and directing the Dominicans to use the Inquisition to root them out. But the repression did not succeed. The Waldensians fled to remote mountain regions in Italy and France until the late nineteenth century when religious toleration finally arrived in Italy.

For many years now the Waldensians have maintained a church, a bookstore, and a seminary just off the Palazzo di Giustizia in Rome, a short walk from the Vatican. I happened to be staying at that seminary in the summer of 1996 when Pope John Paul II issued an unexpected invitation to the "Valdese," as he called them, to meet him for a special gathering in St. Peter's Basilica. The pontiff had just returned from a trip to Slovakia, where he had apparently been touched by the sight of a monument honoring some early Protestants who had been martyred there during one of the region's many eruptions of religious strife. Unable to ignore such an unusual invitation, I joined the "Valdese" to walk along the Tiber to St. Peter's square.

When we arrived, to our astonishment the Vatican staff gathered our small group not in some little reception room as we had expected, but around the high altar in St. Peter's itself. There we stood for a few minutes, some of us gazing up at the biblical text emblazoned around the inside of the dome: "Thou art Peter and upon this rock will I establish my church." After a few minutes the Successor of Peter entered in glistening white papal regalia, walked slowly to the altar, and then told us, in deeply sincere tones, that it was now time to leave our differences behind and search out what we all have in common. He then strolled around and shook hands with everyone, blessed the entire delegation, and left. I am sure this was the first time any pope had ever received and blessed a group of Waldensians. It had taken eight hundred years.

It sometimes surprises me to notice how lightly some Christian leaders, Catholic and Protestant, seem to take creedal articles for which their predecessors were willing to burn people or even to be burned themselves. During the reign of Charlemagne, the Western church arbitrarily inserted a short phrase, called the *filioque* ("and the Son") into the Apostles' Creed. It stated that the Holy Spirit derives (the word they used was "processes") not just from the Father, but also from the Son. Eastern Orthodox Church leaders were outraged. The point may seem trivial today, but to them it clearly meant that the Western church had subordinated the Spirit to Christ, and this threatened the equality of the three Persons of the Trinity. Arguments raged over this insertion for a thousand years, especially since the creed is recited during Mass, and some theologians considered the *filioque* a major obstacle to the reunion of the "two lungs." Then, however, when Pope John Paul II hosted the Eastern Orthodox patriarch in Rome and they conducted an ecumenical Mass together, the pope simply left out the troublesome phrase. Few people even noticed.

Still, in its own way, John Paul II's welcoming of heretics and schismatics is a hopeful sign. It suggests that even within the heart of the Catholic Church the Age of Belief, with its insistence on creedal conformity and doctrinal correctness, is passing, and an Age of the Spirit is stirring. The transition will not be a smooth one, as I learned during a highly informative conversation I had with the man who was to become John Paul II's successor on the throne of St. Peter.

CHAPTER 8

No Lunch with the Prefect

How to Fix the Papacy

The one conversation I have ever had with Joseph Ratzinger, the man who later became Pope Benedict XVI, taught me a useful lesson. I learned that, although the invaluable new knowledge recently gained about early Christianity could have enormous implications for the future, it might not. A change in how we understand the past can often generate a change in how we view the future. But I got a particularly vivid lesson in how it might *not* happen one crisp January day in Rome in 1988.

Since I was planning to visit the Eternal City anyway, I dashed off a letter to then Cardinal Joseph Ratzinger, who was the prefect of the Congregation for the Doctrine of the Faith, the principal guardian of orthodoxy in the Catholic Church. I wrote that, as I hoped to be in Rome, I would be honored to have the opportunity to meet him for an informal conversation. To my mild surprise, there arrived by return mail a large light blue envelope from Vatican City bearing the papal coat-of-arms, containing a letter on embossed, textured stationery informing me that the prefect would be pleased to meet me at 1:00 P.M. I immediately accepted, then hurriedly asked some of my friends who are acquainted with the folkways of Rome if that designated hour meant that the prefect was inviting me to lunch.

"No, not lunch, not in Rome," one of my informants told me. "One o'clock means that if he is enjoying the conversation and wants to invite you to lunch, he will. Otherwise, not."

Having arrived the day before my appointment, I stayed overnight at a residence in Rome run by the Dominicans. But I hardly slept at all on the night before my rendezvous with the prefect. As it happened, some thirty sisters from third-world countries were there at the same time for a brushup theology course. We all ate supper together, and they laughed and looked doubtful when I told them that I had a date to meet Cardinal Ratzinger. The misgivings they voiced about the prefect surprised me. They obviously considered a meeting with him a waste of my time. "Why would you want to see *him*?" one head of a community of sisters in Latin America asked. I told them I thought I would enjoy the exchange, but they seemed skeptical. Inwardly I wondered myself how it would go and lost a lot sleep worrying about it.

It was hard to imagine how anyone could actually *enjoy* a conversation with the "pope's Rottweiler," as he was then sometimes called. He was the church's official doctrinal watchdog, in which capacity he had disciplined and silenced several theologians who, he believed, had strayed over the line into or too close to heresy. Two of these were personal friends of mine, including Ratzinger's former colleague, the German Hans Küng, and his former student, the Brazilian liberation theologian Leonardo Boff.[1] On the morning of our engagement, I woke up early despite a nearly sleepless night, dressed in a white shirt and conservative tie, and then rode a careening taxi through the perilous streets of Rome to the prefect's headquarters.

The "Holy Office of the Inquisition" has undergone a number of name changes, the most recent in 1965 at the Second Vatican Council and is now known as the Congregation for the Doctrine of the Faith. But the city of Rome has never changed the name of the street on which it is located, the Largo Sant'Uffizio. There are ten "Congregations" in the Curia of the Vatican, which in most countries would be called "ministries." Each has its own responsibility, such as education, foreign policy, or family life. But, as happens in secular governments, they sometimes overlap and scrap with each other for influence. Eight of the ten are housed in two massive matching office buildings that line the Via della Conciliazione. The staid, graceless structures contribute nothing to the vaunted elegance of Roman architecture. The "reconciliation" the street refers to is the Lateran Treaty of 1929, in which Mussolini's Italy finally came to terms with the papacy and the Vatican city-state was created. Two of the Congregations, however, are situated elsewhere, one in the Piazza di Spagna and one on the Largo Sant'Uffizio, where I climbed out of the cab. These two, while not contiguous with the main area of Vatican City, are legally a part of it, enjoying a kind of extraterritorial status.

Just across the street from the Congregation, I downed a quick cappuccino at a little snack bar decorated with old fashioned Coca-Cola posters and colored prints of the Colosseum, St. Peter's, and the Trevi Fountain. Then I crossed the street and paused to decipher the inscription on a crumbling stone fountain, placed there— it read—by Pius IX, Pontifex Maximus, whose long papal reign lasted from 1846 to 1878. He was first the pope elected by the liberal wing of the church, but grew increasingly conservative. He is remembered for issuing the Syllabus of Errors, with its stinging denunciation of democracy. It did not seem to be an auspicious omen for my visit.

As I walked through the imposing iron gate of the off-yellow five-story Renaissance palace that houses the Congregation, the thought occurred to me that I was not only crossing an international border; I was also stepping back in time. It also suddenly struck me that I had spent the previous night with members of the

Dominicans, the very order appointed by the pope to conduct the Inquisition in the late thirteenth century. The quietly flowing Tiber has seen many currents.

As soon as I entered the imposing old front door a porter showed me to a high-ceilinged waiting room. It contained three wooden chairs covered with thinning brocade and a table whose gold and ivory paint had begun to chip. There were two albums of photographs on the table. Assuming they were there for visitors to peruse, I thumbed through them. Both were devoted to the many global journeys of John Paul II. Four paintings hung on the wall. One was of a cardinal I did not recognize. Two were of the Virgin Mary, one with her breast pierced by a sword, the other showing her enthroned as the Queen of Heaven. A small one portrayed a broadly smiling John Paul II.

I had barely surveyed my surroundings when Cardinal Ratzinger strode in, welcomed me in English with a smile and a handshake, and ushered me into an adjoining room. He wore a dark cassock trimmed in red piping, a black skull cap, and a medium-sized pectoral cross. His eyes looked tired, but he seemed energetic, if a little brusque. After a few moments of friendly banter, I asked him what he thought were the main sources of "heresy" today. He replied immediately that he had just returned from a trip to Africa and that the problem was really not mainly European liberalism like Küng's or even left wing political theologies like Boff's. Rather, he said, it was the danger of "syncretism," mainly in the non-Western world. It was the fusing of Christian with indigenous local spiritual practices that, he said, obscured the Christian content. The example he offered was the African custom of mixing Christian initiation rites such as Baptism and Confirmation with initiation into the tribe itself. When I asked how one could possibly sort one from the other, he smiled, shook his head, and admitted it was not easy. But then he looked at me calmly and added, "We handle it by working closely with the bishops."

Those few words spoke volumes. Yes, he was saying, the old malignancies on the mystical body are still there. They might be assuming a new form, but they will be dealt with as they always have been: by those who, as the only legitimate heirs of the original apostles, hold the unique right to do so. He the prefect, the pope, and the bishops will "handle it." They possess that power by virtue of being the curators of nineteen centuries of apostolic tradition, and this is the hallmark against which all possible deviations, whether in Brazil, Nigeria, Thailand, or anywhere else in the world, will be measured.

As we talked, it became clear to me that Joseph Ratzinger was a man with a deservedly high degree of confidence in his own scholarly acumen. He gave the impression that in his view many of the errors he was combating were not matters of bad intentions, but of wrongheadedness. He clearly implied that if he could only gather all the theologians and church leaders in the whole Catholic world together at a comfortable spa and talk with them for a week or two, the problems would take care of themselves.

After about forty-five minutes a staff member rapped on the door, looked in, and said, in English (for my benefit?), that someone from the Vatican Secretary of State's office was waiting to see him. The cardinal smiled at me, tilted his head, and held his palms up in a "what-can-you-do?" gesture. He then rose, we shook hands, and as I left he handed me an autographed copy of a small book of meditations on Easter entitled *Seek That Which Is Above*,[2] which he had recently written. The cover shows a page from an eleventh-century codex now in the Cologne Cathedral. On a red-and-gold background it depicts two women, both wearing red robes and bearing anointing oils, their eyes fixed on an angel with red wings and red hair who sits on top of an open coffin in which can be seen rolled up grave clothes. The angel is blessing the women with his right hand raised. At the door we shook hands again. He did not invite me to lunch.

As I walked out the gate onto the Largo Sant'Uffizio, passed the Pius IX fountain, and turned toward the Largo di Porta Cavalleggeri to look for a taxi, I did not suspect, of course, that the man with whom I had been chatting would one day be Pontifex Maximus. When that elevation did occur in 2005, I wondered what kind of pope he would be. Would he still rely on the same control mechanism the church had used for all those years, even though the historical claims on which that apparatus is based are now suspect? Useful fictions were now giving way to historical facts. But Ratzinger still seemed to view the newly globalized Catholic Church as though it were an extension of Europe. A year later he confirmed this attitude in his lecture to his former colleagues at Nuremberg in which he declared that the fusion of the gospel with Greek philosophy provided the most dependable intellectual vehicle for Christianity in today's world.

Ratzinger is a thorough European, born and bred. But the Catholic Church is now more non-European than it has ever been. The situation Christianity faces in the twenty-first century is radically different from the one his predecessors faced during the long era of Constantine, the Age of Belief. He is a professionally prepared scholar and has written articles on the historical development of ecclesial authority in the early church, but his strategy for keeping his far-flung realm in line relies on the same adhesion to creedal uniformity and obedience. Discussion may be allowed, even encouraged, but only up to a point. Finally, as the old dictum puts it, *Roma locuta, causa finite est,* "When Rome speaks, the matter is closed."

As Pope Benedict XVI, Joseph Ratzinger is arguably one of the best-trained theologians ever to occupy the throne of St. Peter. He has not been as severe as some feared he might be. But I still wonder how good a listener he is. If he were able to listen, it would be fascinating to organize the kind of leisurely conversation at a comfortable spa that I surmised he sometimes thought about, but with somewhat different people attending. First, I would want a number of Christians from Asia, Africa, and Latin America, people steeped in their own cultural traditions who might never have set foot in Europe, let alone Rome or the Cologne Cathedral. I would also want to have in the room the scholars from different traditions who are painstakingly reconstructing the actual history of the first centuries of Christianity. If the wine was of a fine vintage and the atmosphere sufficiently mellow, the gathering might end with some elements of consensus about how the Catholic Church and Christianity more generally might help the twenty-first century to be an age of faith and a new era of the Spirit. But if the papacy is to have a place in this new chapter of Christian history, and I believe it should, then its role will have to change. But how?

The high-water mark of the Roman Catholic attempt to define Christianity as creed and hierarchy occurred in 1870 at the First Vatican Council. There Pope Pius IX asked for and obtained, albeit by a mixed vote, the doctrine of papal infallibility. A close parallel to some tenets of Protestant fundamentalism, the doctrine states that when the pope speaks *ex cathedra,* that is in his official capacity as pontiff, and speaks to the whole church on a matter of faith or morals, the Holy Spirit prevents him from erring. Under those carefully delimited circumstances, the pope, as the earthly Vicar of Christ, is infallible. His decrees cannot be questioned or rescinded by any ecumenical council or, presumably, by any subsequent pope. They do not have to be suggested by or approved by the church as a whole. Although this power appears awesome, in fact it has only been exercised once since 1870. That was in 1950 when Pope Pius XII declared that the Assumption of the Virgin

Mary—that she ascended bodily directly into heaven without passing through the portal of death—was henceforth to be a dogma accepted and believed by all Catholics.

The enunciation of this doctrine, which had been recognized as a "pious belief" for centuries, caused considerable concern among Protestants and Orthodox Christians, if for different reasons. It was also received coolly by many Catholics. But since then, although there have often been rumors about new doctrines to be announced, such as the idea that Mary should be revered as "Co-Redemptrix" with Christ, none has been forthcoming.

Catholic theologians are allowed to argue about the degree of authority possessed by this or that papal statement or encyclical. But this misses the point. The flaw in the idea of infallibility lies not in whether the pope should have it or not, but in another direction. The very concept of "infallibility," no matter who has or does not have it, is itself misleading. Infallibility applies in the area of ideas, teachings, and propositions. It means that such propositions are accurate and must be assented to as true. It requires not faith, but belief. It was at this point in Christian history, in 1870, that the central and original impetus of Christianity—a basic life orientation to the coming Reign of God as exemplified in the life of Jesus—almost completely disappeared from view. It seemed that, at least in one church, belief had vanquished faith completely. Hierarchy and creed had triumphed.

I say "almost" and "seemed," because this is not what really happened. Instead, the popes who followed Pius IX, with a single exception, never wielded the ultimate weapon of infallibility. Some turned to persuasion and reasoning, listened more carefully to the laity, and even—beginning with Pope John XXIII—embraced the fellowship of non-Catholic Christians. In the hundred and forty years since the First Vatican Council, the Catholic Church has nurtured numberless saints, scholars, and martyrs. They are a testimony to the sheer resilience of a Jesus-centered, Kingdom of God faith even in an ecclesiastical structure that continues to define itself with such emphasis on hierarchical authority and correct doctrine.

I freely confess that, as an outsider, I have been fascinated by popes and the papacy for most of my life. I have met three of them personally. One of whom (Paul VI) commended me on my first book and another of whom (Benedict XVI, while he was still only a cardinal) quoted me favorably in one of his articles. I also met John Paul II. I describe a couple of these meetings in other chapters in this book, but my deepest regret is that I never met Pope John XXIII, who was my—and many others'—favorite. My limited experience with the popes and the papacy has, however, led me to believe that there is in fact an important role for the papacy in the Christianity of the future. But I also hope that this future place will be secured despite—not because of—claims to infallibility.

It was in February 1939, when I was nine years old, that I first found out there was such a thing as a pope. Walking down our street in the small town of Malvern, Pennsylvania, where I grew up, I noticed that the doors and lintels of the imposing gray stone St. Patrick's Church, which stood almost next door to our two-family brick house and on the same block as the Baptist church we belonged to, were hung with yards of somber black ribbon. When my father came home from work that evening, I asked him what it meant. The non-churchgoing offspring of two churchly Baptist parents, he pursed his lips for a moment before answering. "Well," he finally said, "their pope died. He lived in Italy, but he died, and those are mourning decorations. It's the way they show their sadness."

He may have hoped I would be satisfied with the answer, but of course I wasn't. I wanted to know what a pope was—it was a term I had never heard before—and why anyone from Malvern would be that sad about the death of someone who had lived so far away. He paused and then tried to explain as best he could what the pope meant to Catholics.

Many years later, what impresses me about his reply is how free it was from bigotry or antipapist venom, something I only learned about much later and never heard at all either in church or at home. My parents' attitude seemed to be that if Catholics, whose ways were a bit mysterious anyway, wanted to have an Italian who lived far across the ocean as the head of their church, that was their business. It had nothing much to do with us. The only thing that riled them about Catholics was that some of them seemed to think they were the only ones going to heaven.

That conversation was the beginning of my continuing interest in popes and the papacy. As I grew, I also came to see that the pope, even though we were not Catholics, did have something to do with us. The pope who had died on that cold February day in 1939 was, of course, Pius XI, the librarian-diplomat whose memory tends to be overshadowed by his flashier protégé and eventual successor, Pius XII, whose somewhat sour visage and rimless glasses I came to recognize during my teenage years as the Italian who headed the Catholic Church. I never saw him as a warm or welcoming figure, but I have also discovered that many Catholics didn't either.

Still, as I began to study history, first in high school, then in college, and ever since, I could not help noticing that whatever period or problem I was reading about, at least in the West and for nearly two thousand years, the popes were always there. Try to study the history of political institutions, philosophy, art, science, or literature without bumping into popes everywhere. They did, after all, have something to do with us, because they were significant actors in a history we all share. Besides, whatever you might think about the claims made about the popes, it would be hard to find a more absorbing collection of men (I am leaving out "Pope

Joan," whose credentials and historicity, it seems, are still in some dispute). The bishops of Rome have included saints, rakes, scholars, schemers, administrative geniuses, reformers, egomaniacs, tyrants, art collectors, warriors, builders, and even an occasional personage with an interest in theology.

Somehow, as I plunged deeper into history, then theology and the history of religion, it was the sheer persistence and virtual omnipresence, for blessing or bane, of the papacy that impressed me. I began to see at least a glimmer of plausibility in the hoary Catholic argument that any institution that has survived that long, despite the fornicators and four flushers who had actually occupied the office, must be taken with some degree of seriousness. If the God of the Bible, as I believe, acts in and through human history, then it has to be conceded that the papacy occupies a not inconsiderable chunk of that history, and not just in the West.

I was already a doctoral student in the history and philosophy of religion at Harvard in 1958 when Pius XII died and a roly-poly cardinal named Roncalli was elected to the throne of St. Peter and took the name John XXIII. His choice of this name was a bit puzzling to those of us who knew a bit about papal history, since the previous John, who had reigned seven hundred years earlier, had become a slight embarrassment to the church. The former John had reigned from Avignon in southern France and thus represented an episode in church history some Catholics would prefer to forget; he had worried sober theologians by talking about his elaborate mystical visions of what would happen after the final judgment. But there you had it again: persistence. The Catholic Church had waited seven hundred years, but 1958 seemed an opportune time, at least to Roncalli, to retrieve and refurbish a perfectly good biblical name.

It is touching to have been reminded recently—in Peter Hebblethwaite's biography of Angelo Roncalli[3]—of something I had read but nearly forgotten: that virtually the last words he uttered on his death bed were *ut omnes unum sint* ("that all may be one," Jesus's prayer in John 17:21). I think it is safe to say that, given Roncalli's short but spectacular papacy, the name John has now been fully restored and vindicated. The Catholic Church, it seems, is not in any particular hurry about these things.

John XXIII did far more than reclaim a papal name. He demonstrated, in a thrilling and imaginative way, the kind of freedom a pope has if he is willing to exercise it. John XXIII not only issued encyclicals, like *Pacem in Terris,* that still reverberate and not only assembled a council that changed the church forever; *he also redefined the religious, cultural, and moral meaning of the papacy itself.* He did this, moreover, not through any sweeping juridical reforms, but simply by the way he lived. I continue to be astonished when I remember how not only Protestants, Jews, and members of other religions, but also atheists, skeptics, and agnostics seemed to admire and even love him and how genuinely sad hundreds of millions of people were when he died.

I am also somewhat baffled by it. Why should so many people who, like my parents, think of this pope business as an odd but harmless Catholic thing have any interest in whether a pope is generous, expansive, and humble or not? It almost suggests that there was, and is, something deep in even the most unpapal (as opposed to antipapal) soul that hopes for a pope we can all feel fond of. It is the evolution of this cultural, spiritual, and moral dimension of the papacy that is left out of most of the suggestions I see about the future of the papacy. Maybe the omission occurs because most of those who engage in the discussion are Catholics, and since they tend to be preoccupied with other aspects of the papal office, they miss this one. Perhaps one almost has to be something of an outsider, and therefore not so wrapped up with issues of collegiality, infallibility, and curial power, to appreciate it.

The first pope I met personally was Paul VI. It happened at a consultation in Rome sponsored by the Vatican's then newly established Secretariat for Nonbelievers, whose president was Cardinal Koenig of Vienna. It was a meeting that altered forever my ideas about the papacy and what its future course might be. I was not, however, invited to the conference as a nonbeliever. Vatican II had made it clear that Protestants were now to be viewed in a much more favorable light, and a Secretariat for Christian Unity had just been established. I was invited because it was shortly after the appearance of my book *The Secular City,* and someone at the Vatican, possibly even prompted by the pope, thought I knew something about secularization and modern unbelief. When at the conclusion of our talks Pope Paul VI received the scholars who attended, he took my hand and, with gentle eyes looking over his hawklike nose, told me that he had been reading my book and that, although he disagreed with some of it, he had read it "with great interest." I was immensely pleased, but also sorry the next day that I had not asked him to put it in writing. It would have made a marvelous blurb for future editions.

What was important about that consultation, however, was not meeting the pope. ("It's like visiting the Statue of Liberty when you go to New York," the monsignor who administered the Secretariat told us before the audience.) The important thing was that this was a meeting sponsored by an official organ of the Vatican Curia to which not only Protestants and Jews but nonbelievers and even Marxists were invited. It suggested a boundless new arena for papal leadership, a transformation of the Vatican itself into an open meeting ground where representatives of various contending worldviews could come together for uncoerced and honest conversation. This hope is voiced by historian and Vatican watcher Giancarlo Zizola when he suggests the possibility of the Vatican becoming "such a point of concentration of spiritual authority in the eyes of all Christians and of all peoples as to become a kind of agent of unification of all forces that tend toward the good, without losing at the same time continuity with what had previously been considered good."[4] This represents a truly catholic vision of what Christ's prayer *ut omnes unum sint* could mean.

That meeting in Rome was a genuinely remarkable gathering, but I regret to say that the Secretariat for Nonbelievers soon fell upon hard days. Perhaps it was just a little too daring, a bit in advance of its time. Still, I like to think of its courageous work almost as an eschatological sign, a token of future possibilities. After all, the authority of the bishop of Rome in the early years of Christian history arose when he was looked to as the one to hear out and settle otherwise intransigent disputes between contending parties within the church, so the kind of meeting I attended would represent a logical extension of that practice. Someone reported a few years ago that the reason the Secretariat for Nonbelievers eventually declined into insignificance was because neither Cardinal Koenig, who died in 2004 at the age of ninety-eight, nor the clergy who administered it in Rome were cagey enough to deal with the hardball of internal curial politics. This may well be the case, but again, maybe one has to be a non-Catholic, or at least blissfully uninvolved in the internecine power struggles of Rome, to appreciate just how powerful and promising that historic gathering was. I still believe, despite more recent reverses, that it presages a role the papacy—and quite possibly only the papacy—could play as we open the next chapter of Christian history.

Meanwhile the Protestant struggle to move beyond fundamentalism is also under way, as we are about to see in the next chapters.

CHAPTER 9

Living in Haunted Houses

Beyond the Interfaith Dialogue

One rainy winter day when I was a boy of eight or nine and feeling unusually restless, I decided to rummage through the attic. There, tucked behind some dusty suitcases and chipped blue French provincial bedroom furniture, I uncovered a stack of old encyclopedias. I thumbed through them distractedly until suddenly coming upon a foldout map, "The Religions of the World." I stared at it with mounting curiosity. It was color-coded. It showed "Hinduism" in red occupying the Indian subcontinent. "Buddhism," appropriately orange, was spread across Southeast Asia from Thailand and Cambodia up to Japan. Since the map was an artifact from before the Maoist revolution, China was designated "Confucianist" and tinted in light gray. What the editors called "Mohammedanism" constituted a long yellow splash across North Africa, through the Middle East, and into Indonesia. Christianity sprawled comfortably across both Americas and Europe. I was amazed. In our small town we had Presbyterians, Methodists, Baptists, Quakers, and Catholics. But, I wondered, who were all these other people, and what were their religions like? I date my lifelong interest in theology and comparative religion to that drizzly afternoon.

The multihued map, however, is now totally outdated. Today all these religions are everywhere. Just as Christians are rediscovering their genuine origins, they also find themselves bumper to bumper with other traditions in areas where Christianity is a small minority. The other religions are here, not just there. All are now crammed into a shrinking world as well. Immigration patterns have transported large Hindu, Buddhist, and Muslim populations to Europe and America. Pagodas and mosques nestle among churches and synagogues. Adherents of the different world religions can no longer avoid each other, so understanding each other is no longer merely an option, but a necessity. The sobering truth, however, is that proximity has not always bred respect. In many places it has spawned suspicion and contempt, and just as religion has become more rather than less of a force in our time, the relationships among the different traditions have reached a new moment of crisis.

As human beings we live in both nature and history. We fuse two modes of existence. We all inhabit bodies, but we clothe them with everything from loincloths to Prada. We all speak, but in hundreds of different languages from Bengali to Serbo-Croatian. Likewise, we are all "faith-ing" animals. We cannot live without some degree of confidence in whatever lends coherence and purpose to our lives. It can be good luck, our ancestors, our money, brains, or contacts. It can even be a confidence that none of the above can be trusted, and it can change from year to year or from one hour to the next. Still, it has to be something. We are all "faithers," but we direct our faithing toward a myriad of different entities.

The religious and cultural patterns we live in shape our languages and our thought forms in ways that are almost impossible to escape. Jews and Christians who come to deny the existence of "God" inevitably deny the God they learned about through the

Jewish or Christian tradition. Even conversion to another religion does not solve this problem. Christians who embrace Buddhism cannot help but understand the *dharma* in part through the lens of the faith they are leaving. I have met a number of people from other faith traditions who have become Buddhists. But without exception they either extol the virtues of their new faith at the expense of the one they have left, usually Christianity or Judaism, or suffuse their Buddhism with Christian or Jewish overtones. Our traditions, whether we like it or not, permeate the language, thought forms, institutions, and values of our societies. They seep into the marrow of our bones and the synapses of our brains. They lodge not just in our conscious thinking, but also in our instinctive responses. I once heard Professor Arvind Sharma, the noted scholar of Indian religion, parse this unavoidable element of human existence in a whimsical reply to a reporter's question. Asked if he was a "believing" or a "practicing" Hindu, Professor Sharma smiled and responded, "Well, if you live in a haunted house, does that mean you believe in ghosts?"[1]

To some extent we all live in haunted houses. But although the houses may be in one shrinking global village, they remain separate houses. We all share a common need for a faith, whether it is a religious one or not, but we find ourselves amid a bewildering array of different ways of symbolizing both faith and its object. The chart of world religions still has many different colors, even though they are now striated and marbled. The map now looks less like a Joan Miró painting, with the colors clearly delineated, and more like a Jackson Pollock, with large swatches here and there, but spots and driblets splattered all over the canvas.

More than that, historically the contrasting tints have fueled an endless succession of crusades, jihads, inquisitions, and persecutions. It has been said that people are willing not only to "die for the faith," but also to kill for it. After the twentieth century, however, we have to add that not only have religious people killed atheists and heretics; atheists have been willing to kill religious people because of their religion. It is an ugly history, and among the various religious traditions Christianity has amassed one of the goriest records. But there is some evidence that Christianity's current retrieval of its core faith, especially in parts of the world where Christians live as minorities among those of other religions, could generate a more respectful, cooperative, and compassionate attitude.

Christianity began as a loose gaggle of Jews, soon joined by Gentiles, who were trying to follow Jesus by continuing his life work, best stated in the prayer he taught his friends, that God's reign of peace and justice, his "Kingdom," should "come on earth as it is in heaven." But Jesus never met a Hindu, a Buddhist, or a Muslim. He left no clear precedent for how to live with people of other religions. Consequently, the question of what the current rebirth of faith means for relations among these different pathways requires some original thinking. But as the new century begins we face a curious paradox. It is the best of times and the worst of times. On the one hand, there are more organizations, conferences, and seminars devoted to interreligious dialogue than at any time in previous history. However, we also live with terrifying animosity between—and within—religions. Hindus and Muslims slaughter each other on the Indian subcontinent. Ultra-Orthodox Jews and radical Muslims aggravate rivalries in Israel and Palestine with claims that Yahweh or Allah has given them the land. Meanwhile, Jews kill Jews and Muslims kill Muslims.

Maybe these two contradictory trends have a common explanation: we can no longer avoid each other. There was a time when most of the adherents of any religion (with the exception of Jews) could live their whole lives in blissful ignorance even of the existence of any other one. Now all that is changed. Due not only to tides of immigration, but also to jet travel, the Internet, and films, the dispersion of religions all over the globe now makes us all each other's neighbors, whether we like it or not. In this testy new planetary neighborhood, an honest assessment of relations suggests that we can no longer avoid dealing with the "religious other."

I became increasingly aware of the urgency of "interfaith dialogue" when I was in college, where I met Hindus and Muslims at a club for international students. Then as soon as I began my teaching career, I became an enthusiastic participant in dialogues in several different venues, some of them deliciously exotic. I lived for a week in a Vaishnavite Hindu compound in Vrindavan, India, and sat on the floor in bare feet exchanging ideas for hours with sadhus from the adjoining region. I attended a conference in the temple city of Kyoto, Japan, sponsored by a Buddhist organization. Later I hunched over old texts in three-way study with Muslims and Jews at the Shalom Hartman Center in Jerusalem. I taught a course on Jesus for two summer terms at the Naropa Institute, which was founded by the Tibetan Buddhist lama Chogyam Trungpa, in Boulder, Colorado. At home in Cambridge, I often visited the local Zen center and ate lunch with numerous visiting scholars who lived at Harvard's Center for the Study of World Religions.

I was getting to be a real jet-setting interfaith adept with shelves of exotic souvenirs. But I was also becoming increasingly aware that the people I met were much like me. They belonged to the "dialogue wing" of their traditions. The other wing was always missing. It was evident that continuing in this direction would inevitably lead to a cul-de-sac. We also needed to talk with the "fundamentalist wings" in our own and other traditions, especially since a lot of the religious animosity that sometimes flares into violence today occurs within religious groups, not between them. Although spokespersons for the American religious Right attack what they call the "liberal media," Hollywood, "activist judges," and stem-cell research, they reserve their most potent fusillades for other Christians who disagree with them on these and a host of other issues. The questions that concern the religious Right most are not now—as they once were—biblical inerrancy or the doctrine of the atonement, but rather what they call "social issues," matters of politics and culture. The proper place of gays and lesbians in the church is one of the most divisive issues currently tearing some denominations apart.

The passions enflamed by these internal struggles within particular traditions can lead to mayhem and death. The American Christian convicted of killing staff members at a clinic that provided abortions never repented, because he believed he was obeying God's Word and saving the innocent lives of unborn children. Prime Minister Rabin was assassinated not by a Palestinian, but by a devoted Jew acting on what he believed the Torah instructed him to do to both save Jewish lives and prevent the surrender of land God had given to his people. It was not a Muslim who killed Gandhi, but a fellow Hindu. Pakistan's Benazir Bhutto was murdered by a fellow Muslim. Everywhere in the world, a "circle-the-wagons" wing has materialized within each religion that defines itself at least as much against its coreligionists as against outsiders.

The eruption of these "fundamentalist" movements puts the interfaith conversation in a difficult bind. Whatever else they may disagree on, fundamentalists in every tradition concur on one thing: they vociferously oppose interfaith dialogue. They see it as a clear evidence of selling out. Their refusal to come to the table is aggravating to anyone trying to build peace among the religions. But the response to their refusal is also disappointing. Most of those participating in interfaith dialogues—although there are a few exceptions—are content to stay with the easiest elements of the conversations. Christians who take part in dialogue strongly prefer to converse with sympathetic Jews, Muslims, Hindus, and Buddhists. They rarely try to communicate with the most refractory wing within their own camp. This is understandable. What dialogically oriented Christian would not rather spend an afternoon with the Dalai Lama than with Pat Robertson?

Of course in conversations between people from differing traditions, for example, between Christians and Buddhists, differences always come up. Indeed, that is one purpose of the conversation. But the differences seem to be at a safe remove, since the participants are not a part of the "family." They can be registered and dismissed as "interesting." This is not the case, however, with the discrepancies that inevitably arise when those in the interfaith wing of a religion try to converse on a serious level with those from the circle-the-wagons wing of the same affiliation. In these encounters, things get tense, tempers often flare, and people sometimes stomp out of the room. More seems to be at stake. Many people try and then just give up. But quitting merely propels the whole interfaith enterprise toward a dead end. It creates the unpleasant prospect of a future in which, while open-minded members in each religion enjoy cozy colloquies with each other, the ultraconservative wing in each becomes more isolated and truculent.

As I became convinced that something had to be done about this stalemate, a drastic idea came to me. I suggested to my colleagues in 1983 that we invite Reverend Jerry Falwell and some representatives of Liberty University, the institution he founded and headed in Lynchburg, Virginia, to visit us at Harvard. Falwell, who died in 2007, enthusiastically styled himself a "fundamentalist" and boasted that his theology and political stance were "as conservative as you can get." Some faculty and students were aghast at my idea. They strenuously opposed inviting him to the campus and warned me against the danger of "giving him a platform." But I persisted, and even enlisted the support of colleagues from the

John F. Kennedy School of Government, who were accustomed to entertaining controversial guests. After considerable negotiation, we eventually agreed on a jointly sponsored event at which I would introduce Falwell and two graduate students in religion would respond to him briefly, followed by a question-and-answer period and then a dinner in the splendid penthouse of the JFK School, overlooking the Charles River.

Falwell's visit was a tumultuous event. Gay and lesbian students, some in imaginative drag costumes, picketed, but did so without much rancor. Falwell's staff members excitedly filmed them. I knew those knobby-kneed men in miniskirts and women in tuxedos would soon be featured on his weekly TV show, *The Old Time Gospel Hour,* together with an ardent plea to keep those checks rolling in because, "just see what we are up against."

The Kennedy School's largest auditorium was filled to overflowing. I made a cordial introduction with time-honored Ivy League restraint. A few individuals in the audience shouted insulting comments at Falwell as he spoke, but I tried, with considerable success, to maintain civility. Some people in the audience apparently expected him to be blundering and inarticulate, but he was not. He was clearly enjoying the day immensely. He gave sharply honed answers to all the questions. For example, when someone challenged him on the racial composition of Liberty University, Falwell waved a piece of paper that he said demonstrated that Liberty's per capita proportion of minority enrollment was higher than Harvard's. One student asked him whether, if he discovered an intruder in his house, he would confront the burglar nonviolently. No, he would not, Falwell responded, bouncing on the balls of his feet. He kept a gun in his bedroom, and he would use it to dispatch the unwelcome visitor to the next world. After the lecture, when we all gathered for wine and cheese and then dinner (Falwell and his people drank mineral water), the conversation was pleasant, if a little tense. Still, after everything was over, no one thought the visit should never have happened.

A few years after the Falwell visit, we entertained a group of faculty members from Regent University, in Virginia Beach, founded by Pat Robertson. Their visit included a private conversation with members of our faculty—on how to make religious values relevant in the public arena—and a well-attended open forum that filled the largest lecture hall in the Divinity School. Neither of these visits created any dramatic breakthroughs, but they demonstrated one thing clearly: the idea that "you just can't talk to those people" was not necessarily true. We not only can; we must, and we did.

Admittedly, this kind of *intra*faith dialogue is often more difficult than *inter*faith dialogue. Both sides understandably tend to avoid it, albeit for different reasons. But the result is that tensions between the wings within each tradition deepen, and instead of communication we fuel confrontation, calumny, and the constant threat of schism. As conditions worsen, we feel ever more uncomfortable talking with coreligionists who—many of us believe—distort and demean what we both share. Sibling rivalry is the nastiest kind. In the first murder Cain killed Abel over the proper way to sacrifice to the God they both worshiped. The rivalry between the brothers was an *intrafaith* dispute.

The future possibilities for such intrafaith dialogue are not, however, as foreboding as they once appeared. They have been improved by the fact that both wings have been touched by the current liberation of the message of Jesus from the creedal cage in which it has been encased. Once again, this liberation stems from both the rediscovery of the biblical Jesus and the emergence of a post-Western Christianity. First, conservative Christians have also heard the news of the overturning of centuries-old fictions about early Christianity; they were never comfortable with theories of "apostolic succession" anyway. The rediscovery of the actuality of the Jesus movement has begun to find genuine acceptance. And as evangelicals incorporate more of this Jesus-centered outlook into their thinking, they find it a little easier to talk with the "liberals" they once looked upon as a fifth column. This development also brings both these wings into closer contact with the Christians of the global South, and it is there that some of the most decisive changes in the attitude of Christians toward people of other faiths are occurring.

The change in the approach to both interfaith and intrafaith dialogue among Christians in Asia and Africa came as a surprise to many observers. During the years when the churches of Asia and Africa and the third world were principally those founded and still administered by American and European missionaries, dialogue with other religions was viewed with suspicion. Christians in those countries wanted to underline their particularity, to make it clear that they represented something new and different. But as these "new churches" matured and as a second and third generation of leadership emerged, that viewpoint began to change. The grandchildren of the first converts became more interested in finding common ground with their neighbors, especially to confront the poverty that still blights their regions.

The Christian Conference of Asia brings together people from an area beginning with Pakistan in the northwest, through Thailand, Cambodia, and China, to Korea and Japan in the northeast. When I attended its annual meeting in the stunningly ultramodern city of Hong Kong in 2003, I was surprised to find that the central concern of the two hundred delegates was how best to work together with their non-Christian neighbors on issues of women's rights, ecology, and peace. It was also clear to me that they thought arguing over doctrines and beliefs was too "Western" and a little boring. Their idea of interfaith dialogue was to work with their fellow Asians of whatever religion to advance the Kingdom that Jesus had inspired them, as Christians, to strive for, regardless of what the others called it. They were neither "fundamentalist" nor "modernist." They seemed more attuned to the element of mystery at the core of Christianity and to its vision of justice. They were also clearly impatient with many of the disputes that preoccupy the different wings of the American churches.

The conservative-evangelical-fundamentalist community is neither monolithic nor immobile. It is divided and subdivided along theological, racial, gender, geographical, denominational, and political lines. These divisions collide and conflict, and the internal rhetoric generated is frequently more intense than the rhetoric they direct toward their external opponents. The splits within the conservative religious community gained widespread attention in February 2005 when Robert Wenzl, then vice president of the National Association of Evangelicals, blasted his fellow evangelicals for having "lost their perspective." Reaching back into history, he condemned Jerry Falwell's Moral Majority, which had been so active in the 1980s, as "an aberration and a regrettable one at that," because it was "flawed by a fatal hubris." He intimated that he hoped the same flaw might be avoided in the growing "megachurches," some of which are comfortably ensconced in the suburbs rather than in urban areas, where the need for justice ministries is so evident. If a spokesperson for the liberal National Council of Churches had voiced such a criticism, it would have gone unnoticed. But this was a high officer in the NAE, and the story in the *Boston Globe* reporting his speech carried the headline, "Official Chides Christian Right."

There is also a fresh theological openness among American evangelicals. They now candidly debate matters that once appeared taboo, such as the nature of biblical authority and the possibility of God's redemptive presence in other religions. A heated dispute has also broken out about eschatology, the theological doctrine of the "last things," and how the world will end. The argument centers on the *Left Behind* series of novels, which have sold fifty million copies and are based on a fundamentalist Armageddon theology. More spats will surely arise about whether bare midriffs and rock music are appropriate for worship services (they appear to be gaining ground) and whether women can be ordained.[2]

Conservative Christianity in America—and in many other parts of the world—is not a phalanx. The Spirit is moving. Faith is becoming more salient than beliefs. Current research indicates that the evangelical and Pentecostal movements in Latin America are not spawning a Latin equivalent of the North American religious Right. In Brazil, for example, evangelicals helped elect Lula (Luiz Inácio Lula da Silva), the candidate of the democratic left Workers Party, as president.[3] Worldwide, evangelical movements are moving, changing, and dividing. They are vigorous in many ways, but often ambivalent about their mission. Many of their leaders who once condemned the "social gospel" are now searching for a social theology of their own that includes peacemaking, striving for racial justice, and combating poverty. The opportunity for useful conversation with the "other wing" may be more promising than ever.

We should seize this opportunity. Unless we do, we face the dour prospect of a future in which open-minded members in each religion devote increasing amounts of time to friendly conversations with like-minded members of others, while the conservative wing in each becomes more inaccessible and hostile. We will end up with more and deeper divisions than we once had, only running along internal rather than external fault lines. Ironically, the *inter*faith movement would then be defeated by its own success.

I recognize the serious objection that is immediately raised to such a suggestion: "You just can't talk to those people." Fundamentalists, it is said, are against dialogue as a central tenet of faith, while dialoguers affirm it as a central tenet of theirs. Therefore, no communication is possible. But the symmetry of this picture does not fully correspond to reality. One of the reasons ultraconservatives are reluctant to talk with those on the other end of their own tradition's spectrum is that they often feel, sometimes with reason, that the "liberals" view them with condescension and disrespect. In America they are often treated dismissively as hicks and rednecks, ignorant and out of step. These stereotypes often make it difficult for them to engage in conversation. But because such intrafaith converse can be difficult is no reason to avoid it; it signals a good reason to try to engage in it.

The paradox of the interfaith enterprise today is that we live in the best of times and in the worst of times. We have more conversation and more conflict than ever. We need to turn our attention to the religious dimensions of political strife and the political dimensions of religious discord. We need to face in three directions: toward other faiths, toward the "other wing" in our own tradition, and toward the complex political context of our fractured world.

CHAPTER 10

Get Them into the Lifeboat

The Pathos of Fundamentalism

Fundamentalism is the current Protestant variant of the toxin of creed making that entered the bloodstream of Christianity early in its history. Fundamentalists collapse faith into belief. They define themselves by their unyielding insistence that *faith* consists in *believing* in certain "fundamentals." This, together with being "saved" or "born again" and telling others about one's beliefs, which is called "witnessing," makes someone a "real Christian." Of course, many fundamentalists are also people of genuine faith who trust God as they understand him and try to love their neighbors. And many people in a variety of spiritual paths experience a formative awakening that can change the way they live, though they might not call it a rebirth. But the fundamentalist obsession with correct beliefs often makes faith, in its biblical sense, more elusive. It replaces faith as a primary life orientation with a stalwart insistence on holding to certain prescribed doctrinal ideas, and this in turn often promotes a kind of taut defensiveness and spiritual pride that are not in keeping with the love ethic of Jesus.

I think I understand fundamentalists pretty well because I once was one, if only for a short time. During the first months of my freshman year at Penn, I was not making the adjustment very well. In high school I had been president of the senior class, an honor student, and a key player in "The Top Hatters," the school's dance band. But in college I found myself with dozens of class presidents, three of them on the same hallway in my dorm, and I was surrounded by honor students. I did get into the eighty-piece marching band, but when we strutted onto the football field at halftime, there were two rows of saxophone players, most of whom could play better than I could. Further, I did not enjoy the rowdy fraternity drinking parties and I felt left out of the bantering and braggadocio about sexual conquests, much of which—I now realize—was more invented than real. Still, the social life of the campus completely revolved around the fraternities, and I knew that if I didn't join one, I would miss out on a major element of college life. In addition, I secretly wondered if any of them would want me, and the prospect of "rushing" but not being accepted in one was just too humiliating to consider.

While I was anxiously pondering what to do, one evening I found a note tacked to the door of my dorm room, inviting me to a weekend outing on a lake in New Jersey sponsored by something called the "Penn Christian Fellowship." The message indicated that some young women from Bryn Mawr and some nursing students were also being invited. It was signed by two friendly older students I had met briefly in the snack bar a few days before. It sounded like an attractive idea, so I called the phone number on the note and told them to count me in.

The weather was balmy that weekend, and for the most part I enjoyed what turned out to be more of a conference than a mere outing. We sang some of the lusty hymns I knew from my church upbringing and engaged in lively group studies of the Bible. We ate well-cooked meals, played softball, and paddled canoes on the lake. When I awkwardly swamped the canoe I was trying to dock, everyone laughed good-naturedly, and one of the other students lent me a pair of dry slacks. The only thing that bothered me was that the roommate to whom I had been assigned wanted us to get out of bed, fall on our knees, and pray together. It turned out he suspected, rightly, that I was not really sure I was saved, and he did not want the night to pass before I felt the "blessed assurance."

I made some friends during the weekend, and when we got back to Philadelphia, I began attending some of the Bible studies the group sponsored, never led by clergy but always by other students. Although I often disagreed with the interpretations being offered, I was an eager seeker, trying to learn everything I could in all my classes, and since there were no courses on the Bible in the catalog, this seemed like an important addition to my education. I also began dating one of the young women I had met at the weekend, but it was a short-lived romance, especially since, even after three pleasant evenings together, she was still not willing to let me kiss her goodnight.

The Penn Christian Fellowship was affiliated with an international campus-based organization that had started in Great Britain called the InterVarsity Christian Fellowship. One of its goals was to bring a kind of intellectual respectability to what was in fact a fundamentalist version of Christianity, which had been accused—often correctly—of anti-intellectualism. The first Inter-Varsity group in America was founded at the University of Michigan in 1938. The idea spread quickly, and by the time I arrived at Penn in the late 1940s, there were over five hundred chapters on campuses across America. By then the movement had succeeded, at least in some measure, in convincing thousands of students that being a conservative evangelical or a fundamentalist did not mean being a redneck bumpkin. But I soon came to notice that the intellectual rigor did not include any critical study of scripture. I was also increasingly troubled by its total lack of concern for the social-justice imperatives of Christianity and by the no-dancing, no-beer, no-necking prudery of most of the members.

The young woman who wouldn't kiss goodnight, I discovered to my regret, was no exception.

Still, the following summer I decided to attend a weeklong InterVarsity conference at a wooded campground in New Jersey called Keswick. There we had more spirited singing, more prayer, more swimming, more Bible study groups, and a bounteous supply of women students from colleges around the area. I also came to know the son of Donald Gray Barnhouse, one of the great fundamentalists of the time. The father was a powerful preacher of tremendous eloquence, and I had begun to attend his Tenth Presbyterian Church on 17th Street in Philadelphia. By that time I had learned how to beach a canoe, and my roommates apparently thought I was on the safe side of Jordan.

But it was during that week at Keswick that I also began to have severe doubts about whether this was really the group for me. Serious struggling with the historical study of the dating or authorship of biblical texts was not only missing. It was suspect. When I mentioned that I had written a term paper on Reinhold Niebuhr, few knew who he was, and those who did considered him to be just another "modernist," the favored fundamentalist epithet for anyone on the other side of the great divide. Further, it was 1948, and I supported Henry Wallace, the third-party (Progressive) candidate for president. Everyone there who saw the Wallace button I sometimes wore voiced immediate disapproval. It was not just that they suspected him of being a Communist, but that they objected to any overt involvement in politics: it merely diverted people from the real task of saving souls.

For InterVarsity, faith, in the last analysis, seemed to be equated with conforming to a strict doctrinal creed, cultivating a regular devotional life, and "witnessing" to unbelievers. But at the Keswick summer conference I also began to detect certain tensions within the ranks. At dinner one evening I overheard one young

man confiding to another that the uncomfortably high tempera-
ture in the open assembly hall in which we gathered was undoubtedly caused by the Holy Spirit hovering so closely overhead. When
I mentioned this comment that evening to a fellow Penn student
who was also attending the conference, he pursed his lips, shook
his head, and rolled his eyes upward. Apparently he too had his
doubts about the calorific efficacy of the Holy Spirit.

It was only several years later, while doing research about fundamentalism, that I began to understand some of the divisions
within the InterVarsity Christian Fellowship that I had first noticed at the Keswick conference. The term "Keswick" itself derives
from a movement that began in England in 1875, with meetings in
a town by that name, that sought to promote a "higher life" among
Christians. The idea stemmed from the theology of John Wesley
(1703–91), the founder of Methodism, who preached that just
being saved or converted was not enough. Christians must have a
personal inner experience with Christ and then strive for more
and more "holiness" and even eventually for sinless perfection.
From the outset, however, such notions were condemned by Christians, more influenced by Calvinism, who believed salvation was a
once-and-for-all gift of God and looked with suspicion on any
kind of gradations or stages in the Christian life.[1]

The friction between the Calvinist and Wesleyan wings of
American fundamentalism has persisted since the movement's in-
ception. Calvinists are often wary of "experience" and more ada-
mant about right doctrine. Wesleyans, on the other hand, assert
that an emphasis on doctrinal correctness is useless without a deep
personal encounter with God. This old argument surfaced in an
ugly way during the first decades of the twentieth century in a
wrangle between doctrinal fundamentalists and Pentecostals,
who, although they hold to some of the "fundamental" doctrines,
put a much bigger emphasis on a direct experience of the Spirit of

God. The fundamentalists recoiled from what they saw in Pentecostalism as excessive emotionalism with not enough sound belief. They suspected Pentecostals of mental disease or exhibitionism or both. Jerry Falwell, a strictly Calvinist fundamentalist, once remarked that when Pentecostals shout, groan, and speak in tongues, it is probably because they have eaten some badly cooked fish. The antagonism has never been resolved.[2]

There was little evidence of this tension within the Penn Christian Fellowship. Still, over the next months I drifted away, although I continued to be friends with many of its members. But I have never harbored the animosity toward the group that some ex-members of "cults" often do. It was *not* a cult. No one ever misled or deceived me. The motives of those who had invited me were genuine and unselfish. Rather, the Penn Christian Fellowship and the larger InterVarsity Christian Fellowship were authentic expressions of a certain strand within the wider fundamentalist movement. I learned a lot while I was with them and still appreciate it. I have moved far away from the tight parameters of their worldview, but I understand what motivates them better than those who have never profited from that exposure. Ever since those college years I have followed the twists and turns of the fundamentalist movement with keen interest, often with disappointment and sometimes with anger, but never without a degree of sympathy.

One issue on which I have come to disagree most emphatically with a particular strain of fundamentalism is its destructive and self-serving view of the "end time." The belief that Christ will come again soon has woven a jagged course throughout Christian history, but it surfaced with a vengeance in the nineteenth century in America and the United Kingdom as anxious people wrenched isolated verses out of their contexts in Ezekiel, Thessalonians, and Revelation in order to contrive an exact schedule of the "signs of the end," the events preceding the return of Christ and the Last Judgment.

An Irish Anglican, John Nelson Darby (1800–1882), invented a particularly precise version of this scheduling called "dispensationalism," which held that all history was divided into seven dispensations, of which the present one was the last. He and his followers also added that true believers need not fear the awful times of tribulation that were coming because, before the worst of it, they would be "raptured," taken to heaven without dying. The *Left Behind* series of novels, with their horrific descriptions of the "rapture," the "great tribulation," and the bloody battle of Armageddon, are based on this dubious theological scheme.[3]

One of the worst features of dispensational fundamentalism is the foreshortened time it assigns the earth before the end comes, which makes any concern for the health of the planet's oceans and air and forests superfluous. Another is the belief that Christ will not come until a titanic battle is fought in Palestine between Christ and the Antichrist. This fatalistic conviction undercuts efforts to arrive at a peaceful solution to the conflict between Israelis and Palestinians. Fortunately, not all fundamentalists hold these extreme views, but enough do to jeopardize the ecological and peacemaking efforts of other Christians and other concerned people.

Fundamentalism had roots elsewhere, but it was born in America. When it first appeared in the early decades of the twentieth century, it was generated by people who believed both the church and the society were heading for catastrophe, because Christians were losing, indeed squandering, their faith. Their fears were not entirely groundless. In 1910 Charles Eliot (1834–1926), then a professor emeritus at Harvard, delivered an address entitled "The Future of Religion." He advocated a new version of Christianity that would have only one commandment. It would require simply the love of God expressed in service to others. There was no further need for theology, churches, scriptures, or worship. Eliot's ideas—and he was not alone in propounding them—horrified almost all

Christians, but the fundamentalists fought back in a particularly forceful and organized way.

Starting in 1910, they opposed this "modernism" by publishing a series of twelve widely circulated booklets called *The Fundamentals*, which asserted that many people who called themselves Christians had slipped so far into accommodating Christianity to modern culture that they had lost its essentials. These core "fundamentals" constituted the nonnegotiable beliefs one must absolutely hold to in order to be a Christian. There were five. The first and most prominent "fundamental" was the divine inspiration and total inerrancy of the Bible. This conviction was the cornerstone on which everything else was built. Second, they listed the Virgin Birth of Christ as a testimony to his divinity. Next, they included the "substitutionary atonement" of Christ on the cross for the sins of the world, and his bodily resurrection from the dead. Finally, they asserted that belief in the imminent second coming of Christ "in glory" was in no way optional, but just as "fundamental" as the other beliefs in their creed.

At first glance the choice of these five beliefs seems arbitrary, even peculiar. Notice that there is no reference to the *life* of Jesus. His feeding the hungry and healing the sick are not mentioned. The parables and the Sermon on the Mount are missing. His opposition to the political and religious elites of the day—undoubtedly the reason for his arrest and crucifixion—does not appear. Why did the fundamentalists pick out the five doctrines they did as the indispensable nucleus of Christianity and not others?

Given the cultural and religious atmosphere of America in the early twentieth century, however, it is not hard to see why they chose these five "fundamentals." Inflexibility on the inerrancy of the Bible was intended to counteract the growing application of historical methods to the study of scripture, which had already resulted in doubts about whether Moses had really written the

Pentateuch and the authorship of some of the letters attributed to Paul. Emphasizing the Virgin Birth and the atonement was directed against understanding Jesus simply as a great spiritual teacher or an ethical exemplar. Highlighting the imminent Second Coming, to be initiated according to this view by plagues, famines, and a steep degeneration of conditions around the world, was intended to undercut any idea of progress, however gradual, toward the Kingdom of God. Things would get worse, much worse, before the end.

Financed by conservative businessmen, the *Fundamentals* pamphlets were widely distributed free to Protestant ministers and lay leaders across the country. In 1920, an article in the *Baptist Standard* suggested that the courageous Christians who defended these focal principles should be called "fundamenta*lists*." The label stuck. Even though it is now widely and loosely applied to radically conservative movements in many different religious groupings, including Islam and Judaism, and often carries a pejorative overtone, it was American Protestants who invented it and proudly applied it to themselves.

Fundamentalists have always regarded their beliefs as under attack, and therefore have engaged in counterattack, on two fronts. First, they believed the whole world, but America in particular, was caught in a downward spiral of decadence, depravity, and heterodoxy. They ridiculed the idea of any "social gospel" as a futile effort to refurbish a fatally punctured liner that was already sinking. As the great revivalist Dwight Moody (1837–99) put it, "The Lord told me, 'Moody, just get as many into the lifeboat as you can.'"[4] But they also fought against an even more dangerous enemy within, namely, those current theological trends that seemed to them a rank betrayal of Christianity by "modernists" in their vain effort to adjust a timeless message to the shifting sands of a fallen world. Leading fundamentalist preachers often lashed out against the loose morals of the Babylon around them, but they reserved their most vivid polemics for other preachers who were selling the faith for a "mess of pottage".

Contrary to the image they have had, fundamentalists were not mostly rural; nor were they an uneducated or semiliterate gaggle. They boasted within their ranks several prominent scholars, and one of their principal arguments was that modernists and liberals were intellectual slouches who were just not thinking with enough rigor and clarity. In this debate, the authority of the infallible Bible became the touchstone. The highly respected Princeton Greek and New Testament scholar J. Gresham Machen (1881–1937), in his *Christianity and Liberalism* (1923), firmly maintained that only belief in a totally inerrant Bible could save Christianity from sliding into an abyss of emotional confusion. The Bible, he argued, was authoritative not only in matters of faith, but also in moral standards, history, and cosmology. He also contended that the Bible, as the grid through which everything else is interpreted, needs no interpretation itself. It is clear and sufficient. It says what it says, and that is what it means. Interpretation, he asserted, would lead to disagreements about what it says and inevitably to the weakening of its authority. He flatly dismissed the emphasis on "religious experience" that he found among modernists—and even among many evangelicals—as vague and anti-intellectual. Experience was a slender reed, a vagrant and unreliable basis for authority. Only the Word of God was constant and unchanging.

Their willingness to do battle not only against the barbarians at the gates, but also against the Trojan horse within quickly gained leaders of the movement the designation "fighting fundamentalists," a title most of them relished. From its launching, American fundamentalism was an aggressive and argumentative affair. There was, indeed, so much to be against. But their argumentativeness often spilled over toward each other. Fighting fundamentalists fought other fighting fundamentalists over how the fight against the enemy should be waged. Some took the scriptural admonition to "come out and be separate" (2 Cor. 6:17) literally and seceded from the denominations they belonged to. Others opted to stay and carry on the fight within the halls of the modernists. But then those who left had to decide whether to continue in fellowship with those who stayed, and then the pull-outers argued with those who stayed in about that.

On the eschatological front, some held to one or another timetable for the "last days" they believed were already ushering in the Second Coming. Others were skeptical about any such schedules. Even the question of what inerrancy means did not escape dispute. What was inerrant—the words, the ideas the words expressed, or the content of an entire letter or gospel taken as a whole? Some fundamentalists even dared to suggest that the original context of a scriptural text might in fact be relevant. After all, Paul had specifically written to the Romans or the Galatians, not to Chicagoans or Clevelanders. Shouldn't understanding that help us grasp what he was saying to them (and therefore presumably to us)? But others saw in this strategy as inviting the emergence of the specter of endless disputes over interpretation, with a consequent loss of confidence in "what the Bible plainly says."

These disagreements may sound puny or precious to some people today, but fundamentalists fought each other savagely over them, frequently "separating" from those with whom they did not agree. One result of this internal bloodletting was that it undermined the primary objective of the whole fundamentalist movement, which had been to quell the slide toward doctrinal cacophony by insisting on one unquestionable source of authority, the Word of God.

Despite its continuing internal fractiousness, as the twenty-first century begins, Protestant fundamentalism, though declining, has not yet disappeared. And although there are important differences between the original meaning of the word and the various, disparate movements to which the label is applied today, they all evidence a kind of "family resemblance." Each engages in a highly selective retrieval of texts, rites, practices, and sometimes organizational patterns from the past and then deploys them in a current battle. Those some now call "radical Islamists" refuse to be called "fundamentalists," viewing it as yet another attempt to impose on them a foreign, Western category. But they do attempt to revive the earliest period in Muslim history, that of the "rightly guided caliphs," as a model for reforming modern society. Those Jews who stake their claim to all of Palestine on a literal reading of the "promised land" passages in the Bible are sometimes called "land fundamentalists." There is a similar tendency among those Catholics who call themselves "traditionalists." They seize upon the declining use of the Latin Mass as the main symbol of what has gone wrong with their church.

Each of these movements combats an outside threat, but is much more concerned with the "fifth column" within. Radical Islamists oppose the West largely because of its support of what they believe are counterfeit and illegitimate so-called Muslim regimes in many of their countries.[5] The "land fundamentalists" of the Jewish settler movement lash out with particular ferocity, and some with violence, against fellow Jews who do not share their religiously based claim to Palestine.[6] Catholic traditionalists waste little energy criticizing Protestants, but pile their passionate polemics on the current leadership of their church, sometimes including the pope.[7]

Having once experienced at least a hint of the vigor that drives Christian fundamentalists, I am always fascinated by their movements and still feel a touch of empathy with them. I cannot help but admire their commitment and drive. I still find myself at times humming the soaring hymns I learned with them. Still, I also know how much effort it requires to be a fundamentalist. It can get tiring. You must constantly fight not only the skepticism of those around you, but the doubts that arise within yourself. Mainly fundamentalists evoke from me a sense of sadness. Their pathos is that they expend such energy on such a losing cause.

Meet Rocky, Maggie, and Barry

*Which Bible Do the
Bible Believers Believe?*

When the late Jerry Falwell introduced Ronald Reagan to a group of his fellow pastors, he told the president, with a radiant smile, that they were all "Bible-believing preachers." Reagan looked pleased. Protestant fundamentalists like to call themselves "Bible-believing Christians."

During the last decades of the nineteenth century especially in America, "believing the Bible" began to become a kind of litmus test of whether one was a "real Christian." Given all the upheavals and uncertainties of the times, it is understandable that some people felt they needed an absolutely dependable, indeed infallible, authority. The declaration of papal infallibility in 1870 had responded to the same yen among some Catholics. References to the fundamentalist view of the Bible as a "paper pope" are historically quite apt. However, the result in both cases has been ruinous, degrading faith into a kind of credulity.

It might be impolitic to ask such "Bible believers" *which* Bible they believe, but the question is a useful one to understand the appropriate place of the Bible in a community of faith. The answer must begin by recognizing that there is no such thing as *the* Bible. There are number of different ones. What Jews, Catholics, and Protestants call "the Bible" are different books. The Jewish one, called the Tanakh and first written in Hebrew, incorporates the five "Books of Moses" (Genesis, Exodus, Leviticus, Numbers, and Deuteronomy), the Prophets, and the Writings. The Protestant "Bible" includes all of these, though arranged in a different order, plus what Christians refer to as the "New Testament," originally written in Greek. The Catholic Bible has all of the above plus the "Apocrypha," which incorporates such books as Judith, Ecclesiasticus (Sirach), 1 and 2 Maccabees, and several other, shorter books. Protestants excised this whole section during the Reformation, when—it is reliably reported—Luther would like to have torn the Letter of James out of the New Testament as well. It does say, after all, that "faith without works is dead," so the testy Wittenberg theses-nailer called it a "straw epistle." A champion of salvation by grace, he feared that the Letter of James might mislead people into thinking it might be gained by good works.[1]

Since what we mean by "the Bible" has been changing from century to century, with various books being included and excluded depending on the theological climate, it would be useful for "Bible-believing" Christians to engage in an imaginary experiment. What if they were Bible-believing Christians in the second century CE? At that time the only Bible Christians had was the Old Testament. The New Testament had not yet been compiled. What if they lived at a time when books like *First Clement* and the *Apocalypse of Peter* were still being read in many congregations along with the various letters of Paul? Many Christians at that time wanted to include them in the New Testament, but eventually they were not. What if our Bible believers lived in the fifteenth century when the "apocryphal" books that Protestants excluded a few decades later were still considered to be Holy Scripture and still read in the churches (as they are in Catholic churches today)? The idea that "the Bible" has always been the same book year in and year out and you either believed it or you did not may be comforting, but it has no basis in reality.

Having settled which Bible they believe and when, another query one might put to our self-described Bible-believing Christians is: Which translation do they believe? There are shelves of translations, even in English, and at points they vary widely on how to render particular verses.[2]

This explains why such a flurry arose among fundamentalists when the Revised Standard Version of the (Protestant) Bible first appeared in 1952. In the King James edition, dating from 1611, a familiar verse in the Old Testament reads, "Behold, a virgin shall conceive, and bear a son, and shall call his name Immanuel" (Isa. 7:14). In keeping with the common Christian approach to the Hebrew scriptures in those days (and in some quarters today as well), this text was often interpreted as an obvious prediction of the birth of Jesus Christ from the Virgin Mary. It is a favorite for Christmas season readings. But the scholars who prepared the new translation noticed that the Hebrew word in question (*almah*) actually means a young woman who has reached sexual maturity, but does not indicate whether she is a virgin or not. Part of the confusion stems from the fact that the Greek translation of the Old Testament (the Septuagint) uses the word *parthenos,* which does mean "virgin." The RSV translators, however, rightly wanted to use the original Hebrew version. But they noticed that when the word *almah* appears in the Hebrew scriptures, it always means "young woman," so that was how they decided to translate it. They based their decision on linguistic grounds, not on theological proclivities.

But as soon as the "new Bible" rolled off the presses, outrage erupted among fundamentalists. They viewed the RSV as blasphemy.

Some, noting it had been published in a red cover instead of in the usual black imitation leather (or white imitation leather for brides to carry at weddings), began to brand it the "red Bible." Since the Cold War between the United States and the Soviet Union was raging at the time, the hint that there was something both sinister and subversive about the new Bible was not subtle. This translation was part of a Communist plot.

The scholars who had made the translation were surprised by the fierce reaction. Perhaps somewhat ingenuously they thought they were merely applying their best philological insights to their work. They had translated the Hebrew word *almah* quite literally. But this quite literal translation threatened the theological preconceptions of the fundamentalists, who nevertheless vehemently insisted that they believed the Bible "literally." They had no problem deciding which Bible they would believe, and it was not the red one.

Translation has stirred up both linguistic and theological issues since the early years of Christianity. In the third century Origen tackled it, assembling an edition of the Old Testament that set six different versions in parallel columns. A huge tome, it included the original Hebrew text, then a phonetic transcription of the Hebrew in Greek letters, similar to the English phonetic notes found today in some Conservative and Reformed synagogue prayer books. Next came a very literal translation of the same text in Greek, then another Greek translation in more idiomatic Greek. Next to that was the Septuagint and finally yet another translation into what was then "modern Greek." The whole work is called the Hexapla ("Sixfold"). It required an immense expenditure of labor, but Origen placed the columns side by side so that readers could compare them. He wanted to demonstrate as clearly as possible how disparate the different translations of the same passage can be. Which of those six columns do our Bible believers to believe? The Hexapla was a monumental accomplishment, and it represents a formidable challenge to anyone who contends, as the fundamentalists still do, that the words and sentences of "*the* Bible" contain one self-evident meaning.

The disputes still go on. The young woman/virgin question is not the only one on which there continue to be serious disagreements about translating certain phrases. This is especially true in Hebrew books in which there are passages with words that do not appear anywhere else in the Bible, so comparing contexts to discern the meaning is not possible. Most of the last chapter of the book of Job, for example, stumps even the best Hebrew scholars, and this leads to wildly differing views of how the story ends. Does Job really repent and eat his previous rebellious words, or does he remain defiant to the end? Does God commend him for his fierce insistence on his innocence, or does God condemn him? No one knows for sure. There are numerous cases like this, and often what translators do is to make their best educated guesses. Sometimes they indicate a guess in a footnote, but sometimes they do not, thus leading readers to think they are reading "what the Bible says," when that might not be the case at all. Plainly, as we pursue the question of what it means to "believe the Bible," the plot constantly thickens.[3]

Sophisticated fundamentalists, of course, know Greek and Hebrew and are familiar with the translation problem. What Bible do they believe? Their usual answer is that they do not fully believe in any translation, but only in what the text says in the original Greek or Hebrew. But this means they believe it even when, as with the example of Job, they do not know for sure what it says, which seems a bit odd. They defend their position by explaining that, since they believe every word in all the biblical books (at least in the Protestant Bible) was literally inspired by God, they believe whatever it says "on faith." But here "faith" is once again debased into accepting as true something for which you have no evidence. Thus to "believe the Bible" in this sense does not foster the biblical understanding of faith; instead, it is at best a diversion, and at worst a betrayal.

To push the controversy another step back, it is important to recognize that no one anywhere has the original manuscript of any of the biblical books. All we have are copies of copies. This includes even the oldest copies, like the ones found in the Dead Sea caves. In many cases the several copies of a given text differ from each other, sometimes quite markedly. The oldest manuscripts in existence of the Gospel of Mark, for example, have radically different endings. If you piled them all on one table, you would have a fascinating choice of how you think the gospel ends or perhaps how you think it should end. One manuscript has only Mary Magdalene and Mary "the mother of James" (not, interestingly, the mother of Jesus) coming to the tomb where the body of Jesus had been laid. Another version of the same gospel has Salome with them. One ends abruptly with the women who come to the tomb trembling with amazement, so afraid they are unable to say anything to anyone. Some scholars think that this ambiguous ending is just the way Mark wanted it, but others believe there was once additional material, which was subsequently lost. Yet another manuscript of the same Gospel of Mark has the women reporting to Peter and the other disciples. What is a translator to do when confronted with this embarrassment of manuscript riches?

The King James translators more or less ignored the problem. They simply pieced together how they thought the story should end. Three hundred and fifty years later, and more humbly perhaps, the scholars who translated the Revised Standard Version included them all, allowing readers to take their pick. Incidentally, in recounting the same story of the Resurrection, the Gospel of Matthew has only Mary Magdalene and "the other Mary" at the tomb, while the Gospel of Luke includes a woman named "Joanna," and the Gospel of John mentions only Mary Magdalene. These are significant discrepancies, and not on some marginal passage, but on one of the most significant texts in the New Testament, making it even harder to know just what "believing the Bible" might mean.

But the difficulties do not end there. In recent years the bullish Bible market has been flooded with a variety of new translations that try to render the text into modern street argot. One that has attracted its share of controversy is entitled *Good as News,* the work of a former Baptist minister named John Henson. According to one admirer: "The translation is pioneering in its accessibility, and changes the original Greek and Hebrew nomenclature into modern nicknames. St. Peter becomes 'Rocky,' Mary Magdalene becomes 'Maggie,' Aaron becomes 'Ron,' Andronicus becomes 'Andy,' and Barnabas becomes 'Barry.'"

This neighborhood-pub approach to names might not turn fundamentalists off. After all, the disciples could well have used their Aramaic equivalents when chatting with each other in their fishing boats. But what Reverend Henson does with some of the passages in the letters of Paul, especially those touching on sexual ethics, will not pass unnoticed. For example, the seventeenth century King James Version renders 1 Corinthians 7:1–2:

> Now concerning the things whereof ye wrote unto me: [It is] good for a man not to touch a woman. Nevertheless, [to avoid] fornication, let every man have his own wife, and let every woman have her own husband.

This new street-talk version puts it this way:

> Some of you think the best way to cope with sex is for men and women to keep right away from each other. That is more likely to lead to sexual offenses. My advice is for everyone to have a regular partner.

In the KJV, the well-known passage 1 Corinthians 7:8–9 reads:

> I say therefore to the unmarried and widows, It is good for
> them if they abide even as I. But if they cannot contain, let
> them marry: for it is better to marry than to burn.

The new translation gets right to the point:

> If you know you have strong needs, get yourself a part-
> ner. Better than being frustrated.

It is hard to imagine that those who found "young woman" sac-
rilegious in the "red Bible" will readily accept this wording. But
there are many people who will. Just after its publication, Rowan
Williams, the archbishop of Canterbury, commended *Good as
News* and said he hoped it would spread "in epidemic profusion
through religious and irreligious alike." But there will be many
"Bible believers" who will indeed treat it more like a flu epidemic
and do everything they can to vaccinate their people against it.[4]
But prophylactic measures against new adaptations, para-
phrases, and up-to-date renderings of the Bible have little chance
of success. In addition to *Good as News,* a "Bible magazine" called
Revolve, aimed at "teenage girls," has recently appeared. It takes
the next obvious step toward penetrating popular culture: a comic-
book format. The text of the New Testament, although printed on
nearly every page, shares the space with pictures and snippets of
advice meant to appeal to its intended audience. Its covers feature
attractive and fashionably dressed girls, all smiling widely. It includes sections on beauty hints and dieting. It also carries a regular column on what boys think ("Guys Speak Out") and what they
like and don't like about girls. It asks readers to pray for celebrities
like Mel Gibson and Justin Timberlake.

Like the "Cosmopolitan girl," the "Revolve girl" is called upon
to have certain traits, of which the first one is that she does *not*
initiate phone calls or text messages to boys. As one researcher discovered, however, the counsel and the pictures sometimes contra-
dict each other. The sidebars advise the young women not to use
cosmetics and to dress modestly in order to avoid tempting boys
into sinful thoughts. But the pictures focus on young women with
figures like models who are obviously wearing makeup, and the
covers show more than a little cleavage. It is also significant that
some conservative critics have chastised *Revolve* for playing down
how sinful homosexuality is. But the magazine's position on this
issue merely reflects the more tolerant attitude nearly all younger
people, including evangelicals, have on this issue, often in opposition to their parents.[5]

The Bible in all its multitudinous versions remains the number-
one best-seller in the world, year after year. The market is just too
inviting, and there are sure to be more such attempts to reach it.
Already among many evangelicals and fundamentalists a translation called *Good News for Modern Man,* admittedly considerably
less racy than *Good as News,* has gained enormous popularity. One
publishing house recently listed twenty different versions of the
Bible now in print and selling well. Another publisher offers a
"Bible Translations Laminated Wall Chart" for the price of $13.95
to help understandably confused customers make a more informed
choice.

All of these "Bibles," however, contain only the books of the
traditional "canon," those that have at one point or another been
approved for inclusion by church authorities. Usually this has
meant Protestant approval, although a new translation of Maccabees, which as we have noted above is in the Catholic but not the
Protestant canon, has appeared.[6] But now, in addition to all
these variants of the traditional scriptures, a growing array of

"noncanonical" gospels has captured the public's attention. By far the most popular is the *Gospel of Thomas* (discussed in Chapter 4). It is a fascinating text containing 114 alleged sayings of Jesus. Discovered only in 1946 in Nag Hammadi in Upper Egypt, the manuscript claims that its author is the well-known "doubting Thomas," who is mentioned in all four canonical gospels. But since it is written in Coptic, most scholars have dated the Nag Hammadi find at around 140 CE, decades later than them. However, fragments of what appears to be the same text, but in Greek, had been discovered as early as 1897, also in Egypt, so the Nag Hammadi manuscript is now thought to be a copy of an original Greek text that is just as old as the other four gospels.[7]

In any case, the *Gospel of Thomas* can now be found in the Bible section of many bookstores, and its mystical allusions to a spirit within as well as its Zen-like flavor have made it a favorite of numerous, mainly unconventional Christians. Some years ago I spent a few days with a small group of young people in New Mexico whose only text was this gospel and who spent their time feeding and sheltering poor people and living as simply as possible. They also eschewed marriage, but encouraged sexual sharing among themselves. Apparently they took quite seriously the words attributed to Jesus found in Saying 22 of their favorite gospel:

> Jesus said to them: When you make the two into one, and when you make the inner like the outer and the outer like the inner, and the upper like the lower, and when you make male and female into a single one . . . then you will enter the kingdom.[8]

The discovery of the *Gospel of Thomas* and its unexpected popularity, not just as an ancient curiosity, but as an inspirational text (due in no small measure to the brilliant translation and commentary of Elaine Pagels), have opened the door to a deluge of such "apocryphal" gospels and letters. There are, for example, the *Gospel of the Egyptians,* the *Epistle of the Apostles,* the *Gospel of Truth,* the *Gospel of Philip,* and the *Gospel of Judas.* The antiquity and "authenticity" (whatever that term means) of each of them is constantly disputed. But they serve the positive purpose of demonstrating that a wide variety of different versions of Christianity, not just one, flourished during those early centuries. The enormous interest in them today suggests that they offer an alternative spirituality that is attractive to many twenty-first-century people.

This is not something new. Ever since Thomas Jefferson (1743–1846) sat at his desk at Monticello, scissors in hand, and combed through his Bible snipping out all the verses he considered supernatural and therefore not in keeping with his deistic proclivities, people have tried to improve on the Good Book for reasons they all considered worthwhile. In 1895 activist Elizabeth Cady Stanton (1815–1902) and a committee of other women published *The Woman's Bible,* an early attempt to correct its antifeminist elements. Quoting Paul's familiar statement, "There is neither Jew nor Greek, slave nor free, male nor female, for all are one in Christ Jesus," Stanton's version condemned the second account of creation in Genesis, because it subordinated women to men.

Today, in addition to the new "gospels" mentioned above, there is also a version of the Bible in circulation that is tilted to appeal to a New Age sensibility; another tries to compress excerpts from the scriptures of several religions into a kind of "world Bible."[9] Still another translation, in order to minimize offending Jews, softens the anti-Jewish rhetoric in the New Testament by judiciously substituting the word "Judeans" for "Jews." All this makes it more difficult to know exactly what a "Bible believer" is, and there is no end in sight. It is time to come to terms with the stubborn fact that we have no single and indisputable book we can confidently call *the* Bible, which we can either believe or not believe. We have many of them, and now that they appear on film, online, and in comic-book form we are sure to have many, many more.

I do not think this is a deplorable development. The truth is we do not have the original manuscript of one single word of the Bible. All the Bibles we now have are copies, which are therefore prone to errors and insertions, or translations, which by their nature are also always interpretations that always bear the telltale marks of the eras in which they were done and the theological biases of those who did them. But I think this is vastly better than having, perhaps preserved under glass somewhere in a temperature-controlled room, *the* Bible. If we had such a document it might mislead people into thinking that believing *it* is what "faith" is about. This is, of course, exactly the view fundamentalists hold of "the Bible." Now, however, since what we have is not *the* Bible, but interpretations, and interpretations of interpretations, we are forced to look beyond and through the texts to the people who wrote them and to the mystery they are pointing to. It should help us not to bite into the package instead of into what the package contains.

Does it ever trouble fundamentalists that their attitude toward the Bible, a relatively recent one in the history of Christianity, is exactly the same as that of most Muslims who believe the Qur'an was dictated word for word to Muhammad by Allah? I doubt it. But with Muslims and Buddhists and Hindus now down the street and around the corner in America, instead of across the ocean, the challenge, even for ordinary people, of understanding neighbors' sacred texts is bound to become more pressing. I sometimes wonder if those who would like to get prayer and scripture reading back into public-school classrooms (which might, under certain conditions, be a good idea) would allow the scripture to be read from the Hindu *Bhagavad Gita* or the prayer to be the Muslim Shahada in classes in which there are students from those traditions, as there are in many

American cities. The religious pluralism of our country today means that there are many different scriptures in play. In addition to the Bible there are also the Hindu *Vedas*, the Confucian *Analects*, and the Buddhist *Tripitaka*. How does the Bible as a moral guide compare to these other ancient, indeed scriptural, sources of ethical insight and spiritual wisdom?[10] The question of how we respond to the variety of "scriptures" among us today is one example of the challenge of living faithfully among a variety of religions. But that is an issue I turn to in another chapter.

Should we then "believe the Bible"? I am confident that it is possible to take the Bible back from its fundamentalist hijacking and make it once again a genuine support of faith, instead of an obstacle.[11] To do this, it is helpful to know something about how we got into the impasse in which we find ourselves. There are four significant turning points in the recent history of how Christians have viewed the Bible. One came in the late fifteenth century when the invention of printing made the wide distribution of the Bible possible and then—with the spread of literacy—eventually democratized it. The second came in the nineteenth century with the application of the historical-critical method, which subjected the Bible to the same scrupulous scholarship about dating, authorship, and audience that is applied to any other historical document. The third was the advent of the fundamentalist view of the Bible, which rose as a counterattack against the historical critics. The fourth was the "liberation" of the Bible from both historical critics and fundamentalists, which is happening mainly—though not exclusively—in the global South.

It might be argued that the first of these, printing, put a Bible in every literate person's hands, while the second, the historical-critical method, snatched it back and handed it over once again to the experts. These specialists were, however, no longer priests and rabbis, but academic researchers with their lexicons and grammatical skills. The third, the fundamentalist strategy, was an attempt to bring the Bible back to the people, but it failed by making the Book itself the object of a deformed and static caricature of "faith." Like the fundamentalists, I too am interested in rescuing the Bible from its scholarly wardens, but I believe the way they have done it has failed miserably and has understandably soured countless people on it altogether. The fourth stage, the discovery of the Bible by those who had not been party to the wrangle between the critics and the fundamentalists, appears to be the best way to reclaim it for the next generation.

Having taught for many years not just graduate and undergraduate students, but church-school classes and forums, I have often seen what damage both fundamentalist literalism and historical-critical skepticism can do to otherwise thoughtful and serious people. A better approach is to take the critical specialists with a grain of salt, realizing they are not experts in what its message means for today. As for the fundamentalists, it might be useful to help them see that their literalistic reading is a modern and questionable one. I advise my students to set aside their preconceptions and to dive into the Bible the way they might into a compelling novel or a good film.

The Bible is more like Shakespeare than an ancient history textbook. Don't look for history in our modern sense, or for geology, or even for quick answers to ethical problems. Some New Testament scholars now believe that the author of the Gospel of Luke and the Acts of the Apostles (a single work called "Luke-Acts") modeled it on Virgil's *Aeneid* in an attempt to compose a Christian epic. The same literary objectives motivated many other biblical writers. The way to read them is to let their sheer narrative power evoke whatever response it can without relying on an externally decreed authority to either sanctify their status or pick apart their accuracy. Reading the Bible with this kind of imaginative leap puts us into the company of our spiritual forebears. Some of them were rascals, others were saints. Most of them were a mixture of both. But we all share something in common: our awkward attempt not just to respond to the great mystery, but to respond to it—negatively or positively—with the myths and symbols of our own particular tradition.

Even if we want to shake off that tradition, as many people do, it is that tradition that supplies us with the weapons of our revolt. Even the most zealous atheist denies the existence of "God" as the biblical tradition has defined God. The Bible is the wellspring of our intellectual heritage. It is, as the literary critic Northrup Frye (1912–91) writes, our "great code," and wiggle as we may, we can never fully escape it. Even people who decide to embrace another faith tradition carry it with them in their corpuscles.

It is often argued that high-school and college students simply have to become familiar with the Bible if they are not to be at a complete loss in trying to understand the foundational works of our civilization's literature, art, and music from Milton to Melville to Thomas Mann and from Leonardo to Chagall. It is true, of course, that to the biblically illiterate our most treasured cultural prizes remain incomprehensible. They can admire the brush strokes on *The Last Supper* or the meter in Dante's *Inferno*, but if that is as far as they go, they are missing something vital about these works, namely, what they are saying to us. The same is true of the Bible itself. Even people who do not go blank when they look at a painting like *The Binding of Isaac* or *The Prodigal Son* eventually have to come to terms with something else about the Bible: the unavoidable demands its narratives make on our values and worldviews.

But this is where the most serious question about the place of the Bible in our lives today heaves to the surface like some stubborn Moby Dick. Of course much of the Bible consists of poems, legends, and stories, and even many fundamentalists do not take the seven days of creation literally. But why, then, should it make any claim on our spiritual and moral allegiance today? What about some of the morals it depicts, like God's demand to the Israelites that they slay all the Canaanites, including the women and children? Worse, what do we do about those who claim the Bible's authority to damn gays, to plant settlements in the West Bank, or to assassinate a Rabin or a physician who performs abortions? How do we read those texts from both Testaments that seem to justify murder and mayhem?

The only answer to these questions is to use one's imagination, to place oneself in the context within which the Bible emerged, and then to allow it, with all its "texts of terror," to speak for itself. *Macbeth* still speaks to us, even morally, though the stage is strewn with corpses at the end. But in order to do this, it is essential to know something about this old book, the one we often treat more as something to put your hand on when you take an oath rather than what it is: a fascinating record of how people in our own tradition wrestled with the same perennial issues we face, like the meaning of life and love, betrayal, suffering, and death. If war is too important to be left to the generals, the Bible is far too important to be left to either the academic critics or the Bible thumpers. Of course we need to bring to it the same degree of suspicion and expectation we bring to any other primal source. We must know where it came from and how others have struggled to interpret it. We also need to have the courage to let it speak, which I believe it can. But we may need to work hard to hear.

CHAPTER 12

Sant'Egidio and St. Praxedis

Where the Past Meets the Future

In the old Trastevere ("across the Tiber") section of Rome, not far from where I met with Pope John Paul II and the Waldensians in St. Peter's Basilica, stands a small gray nondescript church. It is understandably bypassed by tourists in search of art masterpieces, because it has none. Built in 1630, Sant'Egidio is no architectural gem. Its blue-painted front door is framed on each side by two standard Greek revival Corinthian columns and above by a single window. Once the chapel of an order of Carmelite sisters, it was abandoned by the nuns in 1971. Still, within its aging walls new life is coming to birth. Today this unlikely edifice is the headquarters of a lay association called the Community of Sant'Egidio, a harbinger of the rebirth of a faith founded on actually following Jesus rather than assenting to statements about him.

The community started in 1968 when a cluster of Italian high-school students led by a young man named Andrea Riccardi began meeting to discuss how they could put the examples of Jesus and St. Francis of Assisi—becoming peacemakers and friends of the poor—into actual practice. Since the students came mainly from middle- and upper-middle-class backgrounds, they were especially impressed by how St. Francis had shunned his family's wealth to embrace a life of poverty and cheerful simplicity. Talking, praying, arguing, and reading the Bible together, they eventually settled on the first-century Christian communities who shared their goods (described in the Acts of the Apostles) as their model.

When the group began to grow, it moved, in 1973, into the disused church and took the name "Community of Sant'Egidio." The old church is now the headquarters for a worldwide organization of over fifty thousand members in seventy countries. They have started soup kitchens, homeless shelters, and AIDS prevention programs in several African countries. They organize peace marches, campaign against the death penalty, and in recent years have participated vigorously in dialogues with Muslims. Still, most people had never heard of the Community of Sant'Egidio until 1992 when, to the astonishment of seasoned diplomats, they succeeded in brokering an agreement between the government of Mozambique and the Frelimo guerillas, ending a bloody sixteen-year civil war. Now the community is recognized as a model of what "citizen diplomats" working outside of official channels can accomplish.

The Community of Sant'Egidio is both a forerunner and an example of many thousands of similar locally based congregations with a worldwide reach. Its members not only travel around the globe and bring people to Rome to negotiate peace agreements; they also make friends with the poor, the mentally disabled, and the lonely elderly in Rome itself. The original St. Egidio is the patron of beggars and lepers. The community is a model of how a living faith can emerge from a crumbling ruin. Like many other examples of the current rebirth of faith, they look to the first Age of Faith for their inspiration, but they do not try to return to it. They also admire St. Francis, but they inhabit the contemporary world with joie de vivre, traveling on Air Italia and making use of the latest negotiation techniques and the Internet. The group is not explicitly anticlerical, but it is self-governing and lay led. Its members take no vows, but like St. Francis, they sought the approval of the Catholic Church and are officially recognized as a "public lay association," demonstrating how the new can grow out of the old without wasting time trying to dismantle it. The Sant'Egidio community has many parallels. It strongly resembles the Latin American "base communities" and other groups like them all over the world.

The Sant'Egidio community lives in Rome, but the renaissance it embodies is even more evident in the global South. One reason for this is that during the past few decades the demography of Christianity has changed, shifting dramatically to the south and east. The population numbers tell the story. In 1900, fully 90 percent of Christians lived in Europe or the United States. Today 60 percent live in Asia, Africa, or Latin America, and that figure will probably rise to 67 percent by 2025. About 1975, Christianity ceased to be a "Western" religion. Reversing Hilaire Belloc's famous dictum, the faith now is *not* Europe, and Europe is *not* the faith. The majority of followers of Jesus no longer reside in the old region of "Christendom," but in the global South, where the Christian movement is growing most rapidly. Most of them are black or brown or yellow, and many live in poverty.

This "de-Westernization" of Christianity has produced a wave of new forms of religious life and a variety of liturgies and creative theologies. It also highlights the remarkable similarities between the first three centuries and our own times. In that first period a growing Christian movement, living in a powerful world empire, faced a host of knotty tests. During those early years, a faith that sprang up among Aramaic-speaking Jews in Palestine was spreading swiftly among both Jews and Gentiles throughout a multicultural and linguistically polyglot world, where its new followers adapted and modified it in a medley of different ways. Something similar is going on today. Fifty years ago Christianity was a religion associated in many people's minds with the "West," but today that is no longer the case. It is expanding most rapidly among millions of people whose cultures are steeped in millennia of Buddhist and Hindu motifs, Confucian values, and indigenous African and shamanic rituals.

During the first three centuries, the Age of Faith, Christians constituted a minority among worshipers of Isis and Osiris, Mithra adepts, and those who venerated the gods of the Greek and Roman pantheons and participated in the cult of the divine emperor. Today, both in the world at large and in the places where they are spreading fastest, Christians are once again minorities and will continue to be for the foreseeable future. In those early centuries, as today, there was no central hierarchy, no commonly accepted creed, and no standard ritual practice. In those first centuries Christianity was *not yet* "Western"; today it is *no longer* Western. Christians then were united by their celebration of Jesus as Lord, by the exchange of visitors, gifts, and letters, and by a vibrant confidence in a shared Sprit. They were known as the "people of the Way." Although trends toward centralization and standardization were already visible, it was Constantine's political deployment of Christianity as an imperial ideology that sanctified those developments.

Today, as a new page is Christian history is turned, hundreds of thousands of different congregations with a vast range of practices and doctrines are again united mainly by their faith in Jesus, a shared Spirit, and a sprawling skein of organizations for mutual help, education, and social outreach. Even the Roman Catholic Church, which is theoretically organized as a severely top-down pyramid, must now constantly try to rein in unconventional African bishops and activist Latin American priests and adjust to a restive American laity demanding its right to share decision making, like the "Voice of the Faithful."

Christianity has never been the strictly "Western" religion of the textbooks. The Christian church in Ethiopia goes back to the earliest centuries. There were already Nestorian Christians in China when Jesuit missionaries carried their message to the emperor at about the same time monks reached the north of England. Central and western Africa had fifteen centuries of unbroken Christian history before the first European missionaries stepped ashore.[1] Still, because of the recent explosive growth, many of the Christians in the global South are first- or second-generation followers of Jesus, and this has suggested a useful idea to some historians. They believe it possible to get at least a few hints to illumine "what it was really like then" in first-century Ephesus or Corinth by becoming more familiar with the "new Christians" in twenty-first-century Africa and Asia. When scholars of early Christianity visit these non-Western congregations, they are often amazed at their similarity to those they have been reading about in ancient texts. They exhibit the same liveliness, cheerfulness, and often the same testiness. Maybe the past and the present are not as remote from each other as we sometimes imagine.

Christianity today is more planetary than it has ever been. It is also more culturally heterogeneous, and—as we have seen—its center of gravity now lies in Africa, Latin America, and the Asian Pacific region. It is growing rapidly in China. One of the great paradoxes of modern history is that this seismic change took place because of the actions of the Western "Christian" world. Some of it, of course, is attributable to the work of conquerors, traders, and missionaries. Religion often follows the money and the sword. But most of it is the result of unprecedented population movements. From 1500 on, millions of Europeans quit their "old countries" and settled in every corner of the globe. They pulled up stakes and shipped out for many different reasons. They sought adventure, land, wealth, or the "greater glory of God." Some combined all these motivations. As Hernán Cortéz (1485–1547), the Spanish vanquisher of Mexico, candidly put it when he landed at what was later to be called Vera Cruz ("True Cross"), "We have come here to win souls for our Holy Mother Church, and to get much gold." Others were driven to launch their arduous journeys to escape famine, the military draft, or religious persecution. Some were trying to escape law-enforcement officers. Others were dispatched halfway around the world as a criminal punishment. They were, as Australians today wryly remark about their forebears, "selected by the best judges in England."

The Europeans carried with them an assortment of different kinds of Christianity. They brought Counter-Reformation Catholicism to "New Spain," a relaxed deist Anglicanism to Virginia, and a zealous Calvinist Puritanism to New England. But theirs was not the only kind of population movement. Not long after they had settled in, Europeans began to ship other peoples, often against their will, across the same seas. Even before the pilgrims arrived in Plymouth, a previous English settlement in Virginia had begun kidnapping and importing Africans as slaves. Then inhabitants of the Indian subcontinent were dragooned into ships to toil in the cane fields of the Caribbean, and later boatloads of Chinese were transported to North America to build the railways across the continent.

One result of this massive series of dislocations was that large numbers of non-Western people, usually under less than favorable circumstances, learned about and embraced Christianity. The demographic balance between Christians in the West and Christians in the global South began to shift. One might have thought that the dissolution of the European empires after World War II would have the ended this displacement, but it did not. Instead, the non-

Western portion of the Christian population continued to wax while the Western portion waned. Today the empire has "struck back." Black African priests serve parishes in London and Manchester. The era of Christianity as a Western religion is already over. Instead of "Western Christianity," we now witness a post-Christian West (in Europe) and a post-Western Christianity (in the global South). America is somewhere in between.

This is not just a geographical issue. It means that the new homelands of the faith of Jesus of Nazareth are not the inheritors of either Greek philosophy or Roman civilization. They have minimal interest in the metaphysical issues that obsessed such early Christian theologians as Origen and Athanasius. In Asia their cultures have been nurtured not by Homer and Plato, but by the *Ramayana,* the *Sutras,* and the *Tao Te Ching.* In Africa they have been maintained by a congeries of local rituals, customary healing rites, and the veneration of ancestors. Nor is this recent dislocation only cultural or religious. It also has to do with justice. Since the vast majority of people in this "new Christendom" are neither white nor well-off, their theological questions center less on the existence or nonexistence of God or the metaphysical nature of Christ than on why poverty and hunger still stalk God's world. It is little wonder that liberation theology, the most creative theological movement of the twentieth century, did not originate in Marburg or Yale, but in the tar-paper shacks of Brazil and the slums of South Korea.[2]

As we explore the similarity between the first Age of Faith and the Age of the Spirit that is just coming to birth, it is important to remember that the first three decades of Christian history were no Garden of Eden. As the New Testament itself makes painfully clear, early Christianity was in no sense free of internal conflict. The letters of Paul to the congregations in Corinth and Galatia bristle with stern advice about coping with their arguments. Still, one congregation rarely intervened in what was going on in another. At first most of them simply accepted the diversity. But as my previous chapters have shown, eventually some parties within the nascent movement strove to impose their way of doing things on the others. One such faction, with a hefty assist from the Roman emperors, ultimately won this battle. Then, by purging its rivals, branding them as heretics, burning their books, banishing their leaders, and rewriting the history, the winners assumed the title of "catholic," or "official," Christianity.

Today's emerging new Christianity also suffers divisions, and the tensions do not follow geographical boundaries. As in the early church we see comparable efforts to enforce creeds, pull people into line, and impose uniform practices. Some of these take surprising turns. Traditionalist Anglican bishops in Africa who oppose the ordination of gays "adopt" wealthy American Episcopal parishes that agree with their unbending beliefs. At the same time conservative North American Pentecostals try without success to discourage the left-leaning social action of their Latin American sisters and brothers. At the heart of these attempts to goad people into line, however, there lurks a contradiction. They are carried out in the name of some version of "official" Christianity—called "authentic" or "traditional" or "classical," depending on the denomination. Whatever its label, it remains an expression of the passing Age of Belief, which won its first ambiguous victory centuries ago.

But, with our new knowledge of that early period, the dubiousness of the victory becomes clearer every day. What will happen when the cat is completely out of the bag? How will things change when it becomes known in every pew that the "official" version of early Christianity—whether it is deployed by Catholics or Protestants—was a work of fiction and is no longer credible? Clearly the current discussions about what Christianity "really was," what it "really is," and what it "should be" in its contemporary global incarnation must now unfold in a different idiom.

A key element in the new idiom is the regaining of the original meaning of "faith." It has now become evident that the adulteration of Christianity from the way of life of a vigorous but persecuted minority into the ideology of an empire produced many changes. It not only defaced the institutional profile of the church, but disfigured the meaning of its vocabulary. Students of linguistics know how the context in which words are used inevitably alters their meaning, and this was no exception. At its outset "faith" meant a dynamic lifestyle sustained by fellowships that were guided by both men and women and that reflected hope for the coming of the Reign of God. But when Christianity became swollen into an elaborate code of prescribed beliefs and ritual obligations policed by a hierarchy, the meaning of "faith" was warped almost beyond recognition. Initially faith had meant a primary life orientation, but the evolving clerical class now equated "faith" with "belief in" certain specified doctrines and patterns of authority, which, in any case, themselves changed periodically depending on who held the ecclesial scepter. The result was a disaster for dissent and open discussion. Yesterday's heretic may be tomorrow's saint, but the heretic is still dead.

The clerical seizure of power in the church not only altered the meaning of words; it tainted the capacity of Christians to know their own history. The revised account of the first several decades that male bishops concocted was especially dismissive of women. Only in recent years have both male and female historians been able to correct this men's-club version. It now turns out that women played a significantly larger leadership role than had previously been thought. But the power of false history to shape present perception goes even farther. Since the priestly elite insisted that women had always been subservient and marginal, people were unable to see clear evidence to the contrary.

A ninth-century mosaic in the Church of St. Praxedis in Rome provides a poignant example of this myopia. It shows a certain Theodora with the word *episcopa* ("bishop") etched above her head. The church is located only a ten-minute stroll from the main train station in Rome, but when I first walked through its doors, I found that I had stepped into one of the hottest skirmishes between current historical research and received practices and traditions. This one concerns the leadership of women during the first few centuries of Christianity. The mosaic is in a side chapel. Theodora is pictured with Mary of Nazareth, St. Pudentia, and St. Praxedis, all women leaders of the early church. The controversy centers on what the word *episcopa*, or "bishop," meant in Theodora's day. Was she the convener or president of a local congregation? Or did she have a wider leadership responsibility? Was she "ordained," and if so what did ordination mean then? How does this mosaic fit in with pictures of women leading what appear to be eucharistic services, like the *Fractio Panis* ("Breaking the Bread") found in Catacombs of Priscilla, which has become one of the most contentious images?

These visual depictions clearly accord with the dozens of written accounts of early Christian women leaders catalogued by Sister Carol Osiek and Kevin Madigan in *Ordained Women in the Early Church, 30–600: A Documentary History.*[3] Some skeptics assert that Theodora's title of *episcopa* was merely an honorific one, bestowed on her because she was the mother of Pope Paschal I, whose mosaic portrait, holding the Church of St. Praxedis in his hands, is in the rounded area above the altar called the "apse." They also contend that the women mentioned in the written texts played only auxiliary roles.

The storm continues to boil over what it means that Theodora was a "bishop." The evidence is inconclusive, and the jury is still out. But when I first saw the mosaic at St. Praxedis, a question came to mind immediately. Remembering this was a ninth-century work, I wondered why, if a male dominated clergy had tried so hard to erase evidence of women's leadership, this dramatic refutation of that opinion was still intact. Someone had tried to scratch out the "a" in Theodora. Still, even the most energetic rewriters of history may be a bit reluctant to scrape whole mosaics off church walls. Also, as I learned later, since many of the visual images of women in early Christianity have only minimal textual material attached to them, it is easier to read something entirely different into the picture than what the artist may have originally intended. It also reminded me of the psychological experiments I have read about showing that we often see what we have been prepared to see, not what is really there.

The displacement of faith by belief had even more ruinous consequences. It became so entrenched in theological reflection and church organization that not even the most dedicated reformers could dislodge it. Luther turned Europe on its head by insisting that salvation was "by grace through faith." But within a few generations of his death, "Lutheran orthodoxy" had frozen his insight into the notion that one had to *believe in* the doctrine of justification by faith to assure salvation. A man of robust passions, Luther taught that we all need to put our trust—our faith—in something in order to live. Idolatry was not a matter of bowing down before statues. Luther in fact, unlike Calvin, wanted to keep the statues in the churches. For him, idolatry meant trusting—putting one's faith—in such "idols" as money, power, and fame.

By the time of the Enlightenment, Christian terminology was impossibly confused. The original meaning of faith had been so thoroughly lost that, when the *philosophes* attacked religion by equating it with blind belief and superstition, they were merely echoing what the church itself taught. But then these dissenters went on to make the same mistake. They resolved that "reason" should henceforth banish belief, and that now people should place their faith in reason. The French revolutionaries even enthroned a "Goddess of Reason" in Notre Dame Cathedral, unwittingly proving Luther's point that everyone needs to have faith in something. But their attack only pushed the church into an even more ferocious defense of "belief."

The rise of natural science initiated the final step in the decline of a Christianity that was a collation of ostensible propositions about the world that one was supposed to accept on the basis of a religious authority. Science gradually evolved a method of testing factual assertions and by so doing discredited one pseudofactual religious claim after another. The trial of Galileo by the Inquisition marked the turning point. He had insisted that the earth moves around the sun, not vice versa, and claimed that what he actually saw through a telescope had to take precedence over what both the ecclesial and the contemporary scientific authorities taught about the motion of the heavenly bodies. He was forced to recant, but walked away murmuring that the earth still moves. Some years ago Pope John Paul II honored Galileo, and rightly so. He and the science he represented actually rendered an invaluable service to Christianity. They dismantled the church's claims to competence in describing the workings of the natural world, thus helping Christianity to regain its original impetus as a movement of faith.

Today there is no basis for any "warfare between science and religion." The two have quite different but complementary missions, the first concerning itself with empirical description, the second with meaning and values.[4] Unfortunately, however, although the war is over, sporadic skirmishes between die-hards on both sides continue. Biblical literalists, who totally misunderstand the poetry of the book of Genesis, try to reduce it to a treatise in geology and zoology. Their mirror image is found among the atheists and agnostics who mount spurious pseudoscientific arguments to demonstrate that the universe has no meaning or that God does not exist. Both parties are fundamentalists of a sort, deficient in their capacity for metaphor, analogy, and the place of symbol and myth in human life. Sadly, battle lines that were drawn years ago continue to cause confusion today. Otherwise thoughtful people still mistakenly view the world as divided between "believers" and "nonbelievers." But that era of human consciousness is almost over. We are witnessing the emergence of a different vocabulary, one that is closer to the original sense of the word "faith" before its debasement.

As we look for this new language, it is important to remember that during the fifteen centuries of the Age of Belief not everyone accepted its garbled version of the life and message of Jesus. Recognizing it as a diluted version, colonies of monks, countless nonconformist groups, movements that were branded as "heretical," and many courageous individuals refused to accept the caricature. Those in charge dealt with them harshly, as documented by the dreary history of inquisitions and burnings. Still, many of these groups survived and even thrived within the boundaries of what had made itself into an imperial church. St. Francis of Assisi retrieved the authentic message of the Nazarene, but had the tactical savvy to seek the pope's approval for his raggedy flock of spiritual troubadours. St. Teresa of Avila, for whom faith was a personal bond, close to a marriage, with Christ, relied on her wits and her charm to keep one jump ahead of the Holy Inquisition in sixteenth-century Spain. In our own time, the Sant'Egidio community and people like Dorothy Day, founder of the Catholic Worker movement, and Bishop Oscar Romero, the assassinated champion of liberation theology in El Salvador, have kept embodied faith rather than belief systems central.

It is fortuitous that our recent awareness of early Christianity is coinciding with its explosive growth in the global South, and fortunately my own life trajectory has brought me into close touch with both. I have worked closely with a number of scholars who by patiently brushing away layers of dust and grit are meticulously clarifying our knowledge of Christian origins. Also, I have traveled, taught, and learned in many places in the world, from Brazil to China and from India to Japan. In my teaching at home I have come to know students and visitors from every continent. These two facets of my career flow together when I realize both how hugely kaleidoscopic early Christianity was and that Christians steeped in ancient non-Western cultures do not have to stuff themselves into any preordained pattern.

The prospect of a dappled and motley Christian community sprawled across five continents may be daunting, but the challenge it poses is hardly new. Christianity came to birth in the midst of a cultural change. A Hebrew and Aramaic message in a Greek and Latin world, it was a movement that was born to travel. In fact, it seems designed to travel, and it takes on new life with every succeeding cultural transition. But for this to happen again, some old wineskins must be discarded, and the incubus of a self-serving and discredited picture of Christian origins must be set aside.

We cannot and should not try to reinstall the first Age of Faith. We live in a different world. But Christianity today bears within it both the cherished gems and the worthless debris it has accumulated during the intervening fifteen hundred years of the Age of Belief, which is now expiring. Can we preserve the jewels and get rid of the junk? It was a period rich with memories and lessons, with good examples and bad ones, with treasures and trinkets. Even though we still live with the scars Christianity has inflicted on itself, we cannot dismantle the soaring cathedrals, silence the music, shred the theological texts, or discard the splendid liturgies. They are ours as well as theirs. As we enter this Age of the Spirit, they can still inspire us, and they have much to teach us. But we need to understand our past in a new way, because we still inhabit a world in which that past exercises a heavy hand and will not easily loosen its grip.

CHAPTER 13

Blood on the Altar
of Divine Providence

*Liberation Theology and
the Rebirth of Faith*

On March 24, 1980, Oscar Arnulfo Romero, the Roman Catholic archbishop of San Salvador, arrived just after six o'clock in the afternoon at the tiny chapel in the Hospital of Divine Providence in that city to say an evening Mass, as he had done many times before. Hurriedly pulling on his vestments, Romero first led the small congregation through the Liturgy of the Word, which precedes the Eucharist. Then he stood before the altar, ready to elevate the bread and wine, when a shot rang out. The well-aimed bullet, fired by someone closely acquainted with firearms, pierced his heart, and he collapsed immediately, his blood splattering across the altar and onto the elements he was about to consecrate. He died almost at once, but with his last breath whispered to those around him, "May God forgive the assassins."

Romero's life story was a parable. Even before his death he had become an incarnation of the emergence of Christianity from its centuries-long Constantinian era and into its new global phase. He personified the dramatic turn away from a religion of creeds and hierarchies toward a newly recovered faith in the divine promise of a reign of justice, as taught and demonstrated by Jesus of Nazareth. Today millions of people all over Latin American venerate him as a saint.

Romero started as a quite ordinary, somewhat colorless priest in a church allied for five hundred years with the landowners and the elite. But he died as a spokesman of a church struggling to be born among the powerless people of his ravaged country. He was born in El Salvador in 1917 and began working as a carpenter, but by his early teens had already enrolled in seminary. He took easily to the clerical life and seemed content to live within its securely confining walls. His fellow seminarians found him remote, overly proper, and not very likeable. But his superiors looked upon him with favor and sent him to Rome to study at the Gregorian University, the widely recognized training school for students with both real mental acumen and unquestioning respect for higher authority, qualities that mark them as likely candidates for leadership in the church. Romero received his licentiate in theology and was ordained to the priesthood in Rome during World War II, when travel to other parts of Europe was impossible. His education was Roman to the core, and he returned to El Salvador ready to be a loyal spokesman for what Catholics call *Romanität,* which means roughly "the way they think and do things in Rome." He was "Constantinian" through and through.

Back in El Salvador, a country named for the "Savior," Romero began his career as a priest firmly ensconced in the closed and inflexible hierarchy that had ruled his country's religious life and shaped its political and cultural history since its conquest in 1524 by Spaniards under the command of Pedro de Alvarado (ca. 1485–1541). His first years afforded him ample opportunity to put his traditionalist views of church, theology, and politics into practice. He became rector of the interdiocesan seminary of El Salvador, where he had the responsibility of shaping the thinking of novice priests from all over his country. Soon, however, he moved into regional administrative duties, becoming executive secretary of the Episcopal (Bishops') Conference for all of Central America. A bright and energetic man, and also obedient and ambitious, he was clearly on the way up.[1]

In 1970 Pope Paul VI named Romero auxiliary bishop to Monsignor Luis Chávez y Gonzales, archbishop of San Salvador. This was a sure indication of the confidence Rome had in him and that it was only a matter of time until he became a full bishop. This happened in 1977, when the same pope appointed him archbishop of San Salvador, succeeding Monsignor Chávez. Traditionalist circles within the Salvadorian and wider Latin American church, already alarmed by the spread of liberation theology, welcomed Romero's appointment with applause and a sigh of relief. Here was a solid conventional priest of the old school, one who would not rock the boat and who would show little sympathy for Catholics— lay or clerical—who were involving themselves in social movements and protests. At least this is what they thought, and the evidence of Romero's life up to that point gave them every reason to think that way.[2]

But things began to change quickly and —contrary to almost everyone's expectations— Romero became in his own person a living sign of the fundamental transformation Christianity was undergoing in the late twentieth century. In his case the conversion came by way of what was beginning to be called "liberation theology." Romero did not learn about it in seminary or at the Gregorian. It was not being taught there. He learned it through grueling experience. No sooner had he become archbishop of San Salvador, than a young priest and friend of his, Father Rutulio Grande, who had been serving among the poorest people in the country, was murdered by a death squad.

Romero was personally shaken. Then, when he officiated at the funeral Mass in the village where Grande had lived, the people who had been devoted to the dead priest asked him, "Will you stand with us as Father Rutulio did?" That began Romero's conversion. Ever since his return to his country, every day he had heard about more murders, jailings, beatings, and kidnappings. And now, this. But the authorities feigned ignorance, and the press was silent. Consequently, Romero took a daring step. Every week he announced the names of the dead and the "disappeared" from the pulpit of the cathedral. Then he warned members of the police and the military that God forbade them to kill innocent peasants who were demanding their God-given rights. He became a voice of hope for his suffering people and a growing menace to those who were clinging to their shaky hold on power. He began to sense that he was a marked man, and once in a sermon he promised, "If they kill me, I will live on in the life of the people." Then, on that March day in 1980, the members of the death squad loaded their guns and drove to the Hospital of Divine Providence.

Romero's violent death also made him the saint and martyr of liberation theology, the most innovative and influential theological movement of the twentieth century, and also probably the most widely misunderstood. Liberation theology is not, as its critics charge, a political movement that deploys religious language. Rather, it is a profoundly religious movement with important political implications. Nor is it a theological trend or school of thought like other twentieth-century ones such as the Catholic "Neo-Thomism" associated with Jacques Maritain (1882–1973) or the Protestant "Neo-Orthodoxy" of Karl Barth (1886–1968). Rather than new ideas or theories, liberation theology represents a whole new way of engaging in theology.

It begins by rethinking the Christian message from the point of view of the poor and the outcast. It did not come to birth in the lecture halls of Tübingen or the libraries of the Gregorian University in Rome. It is not a "trickle down" theology, but one that has "percolated up" from thousands of grassroots groups and move-ments. Originating in Latin America during the 1960s, it quickly mushroomed throughout the global South, where Christianity is now growing most rapidly, in Korea, Southeast Asia, sub-Saharan Africa, and India. Bishop Tutu of South Africa as well as the "Min-jung" theologians of Korea, the "Dalit" (formerly "untouchable") theologians of India, and leaders of the underground church in China acknowledge their debt to it. There are also Protestant, Jewish, Muslim, and Buddhist variants.

Like Romero, I did not learn about liberation theology at Har-vard or Yale. But unlike him, I did not learn it by living in the midst of squalor and oppression. My first contact with the move-ment came when I spent the summer of 1968 at the Center for Inter-Cultural Studies in Cuernavaca, Mexico. I had gone there at the invitation of the center's founder, Monsignor Ivan Illich, when—after the assassinations of Martin Luther King and Robert Kennedy in the spring of that year—I felt so deeply disheartened about the prospects of my country that I wanted to go somewhere else for a while. I had met Dr. King in 1956, during the Montgom-ery bus boycott. We stayed in touch, and then I marched and dem-onstrated, and spent a few days in jail, while working with his Southern Christian Leadership Conference. I had made speeches for Robert Kennedy in Oregon and California during his attempt to gain the Democratic nomination for president in 1968. I flew back from Los Angeles the day his campaign ended, confident that "we had won," only to learn of his assassination when I got home.

Angry and confused, I was so eager to get away that I arrived in Mexico, accompanied by my wife and three young children, with no place to stay. Illich helped us find a small house, hemmed in on one side by a tile factory, which clattered noisily during the day, and on the other by a waterfall, which gurgled and roared day and night. We soon grew to appreciate the sloshing of the falls, like a hundred bathtub faucets all turned on full. But we never quite adjusted to the clanking of the factory and were grateful that the workers took a long siesta every afternoon and never worked at night.

It was a noteworthy summer for me, and little by little I became less dispirited. I learned Spanish at the center's excellent language school and taught a course on contemporary social theology in lieu of tuition. We visited beaches and Aztec pyramids. I learned to savor cheese enchiladas and Dos Equis beer. It was a propitious time to be south of the Rio Grande. The spirit of change was in the air. The Catholics in Latin America were already caught up in new theological and social currents, and many priests had been forced to leave their homes by either church authorities or their governments, but the bishop of Cuernavaca, Don Sergio Méndez Arceo, who sympathized with what they were doing, always seemed to find a place for them in his diocese. Their presence transformed Cuernavaca, a cool summer retreat for the Mexican elite, into a cauldron seething with spirited discussions over cups of coffee and glasses of beer around the *centro*.

When I got back to Harvard, I immediately began teaching courses in liberation theology, among the first offered in North America. Only in retrospect have I realized that if I had known about the ruthless massacre of over one hundred student demonstrators in the Plaza de las Tres Culturas in Mexico City, which took place just before I returned, I might not have felt so hopeful. But the Mexican authorities quickly hid that awful news from the public, which only learned about it weeks later. In fact, it took years for the full horrendous truth to come out.

One of the people who breezed through Cuernavaca that summer was Father Gustavo Gutiérrez, a Peruvian priest, often thought of as the "father of liberation theology." He divided his time between teaching at the Pontifical Catholic University in

Lima, serving an impoverished parish there, and traveling to various places on the continent to teach and speak. We met at Illich's center, and the following year Father Gutiérrez invited me to give a lecture in Lima at his university, the Pontificia Universidad Catolica, which the faculty and students there simply call the *Catolica*. I accepted, and in Lima I stayed with the Maryknoll priests, ate with Father Gutiérrez at an unfussy restaurant in a crowded working-class district, and visited his parish in Rimac a drab and dingy quarter of Lima. He was about to publish his epochal book, *Theology of Liberation*, which appeared in English in 1971, and we talked about it at length.[3]

Father Gutiérrez, like Bishop Romero, is a living example of both the steep decline of a Christianity based on hierarchically imposed beliefs and its current rebirth as faith in the promise of the era of justice exemplified in the life of Jesus. Gutiérrez is a stocky, somewhat rotund man whose brown skin reveals his Quechua lineage. He walks with a slight limp, the result of a childhood illness. His owlish face is softened by a wide grin, which he frequently flashes. He dresses in simple civilian clothes, and when he talks, he looks at his listener over large glasses in plastic frames. I have never seen him in a clerical collar.

"Gustavo," as all his friends call him, started out to study medicine. He wanted to be as helpful as possible to the poor people he knew so well. He soon changed his direction, however, and entered the seminary in Lima to study for the priesthood. As in Romero's case, his teachers recognized his intellectual gifts, but—perhaps not seeing Romero's submissiveness—they dispatched him to Louvain and Lyons instead of Rome. There Gustavo delved into Jacques Maritain's "integral humanism" and Emmanuel Mounier's Catholic personalism and also read some of the books of Pierre Teilhard des Chardin, whose writings had been condemned by the Vatican. He was also drawn to Yves Congar's thinking on the theology of the laity.

He wrote his own thesis on the religious significance of Sigmund Freud. When he returned to Peru, Gutiérrez had accomplished something few before him ever had. He had fused his indigenous roots and his passionate love for the poor with the best theological scholarship available. He was entirely ready for the next step.

Although he is widely thought of as the father of liberation theology, Gutiérrez always tries to minimize his own role. When, during my visit with him in Lima, I once asked him why liberation theology had first appeared in Latin America, he told me the answer was simple. It was because of the potent mixture of faith and poverty there. "The poor people of our continent," he said, "began to understand their poverty from the perspective of their faith, and their faith from the perspective of their poverty." This meant that the first question they asked was not about the "existence" of God, an issue that had preoccupied educated middle-class Westerners, whose concerns were shaped by science, skepticism, and rationalism. The question poor people posed was the much older one of how to justify a God of love and justice with the suffering and deprivation they felt and saw around them. They drew their response directly from their understanding of who Jesus was and what faith in him involved. They found in Jesus not a rationalization of why things are as they are, but rather an unflinching confidence that things need not be this way and that they can and will change. They saw in Jesus a challenge to the fatalism that had often dogged them and an assurance that not even defeat and death can prevent the coming of God's reign of justice.

It is not difficult to see how liberation theology connects the vitality of early Christianity with the emerging profile of Christianity. The centrality of faith-as-confidence in Jesus and the Kingdom of God, which is inseparable from him, provides the link. As Gutiérrez writes: "Reflection on the mystery of God (that is theology) can only be done by following Jesus. It is only possible in this way and in this spirit to think about and announce the Father's gratuitous love for every human person."[4]

Liberation theology is more than just a regionally specific "Latin American theology" or a passing fad. It embodies a momentous leap out of the many centuries in which Christianity was defined as a system of beliefs imposed by a hierarchy. It symbolizes the resurrection of faith-as-trust and represents the retrieval of the core of the gospel message as it was understood and lived in the earliest centuries of Christianity. It is an unmistakable sign of the coming of an Age of the Spirit.

Liberation theology dramatizes the link between the origins of Christianity and the recent shift of its center of gravity from the West to the global South, which has generated a significant change in what it means to be a "Christian." Many more destitute and formerly excluded people are now full-scale participants in the worldwide Christian community. The result of this upheaval is that the Christianity of the twenty-first-century has begun to look more like that of the first two centuries, when streams of women, slaves, and impoverished city dwellers joined the new congregations. The original idea of Christianity as a faithful way of life has begun to displace the enforced system of creeds that defined it during much of the intervening time.

There are many reasons why Latin Americans began to see Jesus this way. First, they read the gospels in small groups, often led by laypeople, in which they discussed ways to respond to the appalling conditions they lived in. Priests and nuns had originally organized these groups, called "ecclesial base communities" (*comunidades eclesiales de base*, CEBs), to complement regular parish worship, especially in areas where clergy were in short supply. But they soon outgrew clerical oversight and took on lives of their own. They met in villages, small towns, and in the shabbier sections of the big cities.[5]

Whenever I visited one the CEBs, I felt a strange sense of déjà vu. They seemed amazingly similar to the descriptions I had read of the tiny congregations of Christians that dotted the Mediterranean basin in the first centuries of our era. The men and women who gathered in the CEBs were usually from the less privileged strata of the society. Their clothes were clean, but worn. Some could barely read. The atmosphere was relaxed and informal. They sang, strummed guitars, prayed, welcomed visitors, shared food, read a biblical passage (usually from the gospels), and energetically discussed the problems their communities were facing in light of the passage they had read. They often made shrewd connections between the biblical stories and their present circumstances. They had clearly not been distracted by either of the two approaches to the Bible that hampered its availability in the West. First, they knew little about historical-critical methods, but listened to the texts as if they were good stories. Second, they were unspoiled by fundamentalism, which has only since then made any impact in South America. They did not view Jesus as a "personal savior" whose mission was to rescue them *from* a sinful world, but as the one who announced and demonstrated the nearness of the Kingdom of God that was to come *to* their world.

Christianity understood as a system of beliefs guarded and transmitted through a privileged religious institution by a clerical class is dying. Instead, today Christianity as a way of life shared in a vast variety of ways by a diverse global network of fellowships is arising. The initial fruits of this resurrection are already obvious. In those countries where the clerical leadership clings to the older model, the churches are empty. Any visitor to Europe can witness these vacant pews at first hand. But in those areas of the world where creeds and hierarchies have been set aside to make way for the Spirit, like the stone rolled away from Christ's grave in the Easter story, one senses life and energy. There is no question that some of this energy spills into directions that might once have been called heresy or schism (and still are by some quibblers). Still, the fact that the most fruitful and exciting movements in Christianity today are taking place on the margins of existing ecclesial structures should not surprise anyone. Historically speaking, "schism" and "heresy" have often heralded the deepening and extension of the faith. Pioneers always step outside of established boundaries. Sometimes they are condemned, sometimes honored, and sometimes both, starting with the first and only later ending up with the second.

The Catholic culture of Latin America is not the only sphere in which new life is blossoming. It is also appearing in what some might consider an unlikely place, in the tsunami of Pentecostalism that is sweeping across the non-Western world. It is to that blustery wind of the Spirit that we now turn.

CHAPTER 14

The Last Vomit of Satan and the Persistent List Makers

Pentecostals and the Age of the Spirit

The tidal shift of the world's Christian population from the "north" to the global South is one of the reasons for the present decline in creed-bound Christianity, the revival of faith, and the birth of an Age of the Spirit. But it is an ambiguous development. Some American and European scholars are afraid that this post-Western "new Christendom" is causing more of a reactionary tilt and may end up strengthening fundamentalism.

But the evidence is mixed and is not all in.

Although outsiders often confuse the two, it is Pentecostalism, not fundamentalism, that accounts for 90 percent of this spectacular growth. The two are not the same. In Latin America Pentecostals are often grouped with evangelical Protestants, and in Brazil the two are given the common label *crente*. The word literally means "believer," but that can be misleading. The *crentes* of that continent are precisely those "people of the Way" for whom creeds are less and less significant. Two or three Latin American countries already have *crente* majorities, and others are headed in that direction. When I visited the religious census office in Rio de Janeiro in 2002, I was told that in the previous year, in metropolitan Rio de Janeiro alone, 327 new *crente* congregations had been established. In the same year, only one new Roman Catholic church and two Umbanda (Afro-Brazilian) temples were built.

The situation in Brazil is one of the clearest indications of an Age of the Spirit. But it also mirrors the extraordinary growth of Pentecostals everywhere. The majority of Christian congregations in sub-Saharan Africa and on the Asian rim are Pentecostal. The largest Christian congregation in the world, the Yoido Full Gospel Church in Seoul, Korea, which claims eight hundred thousand members, is Pentecostal. Reports from mainland China suggest a grassroots Pentecostal/charismatic Christian movement is taking place there as well. In the United States, large numbers of Latin American immigrants are leaving the Catholic Church and joining Pentecostal congregations. Like a forest fire that continues to smolder just below the surface, ecstatic worship has simmered in Christianity from its earliest years and constantly breaks through the barriers that have sought to dampen it. It will undoubtedly continue to do so.[1]

It is easy to see why many people confuse Pentecostals with fundamentalists. Both movements came to birth in America in the early years of the twentieth century. Both involved protests against the established Protestantism of the time. But there the similarities end. Fundamentalists are text-oriented literalists who insist that the inerrant Bible is the sole authority. Pentecostals, on the other hand, though they accept biblical authority, rely more on a direct experience of the Holy Spirit. Fundamentalists consider themselves sober and rational. Pentecostals welcome demonstrative worship and ecstatic praise, which they call "speaking in tongues" and which they regard as the Spirit praying within them. They sway and dance in the aisles. People once ridiculed them as "holy rollers." Fundamentalists insist on a hard core of nonnegotiable doctrines one must hold to unquestioningly. Pentecostals generally dislike doctrinal tests and reject what they call "manmade creeds and lifeless rituals." During the first decades of their histories the two movements often fought each other bitterly. One prominent fundamentalist, C. Campbell Morgan, called Pentecostals "the last vomit of Satan."[2]

The year 1940, however, marked a major change in the American religious landscape that further complicated the picture. An influential group of Protestant religious conservatives under the leadership of Reverend Harold Okenga, of Boston's Park Street Church, formed the National Association of Evangelicals. Its purpose was to draw a sharp line not just between their group and "modernists," but also between themselves and fundamentalists. These self-styled "evangelicals" held some of the same beliefs as fundamentalists, but there were important differences. Evangelicals firmly believed in the religious and moral authority of the Bible, but did not consider it a dependable source for geology or biology. They also rejected the notion of retreating from the fallen world. They wanted to engage it.

But the organizers of this new evangelical association faced a problem. What should they do about the Pentecostals, who were already growing so rapidly? On the one hand, they used some of the same vocabulary, but the evangelicals—like fundamentalists—were distrustful of the Pentecostals' emotionality and their claim that the Holy Spirit sometimes spoke to them in dreams and visions, not always mediated through the Bible. Finally, however, the evangelicals invited the Pentecostals to join their new organization. Now, however, the Pentecostals had to decide what to do. In the end, some joined the NAE, and others did not. The relationship has remained touchy ever since.

Are Pentecostals contributing to the shift from belief to faith, or are they among those holding out for a belief-defined Christianity? Are they heralds of the Age of the Spirit? The answer is that there are, after all, 500 million of them, and they vary widely in their theologies and practices. Some Pentecostals, especially white North Americans, have been heavily influenced by fundamentalism. But in the global South, they are more informed by an ethic of following Jesus, and a vision of the Kingdom of God. They have recently become increasingly active in social ministries, but the hostility they sometimes show toward other faiths limits their ability to cooperate.

A few years ago two scholars set out to investigate this new social awakening within worldwide Pentecostalism. Donald Miller, a sociologist who directs the Center for Religion and Civic Culture at the University of Southern California, and Tetsunao Yamamori, president emeritus of Food for the Hungry, spent four years traveling around the globe to find out about what they eventually called "progressive Pentecostalism." Crisscrossing Africa, Asia, and Latin America, they interviewed hundreds of people and observed Pentecostal outreach efforts to drug addicts in Hong Kong, sex workers in Bangkok and Calcutta, babies with AIDS in Africa, and dozens of other programs. What they discovered puts faces and names on what is quickly becoming the major expression of Christianity in many parts of the globe. Take Jackie Pullinger, for example, whose highly effective ministry to heroin addicts in Hong Kong succeeds, she says, by relying on the Holy Spirit. She foregoes modern management methods and a fund-raising staff. Or Pastor Oscar Muriu, whose Nairobi Chapel runs a clinic, a pharmacy, and a sewing school. Or dozens of others the authors visited from Manila to Addis Ababa to Soweto.[3]

Something highly significant is going on in the Pentecostal movement. Its main focus was once fixed on a strictly otherworldly salvation, but now the example of Jesus's concern for the impoverished, the sick, and the socially outcast has begun to play a more central role. Miller and Yamamori foresee a possible fusion with some of the insights of liberation theology. They foresee emerging "progressive" Pentecostalism, with its flexible structures, its welcoming of the emotional component in praise, its uncanny capacity to be at home in different cultures, and now its emerging commitment to the Jesus ethic. They even note a lessening of their animus toward other denominations.

My own experience of the impact of this new Pentecostalism has taken place mainly in Brazil, which I have been visiting for three decades. During one of my first trips there twenty-five years ago I met a young Brazilian sociologist from São Paulo who was studying the peasant leagues then springing up in the arid, poverty-stricken northeast. The farmers were organizing these leagues so they could buy seed and equipment and market their products cooperatively. During her research this novice investigator, a serious lay Catholic, discovered that indigenous Brazilian Pentecostals, even though they constituted only about 10 percent of the population then (the percentage is higher now), had done the lion's share of the work and provided most of the leadership. Eager to uncover the link between their religious faith and their work with the leagues, she interviewed several Pentecostals and asked what the correlation was. They seemed puzzled by the question, she said, and shrugged their shoulders. This in turn puzzled her, but the more she lived among them, the more she began to understand the connection.

Pentecostals, she explained, are practiced list makers. They are used to compiling records of people they intend to invite to church meetings. They knock on doors, then check off who was not at home, who responded favorably, and who slammed the door. Then they return, sometimes again and again. If the door was opened, they learned how to get their message across quickly and clearly. These skills, the sociologist finally noticed, were exactly the ones needed for organizing peasant leagues. No wonder they had set the pace.

The essential qualities of a religious faith can be discerned most clearly in the shape it gives to the institutions it spawns. Pentecostals give birth to voluntary associations, which are vital to any healthy society and the lifeblood of any genuine democracy. They mediate between ordinary people and the larger structures of economy, government, education, and press. They provide alternative patterns of organization and unofficial networks. They school people in the indispensable skills needed to make democracy work.

Despite the misapprehension of many North Americans, the Pentecostals of Brazil have neither remained aloof from politics nor have they imitated the American religious Right. Careful analyses of their political behavior indicate their voting patterns tend toward the "center left." In the recent Brazilian presidential elections, for example, a large majority voted for Lula and the Workers' Party. Their political trajectory was captured two years ago when a close observer wrote about the *inquierization* (the "leftification") of the Pentecostals.[4]

Historically, Latin America has not been a continent richly endowed with voluntary associations. In general one belonged to whatever one was born into. Be it state or nation or tribe or church, you *find yourself* in a collectivity. You do not *join* it. But to be a *crente* you have to join something. To borrow a famous distinction from William James, most Latin American collectivities are made up of the "once born." Virtually the only exceptions to this rule have been labor unions, sports teams, base communities, and Pentecostal or evangelical religious congregations, which are constituted by the "twice born," people who have made a conscious choice to join something. All this means that the stunning growth of Pentecostals is a critical key to the democratization of the whole region, especially since they are beginning to participate in political life in an active way, hold public office, and seek to formulate a "social theology" of their own. But the continued growth of Pentecostals and their contribution to democracy are in no way guaranteed. They are often fragile, vulnerable to both pressures from without and threats from within. How much they will strengthen democracy is still an open question.

There is an emerging consensus today on what it takes to make democracy work. First, there need to be contending parties with different political projects and regular, free elections in which the losers turn over power to the winners. This condition, however, is the bare minimum and by itself scarcely produces democracy. Second, democracy requires what Jefferson called "an informed and active populace" that is free to participate in policy deliberations and takes the time to do so. A populace that is informed but not active or active but not informed will not suffice (to say nothing of a populace that is neither). Third, democracy necessitates a society in which the human and civil rights of every person is legally guaranteed and actively enforced.

Some writers have suggested that a fourth requirement for democracy is a market economy, but others doubt it. China has a rampaging capitalist economy, but few of the essential elements of democracy. In parts of Latin America, on the other hand, democracy has been gaining in recent years, often with little reference to economies. Some observers of the recent history of Russia believe that the rapid imposition of market capitalism there has actually undermined the chances for democracy. Polls show most Russians now associate democracy with profiteering, corruption, and criminality. In view of these requirements for democracy, what are Pentecostal congregations in Latin America, with their Jesus and

Kingdom ethic, doing to nurture them and thus to influence the shape of the public square?[5]

Without a doubt, Pentecostals, whether in North America or South America, have always been very public about their faith. They preach in the streets and markets. They make lists and knock on doors. It is difficult to stroll through a *favella* (shantytown) in Brazil on any given evening without hearing the local congregation broadcasting its music and message on crackling loudspeakers. But this does not yet mean they have a "public theology" for influencing public-policy decisions.

Until recently the contribution of Pentecostals to democracy has been an indirect one. Their role calls to mind the observation of historian Alexis de Tocqueville (1805–59) in the early nineteenth century that it was American religion that provided the indispensable fertile soil for democracy. Without the myriad congregations and other voluntary associations he found in America, he wrote, there would not be the "habits of the heart" democracy requires. In the religious congregations he visited, Tocqueville observed, people learned to discuss issues, make corporate decisions, compromise where necessary, link moral principles to current events, and, finally, to accept the results these procedural strategies produced. Having absorbed these skills in the congregations, he wrote, they could then apply them in the public arena. In short, the free churches of America, unhindered by state sponsorship or hierarchical control, built networks of responsibility, trust, and an idea of the common good that made America an ideal venue for democracy.[6]

There is a difference between becoming a Pentecostal in Latin America today and joining a religious congregation in the United States that Tocqueville visited in the early nineteenth century. In Latin America choosing to *become* a Pentecostal can exact a high price, evoking the scorn of one's neighbors and family and, until recently, legal persecution. For Latin Americans this initial choice requires more courage. It is risky. But it instills a "habit of choosing" and hence a feeling of not being trapped forever in one's station. Becoming a Pentecostal also endows ordinary people with a sense of dignity: they are important to God and to their fellow human beings as bearers of a vital, life-giving message. To borrow a phrase from North American black culture, they can say, "I am . . . *somebody*." Again, once instilled, this sense of self-esteem cannot be easily eradicated.

Here a cautionary note is necessary. The main purpose of Pentecostals, unlike the Catholic base communities, has not been to influence the realm of public policy. They believe they have been called to love and praise God, receive the gifts of the Spirit, and carry the precious message to the farthest corners of the world. Some preachers even exhort their congregations not to become contaminated in "this world," especially since in any case it may soon pass away with the triumphant return of Jesus. But as their numbers increase and they see that their participation in public life can make a difference, Pentecostals preach less about an imminent return of Jesus and more about how to live in a fallen world and sometimes make it a better place.

One clear and present *inner* threat to Pentecostals' capacity to nurture democracy is a tendency to curtail it in their own congregations. Their emphasis on charismatic gifts can make their leadership arbitrary: "If God has put me in this position of power, why should you question my decisions?" Further, dynastic leadership is not unusual. Fathers often hand their pastorates down to their sons. Such leadership leads to a kind of clientelism, as pastors make deals with whatever ruling powers there may be: votes in exchange for patronage. Multiplying rapidly now and full of rich promise for a democratic future, these congregations could, however, falter and shrivel because of their own internal depotism.

But Pentecostals also face threats from without. Ruling regimes in authoritarian countries do not worry so much about the theology of evangelical or Pentecostal congregations. But they *do* worry about "list makers" who know how to get people together, regionally, nationally, and even internationally. Authoritarian regimes are famously fearful of rival networks of information and organization. The Falun Gong in China are not Pentecostals, but they do form voluntary associations. Still, the Communist government was not much concerned about their somewhat esoteric spirituality until they assembled a hundred thousand people in Tiananmen Square. Then the shocked and fearful powers that be cracked down. In Latin America, during the early stage of Pentecostal growth, these threats from without came from both the Catholic Church and the governments it influenced. But except for a few places, such as the Chiapas province in southern Mexico, this kind of opposition is rare today.

Perhaps the clearest threat to the future of Pentecostals in Latin America is a combination of within and without. It is the danger of their being drawn into what Harvard historian Charles S. Maier terms "the [American] empire of consumption," facilitated by the mass distribution of American media and consumer culture. This is where the complex inside/outside threat to Pentecostal congregations appears. Unlike their forebears in the years before the inundation of their continent with mass media huckstering, today's congregations swim in it every day. They are not Amish. They do not withdraw into enclaves. They live, work, go to school, and shop enmeshed in their societies. But supermarket culture always tends to lure people away from citizenship. It transmutes them from voters into shoppers, from citizens into consumers. This means that the political environment in Latin America has begun to resemble North American mass-marketing, an approach that contradicts the highly participatory style Pentecostals engender when they avoid the authoritarian temptation.

But the consumerist style is not just the wolf at the door; it is also a large camel's nose rather far inside the Pentecostal tent. It finds expression in the "gospel of prosperity," sometimes called the "name it and claim it" theology, derived in large measure from North American sources. This current has begun to influence large numbers of *crente* churches, but it has found its major bearer in the Universal Church of the Kingdom of God (UCKG). It is the fastest-growing denomination in Latin America and has now spread to dozens of other countries. The UCKG promises its adherents that if they contribute generously, they will receive not only salvation and health, but wealth, not just in a world beyond, but in this one. Moreover, the organizational structure of the UCKG, patterned after North American sales campaigns, is wholly different from the congregational style of most Pentecostal churches. Its adherents are more like customers or clients than members. It makes no bones about expecting a price for its blessings and exorcisms. It markets itself on television and owns the second-largest TV network in Brazil. Nearly all the other *crente* churches have tried to distance themselves from the UCKG. Many Pentecostal leaders now refer to it as "pseudo-Pentecostal", but because it continues to grow, some are tempted to emulate it.[7]

This ugly dispute points to possible destructive fractures in the wider *crente* community. But it also suggests that we need another precondition for democracy in addition to the ones noted above. A democracy also needs a populace whose basic creaturely needs are met. People scrambling for the next meal for their children or the rudiments of health care do not have the leisure to be participatory citizens. Even though the UCKG panders to people by providing the wrong answer, it has its finger on a real problem.

What comes next? Pentecostals are known everywhere in Latin America for their straightforwardness and honesty. They are sought out for middle-level clerical jobs because employers know they will stay sober, arrive for work on time, and not steal the petty cash. But they still live in societies in which a huge chasm separates the top peak from the vast base. In a sense Pentecostals find themselves caught *between* the promise of citizenship and the seductive pressures of the empire of consumption. Still, they continue to bring to marginalized and wounded people a message of dignity and hope. At the same time many poor Pentecostals are becoming aware of the painful contradiction between their sense of worth and favored status *within* the congregation and the humiliations they face every day as castoffs in the larger society. Perhaps the most critical question they face is where this growing contradiction will lead.

There are at least two possibilities. Socially marginalized Pentecostals, especially those infatuated by the spurious promises of the prosperity gospel, could become increasingly bitter and cynical. After you have prayed fervently for a better job, a stove that works, or a warm house and contributed as generously as you could to the church, but no job, stove, or house appears, then what? Some will relapse into fatalism or withdraw into religious ghettos and give up on citizenship and participation. Some, however, will begin to see—as many already have—that to live in a society in which their humanity is respected will require vigorous advocacy of structural change. This is why some observers believe that Pentecostals could become the core of fundamental nonviolent social transformation.

No one knows, of course. But two core *crente* beliefs will play a decisive role: conversion ("you must be born again") and holiness ("be not conformed to this world"). In political and cultural terms conversion means that people can change and that therefore fatalism—either personal or societal—is not acceptable. Holiness means that you need not buy into the latest mind-numbing fads of the commodity lifestyle. You can be "in but not of this world."

The question of whether Pentecostals will ultimately help fuel the revolution in Christianity toward a rebirth of faith in an Age of Spirit is still an open one. But if the currents Miller and Yamamori charted keep flowing; if Pentecostals learn to respect their non-*crente* neighbors; and if the persistence of the list makers of the *favellas* continues, they might end up on the side of the angels.

CHAPTER 15

The Future of Faith

In his utopian novel *Island*, a sketch of the future of science and religion published in 1963, Aldous Huxley (1894–1963) ascribes the following prayer to his fictional islanders: "Give us this day our daily faith, but deliver us from beliefs." Although a bit eccentric in some respects, Huxley got this one right. In the preceding chapters I have shown how Christianity, which began as a movement of Spirit guided by faith, soon clotted into a catalog of beliefs administered by a clerical class. But now, due to a number of different factors, the process is being reversed. Faith is resurgent, while dogma is dying. The spiritual, communal, and justice-seeking dimensions of Christianity are now its leading edge as the twenty-first century hurtles forward, and this change is taking place along with similar reformations in the other world religions.

Recent developments in Islam and Buddhism provide good examples. Islam, with over a billion adherents, is the second-largest religion in the world. It has demonstrated a sensational renaissance in the past century. There are many theories about why this resurgence has taken place. Some attribute it to a large a pool of newly educated young men without sufficient employment opportunities roaming the streets of Damascus and Cairo and the housing projects of western Europe. Others claim it is due to the failure of either socialism or market capitalism to satisfy the needs of the people. Still others argue that the new oil wealth has sharpened class divisions. One of the most familiar explanations is that the rapid, jarring changes that modern life brings create an identity crisis that prods people to embrace the old certainties of traditional religion, especially when their leaders present them as the answer to all their problems.

All of these factors are certainly part of the picture, but there is an underlying and more strictly religious explanation. Islam has always emphasized the duty of every Muslim to be concerned about the poor. This is a value it shares not only with Judaism and Christianity, but also with some Buddhist teachings. In Islam, the idea of *da'wa* states that Muslims have the duty to call their fellow followers to behave according to the Qur'an and subsequent Islamic teachings. In the past, however, this duty focused mainly on encouraging people to be more faithful in the exercise of their perschal practice, such as praying five times a day, fasting during Ramadan, and abstaining from alcohol.

During the past century, however, two developments have deepened and amplified the idea of *da'wa*. One is the emergence of lay organizations among Muslims, often bringing together people in similar trades and occupations, in which they could cooperate in strengthening and applying their faith. The other is the recognition that in complex societies individual charity toward the poor is not enough, but that nonetheless a person must have sufficient material goods to be a faithful Muslim. It follows that society itself has a responsibility to attend to these material needs, and social justice becomes a religious duty, not just a political goal.

Western observers sometimes mistakenly believe that the use of religious language in Muslim political speech is no more than window dressing, injected by ideologues to heat up motivation, and that this feeds into the quest for identity in a confusing world. The anthropologist Talal Asad, who has studied the Muslim renewal carefully, disagrees. He claims that most Muslim discourse is not the result of tightening economic factors and is not about seeking cultural identity. It is about how to be a better Muslim. It tries to answer the question, "Since I am a Muslim, how should I behave in accordance with God's commands? And since I live among other people, Muslims and non-Muslims, how should we behave toward one another?"[1]

This twentieth-century thrust in Islamic consciousness first took organizational shape in Egypt in 1928. In that year a twenty-two-year-old elementary-school teacher named Hasan al-Banna founded an educational organization called the Muslim Brotherhood. Al-Banna himself nurtured some anticlerical sentiments and had drunk deeply of the gentle and mystical Sufi stream of Islam. The Brotherhood's basic premise was that Islam is not just a set of observances and beliefs, but a comprehensive way of life. From small beginnings, it grew quickly and expanded its agenda to include political aims. Suspicious of communism, capitalism, and nationalism, the Brothers' objective was to build a society of equality and justice based on the principles of the Qur'an. This brought them into opposition to the Egyptian government, and since they sometimes turned to violence when it seemed called for, they underwent severe persecution. Al-Banna was assassinated by government agents in 1949. Since then the Brotherhood has generated similar movements in other countries, and some, like Hamas in Palestine, have embraced violent means. But the Muslim Brotherhood in Egypt today, which has become a stalwart defender of democracy and especially of an independent judiciary, is still persecuted by the government.

The Muslim world is a divided and fractious one. On the whole, thoughtful Muslims insist that Islam is not just a set of ritual obligations, but a community and a way of serving God and neighbor. In some places radical Islamist groups threaten the ecumenical and democratic currents that are struggling to come to birth. But like fundamentalist movements elsewhere they are swimming against the stream. In Egypt, in 2006, the Muslim Brotherhood publicly announced that its objective was the establishment of a democratic state, not an Islamic one. In November 2008 the American national intelligence agencies issued a report indicating the steep loss of support for Al Qaeda among Muslims, because they are alienated by its "indiscriminate killing and inattention to the practical problems of poverty, unemployment, and education."[2]

During the years of this important change in the Muslim world, a sweeping transformation has also been under way in the Buddhist sphere. The best illustration is what has sometimes been called the "Buddhist Reformation" that has taken place in Japan in the past few decades. It occurred in the Nichiren Shoshu, the largest Buddhist denomination in Japan, the one stemming from the teachings of Nichiren Daishonin (1222–82), who is sometimes compared to the Protestant Reformers of the sixteenth century. Early in the twentieth century, some lay followers of this tradition founded a movement called Soka Gakkai (the word means "value creation") in an effort to move education in Japan away from its authoritarian methods and to encourage students to think creatively. It grew rapidly and now has chapters in 128 countries, where its members work for world peace, women's rights, and interfaith dialogue.

At first the priesthood of the Nichiren Shoshu and its lay affiliate got along well and cooperated in the building of an impressive modern temple at the foot of Mt. Fuji, the sacred mountain of Japan. But tensions grew as leaders of the Soka Gakkai began to suggest that true Buddhism requires lay leadership, equalitarianism, human rights, and the reform of society. As the conflict heated up, in 1991 the Nichiren priesthood, in a colossal act of clerical hubris, excommunicated 11 million Soka Gakkai members. To enforce this decision, the priests banned Soka Gakkai members from entering the temple, and then the high priest Nikken Shonin ordered the splendid building's total demolition. Against the wishes of these members and to the horror all architects, the high priest's directive was carried out. The temple was demolished. But Soka Gakkai, as an expression of what some scholars call "Buddhist humanism," thrived. Perhaps the split was inevitable. As Jane Hurst, a student of this movement, puts it, "the pragmatic, goal-oriented, this-worldly focus" of the members of Soka Gakkai was bound to come in conflict with "the otherworldly focus" of the priesthood.

I first came into contact with Soka Gakkai when its international president, Daisaku Ikeda, gave a lecture at Harvard in 1993. Knowing of my interest as a Christian in dialogue with Buddhists and that I had been a Visiting Intellectual in Japan in 1986, the sponsors asked me to respond. Ikeda spoke about the need for intercultural and interreligious exchange. After the session, he told me he would like to assure some kind of presence of his movement at Harvard, both to learn from proximity to the university and to become the voice of humanistic Buddhism. I suggested they buy a building and offer an "open space" where people from the community and from different parts of the university, who are sometimes at odds with each other, could meet for conversation at a neutral place without arousing departmental jealousies. Today the resulting Boston Research Center, inspired by the principles of Buddhist humanism and the conviction that all life can be made sacred, supports a range of programs in global citizenship. The worldwide organization sponsors similar efforts.

Judaism, although much smaller than the other world religions, nonetheless is undergoing analogous changes. A contemporary successor of the joyous, mystical strand of the tradition, stemming from the Hasidism of the Baal Shem Tov (1698–1760), is growing in popularity. In America Rabbi Zalman Schachter freely adopts spiritual tropes from Eastern sources and is one of those responsible for what has come to be called "Jewish renewal." In Israel Gabriel Meyer mixes generous elements of Hasidic, Asian, and Sufi spirituality, attracting thousands of Israeli young people who are not content with the rigid orthodoxy that is the unofficial established religion of the country. Some American synagogues now characterize themselves as "postdenominational," leaving behind the former labeling as Orthodox, Conservative, or Reformed. Despite persistent tensions between Jewish and Muslim die-hards, dialogue and cooperation between Jews and Muslims on peacemaking is on the increase.

These examples indicate that both the renaissance of spirituality and the transmutation in the nature of religiousness are happening in a variety of traditions. The similarities are striking. One clear Christian example is what is being called the "emerging-church movement." Beginning in New Zealand, far from the old power centers of Christendom, it is now expanding in America. It is nondenominational, decentralized, suspicious of many aspects of the institutional churches, and critical of the suffocating role dogmas have played in Christianity. Like that of the earliest Christians, it is a movement of the Spirit that focuses on following Jesus and striving to actualize the Reign of God. Its participants retrieve elements of the Christian mystical tradition that are often frowned upon by the more conventional churches, and in dealing with other religions they prefer conversation and cooperation to conversion.

In the past two decades the emerging-church movement has spread in mainline churches. Marcus Borg describes its theology as "historical, metaphorical, and sacramental" and its view of the Christian life as "relational and transformational."[3] Emergent congregations are especially well equipped to live creatively in the newly post-Western Christianity. They are careful not to confuse the life and message of Jesus with the "Western" elements in which it has been packaged. They try to assign equal weight to both the message and the context so that a new version of the old story can take shape. They strongly underline "living the message" rather than simply proclaiming it. They experiment with settings, like cafes, in which two-way exchange rather than one-way preaching is possible.

Not only does the present trajectory of Christianity suggest a growing distinction between faith and belief; the trend has been visible for quite some time now. In March 1969 I attended a symposium in Rome sponsored by the Vatican Secretariat for Nonbelievers (mentioned in Chapter 8). The secretariat had been created as a result of the Second Vatican Council. Some forty scholars, including Catholics, Protestants, and even a couple atheists, gathered, read papers, and exchanged views. On the last day Pope Paul VI received us and bestowed his blessing.

The most memorable paper at the meeting, entitled "Religion and Belief: The Historical Background of 'Non-Belief,'" was given by University of California sociologist Robert Bellah. It was a prophetic statement, foreshadowing some of the changes I have documented in this book. Bellah traced the question of "unbelief" back to the split that developed in ancient Greece between the traditional religion of the time and a new way of thinking, namely, philosophy. He pointed out that in Book 10 of his *Laws*, Plato (428–348 BCE), who did not believe in the gods of Olympus, nevertheless argued that the stability of any society depends on certain theological beliefs such as the existence of God and the immortality of the soul. Plato therefore made unbelief in these propositions a crime, punishable by five years of solitary confinement for the first offense and death for the second. Plato was talking about the belief that these theological ideas are true. But, Bellah rightly added, this "belief *that*" has little to do with the biblical concept of faith as trust and confidence, which is not a matter of cognitive assent. Therefore, Bellah went on, when the word "belief" is used to translate the biblical terms for faith, it amounts to a mistranslation and creates a serious misunderstanding.

A scholar of comparative religion, Bellah suggested that this confusion vexed serious thinkers for centuries. Philosophers and theologians were often torn between two convictions. On the one hand, they believed their societies needed religion to maintain order, but, on the other, they themselves could not honestly assent to such mythical propositions. Their uncomfortable solution was usually to defend—at least in public—a set of beliefs for ordinary people, but to reserve for themselves the right to have their private doubts. They knew these public beliefs were "noble lies," but they felt they were needed to manage the restless masses. This tactic was not the sole property of intellectuals. A Mexican landowner candidly remarked during the revolution in his country, "I do not believe in God, but I believe in the priest." Even Jean-Jacques Rousseau (1712–78), two thousand years after Plato, demanded in his *Social Contract* that people subscribe to the "dogmas of civil religion," which for him included the existence of God and the happiness of the just and the punishment of the wicked in the life to come. Not to subscribe was to be punishable by banishment from the realm.

Setting aside its obvious hypocrisy, this two-tiered solution was always fragile. It separated people into the many who *believe* (or are supposed to believe) and the few who *know*. The same strategy took place in the Muslim world as well, where the philosopher al-Ghazzali (1058–1111) worked out a similar Islamic solution. But there was always leakage. The books of the cognoscenti, even when hidden away from the masses, could not be concealed forever. As more people learned to read, the double standard gradually came unraveled. Now, in the past century, the portion of the population that can read and ask questions has become a majority, and the spread of the scientific method, which requires publicly verifiable evidence, has challenged the credibility of propositions that must be accepted on authority. A religion based on subscribing to mandatory beliefs is no longer viable.

Still, for both Christianity and Islam something more than hypocrisy was involved. For both, it was their movement into the sphere of Greek and Hellenistic modes of thought that made the difference. In entering the Greek world, Plato's turf, the early Christians mixed biblical ideas into a Greek framework that often distorted their original meaning. They tried to fashion a Christian philosophy to replace the pagan one, and Christianity gradually slipped away from faith and into ideas. The triumph of the clerical elite under Constantine cemented this perversion into the structure of the church.

It is important to remember, however, that the same garbling did not occur in the Asian religions. This explains why representatives of Buddhism and Hinduism are often hard put to set forth a list of their "beliefs." More than one course on comparative religion in the West has foundered on this reef, as students, and sometimes professors, search in vain for the Hindu equivalent of the Nicene Creed. In Asia religion is a matter of seasonal rituals, ethical insights, and narratives handed down from generation to generation. Ironically, in this sense it is more like the Christianity practiced by most ordinary people both today and throughout its history. Creeds were always something theologians invented, often to stake out spheres of authority. The vast body of lay Christians knew little about them and cared less. Their faith was embodied in stories, saints' days, baptisms, weddings, and funerals. But these everyday people constituted, after all, the vast majority. The priests and theologians always remained a tiny minority. Consequently the recent emergence of "people's history" is facilitating the recovery of Christianity's original faith orientation.

As the revival of religion and the change in religiousness spread around the world, it becomes clearer why the extraordinary growth of Christianity beyond the West is helping Christianity regain its initial impetus. These areas lie far removed from Plato's orbit. To be a Christian in India or Korea or Africa today does not mean to be a Christian *à la grec*. It means to be what is sometimes called a "postdogmatic" Christian. The *content* of the faith of non-Western Christians is much like that of the early church, even though the embodied *style* of their religion often resembles that of their non-Christian neighbors.

When I first visited India, I was surprised to find Christians there sitting cross-legged on the floor to pray and pictures of Christ teaching while seated in the lotus position. The Sri Lankan Catholic theologian Tissa Balasuriya is one among several Asian theologians trying to integrate Christianity into the primal religions of their region. In India Protestant theologians such as Paul Devanandan (1901–62) and M. M. Thomas (1916–96) attempted throughout their lifetimes to understand Jesus in Indian categories. But their efforts have never been easy. In January 1997 the Vatican excommunicated Balasuriya, declaring that his work promoted "relativism," but after a worldwide outcry involving thousands of priests, nuns, and laypeople, he was reinstated a year later. His case dramatizes the growing influence of a no-longer-to-be-ignored laity as well as the ongoing conflict between those theologians who try to work from the ground up and the authorities who attempt— with diminishing success—to rule from the top down.[4] Balasuriya is both genuinely Catholic and authentically Asian. He is a good example of both the resurgence and the transfiguration of Christianity today, especially in the global South.

I began this book by suggesting that a fundamental change in the nature of religiousness is occurring. The change assumes different shapes, but some of them overlap. With globalization, religions are becoming less regional. Christians, Buddhists, Muslims, and Hindus now live on every continent. Religions are also becoming less hierarchical. Lay leadership and initiative flourish in all of them, as the Muslim Brotherhood, Soka Gakkai, and the Latin American base communities demonstrate. In addition many are becoming less dogmatic and more practical. Religious people today are more interested in ethical guidelines and spiritual disciplines than in doctrines. They are also becoming less patriarchal, as women assume leadership positions in religions that have barred them for centuries, sometimes for millennia. Women are publishing commentaries on the Qur'an, leading synagogues, and directing Buddhist retreat centers. There are now women pastors, priests, and bishops in Christian denominations.

As these changes gain momentum, they evoke an almost point-for-point fundamentalist reaction. Some Shinto leaders retort by emphasizing the sacredness of Japan, while the Barata Janata party seeks to "Hinduize" India. Radical Islamists dream of reestablishing a caliphate that encompasses all of Allah's land. Some Israeli settlers on the West Bank want to establish a "Torah state," a holy land governed by scriptural law. The religious Right in the United States insists that America is a "Christian nation." Literalist bishops in Africa and their American allies threaten to split the worldwide Anglican Communion over the ordination of gays and women. Indeed, a core conviction of all fundamentalist movements is that women must be kept in their place. All these, however, are in the true sense of the word "reactionary" efforts. They are attempting to stem an inexorable movement of the human spirit whose hour has come.

The wind of the Spirit is blowing. One indication is the upheaval that is shaking and renewing Christianity. Faith, rather than beliefs, is once again becoming its defining quality,[5] and this reclaims what faith meant during its earliest years. I have described how that primal impetus was nearly suffocated by creeds, hierarchies, and the disastrous merger of the church with the empire. But I have also highlighted how a newly global Christianity, enlivened by a multiplicity of cultures and yearning for the realization of God's reign of *shalom,* is finding its soul again. All the signs suggest we are poised to enter a new Age of the Spirit and that the future will be a future of faith.

Acknowledgments

Many of the ideas that went into this book were nurtured over the past years in courses and seminars I have taught, panels and conferences I have attended, and in collegial conversations. These took place with far too many people to list them all. I would like especially to thank, however, my colleagues Allen Callahan, the late Krister Stendahl, Richard Horsley, Karen King and Helmut Koster whose knowledge of early Christian history I drew on shamelessly. I am indebted to Harvard Divinity School for supporting my attendance at gatherings outside Cambridge, and for generously arranging for me to teach a smaller number of courses so that I could devote more time to this book.

I am also grateful to the man once known as Cardinal Joseph Ratzinger (now Pope Benedict XVI) for the interview he granted me when he was still Prefect of the Congregation for the Doctrine of the Faith. I am not sure how he would feel about that meeting should he read chapter 8 of this book, but the conversation was indeed memorable. It is also based in part on some conversations I enjoyed with Carlo Maria Cardinal Martini of Milan. My old friend Arvin Sharma, of Magill University and a leader in interfaith dialogue, has kept me up-to-date on developments in that field. I first presented the material included here in chapter 9 at the historic conference he planned and led in Montreal in 2006, marking the fifth anniversary of 9/11. I continue to be grateful to my friends among the Latin American liberation theologians, Gustavo Gutierrez, Leonardo Boff, and Jon Sobrino for their inspiration.

The thoughts expressed here in chapter 14 were first tried out at the James Luther Adams Memorial Lecture I delivered at Harvard in 2006. My chapters on Fundamentalism grew out of a lecture course I offered for Harvard College and Harvard Divinity School students in which I was ably assisted by, among others, Dr. Atalia Omer, who is now teaching at Notre Dame.

My wife, Dr. Nina Tumarkin, Professor of History at Wellesley College, both encouraged my thinking and offered candid criticism where she thought it was appropriate (and it usually was).

HARVEY COX
16 May 2009
Cambridge, MA

Notes

CHAPTER 1

1. Andre Corten and Marie-Christine Doran, "Immanence and Transcendence in the Religious and the Political," *Social Compass* 54, 4 (December 2007): 565. The phrase "horizontal transcendence" is used by the French philosopher Luce Irigaray. See her *Key Writings* (London: Continuum, 2004), p. 172.

2. Simone Weil, *Notebooks*, p. 583, quoted in David McLennan, *Utopian Pessimist: The Life and Thought of Simone Weil* (New York: Poseidon, 1980), p. 191.

3. See Kieran Flanagan and Peter C. Jupp, eds., *A Sociology of Spirituality* (Burlington, VT: Ashgate, 2007).

4. Seth Wax, "Placing God Before Me: Spirituality and Responsibility at Work," in Howard Gardner, ed., *Responsibility at Work* (San Francisco: Jossey-Bass, 2007), pp. 133–34.

5. Robert Wuthnow, *Sharing the Journey: Support Groups and America's New Quest for Community* (New York: Free Press, 1994), pp. 18, 345.

6. Mother Teresa, *Come Be My Light* (New York: Doubleday, 2007).

7. *New York Times*, September 3, 2007, p. 16.

8. See Paul Borgman, *The Way According to Luke* (Grand Rapids, MI: Eerdmans, 2006).

CHAPTER 2

1. Quoted in Walter Isaacson, "Einstein and Faith," *Time*, April 16, 2007, p. 47; the article features excerpts from Issacson's book *Einstein* (New York: Simon & Schuster, 2007).

2. Isaacson, "Einstein and Faith."

3. Reinhold Niebuhr, *The Nature and Destiny of Man* (New York: Scribner, 1951), p. 1.

4. See Emmanuel Levinas, *The Levinas Reader*, ed. Sean Hand (London: Blackwell, 2001).

CHAPTER 3

1. Jon Sobrino, *Jesus the Liberator: A Historical-Theological View* (Maryknoll, NY: Orbis Books, 1994), p. 187.

2. For Thomas Aquinas's discussion of faith, see his *Summa Theologica,* pts. I–II, Q 62, in *Great Books of the Western World,* vol. 20 (Chicago: University of Chicago Press, 1941), pp. 61–63.

3. See Joao Batista Libanio, "Hope, Utopia, Resurrection," in Jon Sobrino and Ignacio Ellacuria, eds., *Systematic Theology: Perspectives from Liberation Theology* (Maryknoll, NY: Orbis Books, 1996). See also Rubem Alves, *I Believe in the Resurrection* (Philadelphia: Fortress, 1986).

CHAPTER 4

1. In this respect, I am especially grateful for what I have learned from scholars Krister Stendahl, Elaine Pagels, Karen King, Allen Callahan, and Helmut Koester.

2. For the late emergence of the idea of "apostolic authority," see the classic work *Ecclesiastical Authority and Spiritual Power in the Church of the First Three Centuries* by Hans von Campenhausen (Stanford, CA: Stanford University Press, 1969).

3. Karen King, *What Is Gnosticism?* (Cambridge, MA: Harvard University Press, 2003), p. 152. See also Helmut Koester, *Ancient Christian Gospels: Their History and Development* (Philadelphia: Trinity Press International, 1992).

4. King, *What Is Gnosticism?* pp. 142, 147.

5. Charles Maier, *Among Empires: American Ascendancy and Its Predecessors* (Cambridge, MA: Harvard University Press, 2006), p. 10.

6. Richard Horsley has been the pioneer in introducing the empire into New Testament and early Christian history studies. See especially his *Jesus and Empire: The Kingdom of God and the New World Disorder* (Minneapolis, MN: Fortress, 2002). See also Pui-Lan Kwok, Dan H. Compier, and Jeorg Rieger, eds., *Empire and The Christian Tradition: New Readings of Classical Theologians* (Minneapolis, MN: Fortress, 2007), a superb collection of essays covering the relationship of Christianity to various empires from Rome to the present. See also Elizabeth Schüssler Fiorenza, *The Power of the Word: Scripture and the Rhetoric of Empire* (Minneapolis, MN: Fortress, 2007).

CHAPTER 5

1. Stephen C. Rowan, *Nicene Creed: Poetic Words for a Prosaic World* (Mystic, CT: Twenty-Third Publications, 1991).

2. Quoted in Frances Fitzgerald, "The New Evangelicals," *New Yorker,* June 20, 2008, p. 31.

3. Sara Miles, *Take This Bread* (New York: Ballantine, 2007).

CHAPTER 6

1. Helmut Koester, *Paul and His World* (Minneapolis, MN: Fortress, 2007), p. 217.

2. James Robinson and Helmut Koester, *Trajectories Through Early Christianity,* (Philadelphia: Fortress, 1973), pp. 62, 69, as quoted in Karen King, *What Is*

Gnosticism? (Cambridge, MA: Harvard University Press, 2003), p. 152; emphasis in original.

3. There is considerable controversy about the dating of the Gospel of John, but the consensus puts it later than Mark.

4. Hans von Campenhausen, *Ecclesiastical Authority and Spiritual Power in the Church of the First Three Centuries* (Stanford, CA: Stanford University Press, 1969), pp. 91–92.

5. Jaraslav Pelikan, *The Emergence of the Catholic Tradition (100–600)* (Chicago: University of Chicago Press, 1971), p. 117.

6. Margaret Poloma, *Main Street Mystics* (Lanham, MD: AltaMira Press, 2003).

7. Quoted in Campenhausen, *Ecclesiastical Authority and Spiritual Power*, p. 242.

CHAPTER 7

1. Paul Johnson, *A History of Christianity* (New York: Athenaeum, 1976), p. 88.

2. Eusebius, *Life of Constantine* 3.15, in *Library of Post-Nicene Fathers*, 2nd series (New York: Christian Life, 1990), 1:489.

3. Quoted in Johnson, *A History of Christianity*, p. 88.

4. Quoted in Edward Gibbon, *The Decline and Fall of the Roman Empire, Great Books of the Western World*, vol. 40 (Chicago: University of Chicago Press, 1952), p. 311.

CHAPTER 8

1. See Harvey Cox, *The Silencing of Leonardo Boff: The Vatican and the Future of World Christianity* (Oak Park, IL: Meyer Stone Books, 1988).

2. Joseph Ratzinger, *Seek That Which Is Above* (San Francisco: Ignatius, 2007). See also Joseph Cardinal Ratzinger with Vittorio Messori, *The Ratzinger Report: An Exclusive Interview on the State of the Church* (San Francisco: Ignatius, 1986).

3. Peter Hebblethwaite, *John XXIII: The Pope of the Council* (London: Chapman, 1984).

4. Giancarlo Zizola, *The Utopia of John XXIII* (Maryknoll, NY: Orbis Books, 1978), p. 171.

CHAPTER 9

1. For Arvind Sharma, see *Part of the Problem, Part of the Solution: Religion Today and Tomorrow* (Westport, CT: Praeger, 2008); *Hermeneutics and Hindu Thought: Toward a Fusion of Horizons* (New York: Springer, 2008); *Fundamentalism and Women in World Religions* (New York: Clark, 2007); *New Focus on Hindu Studies* (New Delhi: D. K. Printworld, 2005); *A New Curve in the Ganges* (New Delhi: D. K. Printworld, 2005); *A Guide to Hindu Spirituality* (Bloomington, IL: World Wisdom, 2006); *Hindu Egalitarianism: Equality or Justice?* (New Delhi: Rupa, 2006).

2. See Gary Dorrien, *The Remaking of Evangelical Theology* (Louisville, KY: Westminster John Knox, 1998).

3. John Burdick, *Looking for God in Brazil* (Berkeley: University of California Press, 1993).

CHAPTER 10

1. For a brief account of the Keswick movement, see Ernest R. Sandeen, *The Roots of Fundamentalism: British and American Millenarianism, 1800-1930* (Grand Rapids, MI: Baker, 1970), pp. 176–77.

2. See Harvey Cox, *Fire from Heaven: The Rise of Pentecostal Spirituality and the Reshaping of Religion in the Twenty-First Century* (Reading, MA: Addison-Wesley, 1995).

3. Tim LaHaye and Jerry B. Jenkins, *Left Behind* (Wheaton, IL: Tyndale, 1995).

4. Quoted in George M. Marsden, *Understanding Fundamentalism and Evangelicalism* (Grand Rapids, MI: Eerdmans, 1991), p. 21. See also his *Fundamentalism and American Culture: The Shaping of American Evangelicalism 1870-1925* (New York: Oxford University Press, 1980).

5. The "manifesto" of Islamist movements is Seyyid Qutb, *Milestones* (Damascus: Dar al-Ilm, n.d.). See also Gilles Kepel, *The War for Muslim Minds: Islam and the West* (Cambridge, MA: Harvard University Press, 2004).

6. For Jewish West Bank settlers, see Idith Zertal and Akiva Eldar, *Lords of the Land: The War over Israel's Settlements in the Occupied Territories, 1967-2007,* trans. Vivian Eden (New York: Nation Books, 2007).

7. See Christopher A. Ferrara and Thomas E. Woods, Jr., *The Great Façade: Vatican II and the Regime of Novelty in the Roman Catholic Church* (Wyoming, MN: Remnant, 2002).

CHAPTER 11

1. "Apocrypha, NT," in *The Interpreter's Dictionary of the Bible,* Supplementary Volume (Nashville, TN: Abingdon, 1976), p. 34.

2. Sakae Kudo and Walter F. Specht, *So Many Versions? Twentieth-Century English Versions of the Bible* (Grand Rapids, MI: Zondervan, 1983).

3. See "Job," in *The Interpreter's Dictionary of the Bible,* Supplementary Volume, p. 479.

3. *World Net Daily,* March 22, 2007, p. 1.

4. For this analysis of *Resolve,* I am indebted to one of my students, Kevin Anderson, for his unpublished paper, spring 2007.

5. Howard Rubenstein, *Maccabee: An Epic in Free Verse* (El Cajon, CA: Granite Hill Press, 2004).

6. See "Thomas, Gospel of," in *The Interpreter's Dictionary of the Bible,* Supplementary Volume, p. 902.

7. Elaine Pagels, *Beyond Belief: The Secret Gospel of Thomas* (New York: Random House, 2005), p. 231.

8. See Kenneth Kramer, *World Scriptures* (New York/Mahwah, NJ: Paulist, 1986).

9. See Wilfred Cantwell Smith, *What Is Scripture? A Comparative Approach* (Minneapolis, MN: Fortress, 1993).

10. See Peter Gomes, *The Good Book: Reading the Bible with Mind and Heart* (New York: Morrow, 1996).

CHAPTER 12

1. Philip Jenkins, *The Lost History of Christianity* (San Francisco: HarperOne, 2008).

2. See Andrew Walls, "Christian Scholarship and the Demographic Transformation of the Church," in Rodney Peterson, ed., *Theological Literacy in the Twenty-First Century* (Grand Rapids, MI: Eerdmans, 2002), pp. 166–84.

3. Carol Osiek and Kevin Madigan, *Ordained Women in the Early Church, 30-600: A Documentary History* (Baltimore, MD: Johns Hopkins University Press, 2005). Also Karen Jo Torjesen, *Women's Leadership in the Early Church and the Scandal of their Subordination in the Rise of Christianity* (Harpercollins, 1993)

4. See Stephen Jay Gould, *Rocks of Ages* (New York: Ballantine, 1999).

CHAPTER 13

1. Jon Sobrino, *Archbishop Romero: Memories and Reflections* (Maryknoll, NY: Orbis Books, 1990).

2. See Alfred T. Hennelly, S.J., ed., *Liberation Theology: A Documentary History* (Maryknoll, NY: Orbis Books, 1990).

3. See Gustavo Gutiérrez's seminal *A Theology of Liberation: History, Politics and Salvation* (Maryknoll, NY: Orbis Books, 1973).

4. Quoted in Sergio Torres, "Gustavo Gutiérrez: A Historical Sketch," in Marc H. Ellis and Otto Maduro, eds., *The Future of Liberation Theology: Essays in Honor of Gustavo Gutiérrez* (Maryknoll, NY: Orbis Books, 1989), p. 99.

5. Sergio Torres and John Eagleson, eds., *The Challenge of the Basic Christian Communities* (Maryknoll, NY: Orbis Books, 1981).

CHAPTER 14

1. Eric Patterson and Edmund Rybarczyk, *The Future of Pentecostalism in the United States* (Lanham, MD: Towman and Littlefield, 2007). See also Harvey Cox, "Spirits of Globalization: Pentecostalism and Experiential Spiritualities in a Global Era," in Sturla J. Stalsett, ed., *Spirits of Globalization* (London: SCM, 2006), pp. 11–22.

2. See Harvey Cox, *Fire From Heaven: The Rise of Pentecostal Spirituality and the Reshaping of Religion in the Twenty-First Century* (Reading, MA: Addison-Wesley 1995), p. 75.

3. Donald Miller and Tetsunao Yamamori, *Global Pentecostalism: The New Face of Christian Social Engagement* (Berkeley: University of California Press, 2007).

4. See Andrew Chesnut, *Born Again in Brazil: The Pentecostal Boom and the Pathogens of Poverty* (New Brunswick, NJ: Rutgers University Press, 1997); John R. Pottenger, *The Political Theory of Liberation Theology* (Albany: State University of New York Press, 1989); John Burdick, *Looking for God in Brazil* (Berkeley: University of California Press, 1993).

5. Also, for Africa, see Ogbu Kalo, *African Pentecostalism: An Introduction* (Oxford and New York: Oxford University Press, 2008).

6. See Alexis de Tocqueville, *Democracy in America* (Garden City, NY: Doubleday, 1969). Also see Rowan Ireland, "Popular Religions and the Building of Democracy in Latin America: Saving the Tocqueville Parallel," in *Journal of Interamerican Studies and World Affairs* 41, 4 (Winter 1999): 111.

7. For the UCKG, see Ari Pedro Oro, Andre Corten, and Jean-Pierre Dozon, *Les Nouveaux Conquerants de la Foi: L'Eglise Universelle de Royaume de Dieu (Bresil),* Preface by Harvey Cox (Paris: Karthala, 2000). The same editors have published this book in Portuguese as *Igreja Universal do Reino de Deus* (São Paulo: Paulinas, 2003).

CHAPTER 15

1. Talal Asad, "Comments on the Islamic Revival and Islamic Discourse," paper prepared for a conference on political theologies, Harvard University, 2003, p. 4.

2. Scott Shane, "Global Forecast by American Intelligence Expects Al Qaeda's Appeal to Falter," *New York Times,* Friday, November 21, 2008, p. A13.

3. Marcus J. Borg, *The Heart of Christianity* (San Francisco: HarperSanFrancisco, 2003), pp. 6, 13.

4. Tissa Balasuriya, *Mary and Human Liberation: The Story and the Text,* ed. Helen Stanton (Harrisburg, PA: Trinity Press International, 1997). See also Sathianathan Clarke, *Dalits and Christianity: Subaltern Religion and Liberation Theology in India* (Delhi: Oxford University Press, 1998).

5. Many scholars now suggest that the study of religion should go beyond the emphasis on beliefs, because it often turns into a dead end. Sociologist Andrew Greeley, for example, urges less attention to beliefs, less focus on the "prose" and more on the "poetry" (*Religious Change in America* [Cambridge, MA: Harvard University Press, 1989], p. 129).

For Further Reading

Allen Dwight Callahan's *The Talking Book: African Americans and the Bible* (New Haven, CT: Yale University Press, 2008) reminds readers of the invaluable insights to be gained by discovering how the Bible has been read and applied by those previously not admitted to the scholarly fraternity.

In his fascinating and aptly titled *The Religious Case Against Belief* (New York: Penguin, 2008), James P. Carse draws on history to make the same distinction between belief and authentic religious faith I discuss in the present volume.

Gary Dorrien's *The Remaking of Evangelical Theology* (Louisville, KY: Westminster John Knox Press, 1998) follows the important changes going on in a critical part of the Christian world.

A Sociology of Spirituality, edited by Kieran Flanagan and Peter C. Jupp (Ashgate, 2007), analyzes the variety of ways the term "spirituality" has come to be used and some of the problems it creates, in a variety of settings.

Stephen Jay Gould's balanced and eloquent *Rocks of Ages* (New York: Ballantine, 1999) is in my view still the best single treatment of the much debated topic of the relationship between science and religion.

As Christians and others search for a more solid and effective theology of public life, Eric Gregory's *Politics and the Order of Love: An Augustinian Ethic of Democratic Citizenship* (Chicago: University of Chicago Press, 2008) reaches back to an immensely influential figure and argues persuasively for his relevance today.

Richard Horsley's *Jesus and Empire: The Kingdom of God and the New World Disorder* (Minneapolis, MN: Fortress, 2002) is the best single source for understanding early Christianity in the light of its Roman imperial context.

Philip Jenkins's *The Lost History of Christianity* (San Francisco: HarperOne, 2008) describes the thousand-year "golden age" of Christianity in what is now called the global South.

Mark Juergensmeyer's *Global Rebellion: Religious Challenges to the Secular State from Christian Militias to Al Qaeda* (Berkeley: University of California Press, 2008) thoughtfully explores the link between "fundamentalism," nationalism, and disquietude about the secular state.

Karen King's engaging and groundbreaking *What Is Gnosticism?* (Cambridge, MA: Harvard University Press, 2003) makes it impossible to rule out many expressions of early Christianity as simply "heretical."

Helmut Koester's *Ancient Christian Gospels: Their History and Development* (Philadelphia: Trinity Press International, 1992) is still the most complete and accurate overall guide to the welter of early Christian documents that have reshaped our understanding of that period.

As the dialogue between Christians and Muslims looms larger, David Levering Lewis's *God's Crucible: Islam and the Making of Europe, 570–1215* (New York: Norton, 2008) reminds us that this conversation has been going on in one way or another for a long time.

For the most recent and comprehensive analysis of the exploding Pentecostal movement, see Donald Miller and Tetsunao Yamamori, *Global Pentecostalism: The New Face of Christian Social Engagement* (Berkeley: University of California Press, 2007). The book includes a fascinating DVD.

Are We Rome? The Fall of an Empire and the Fate of America, by Cullen Murphy (Boston: Houghton Mifflin, 2007), draws some fascinating comparisons and contrasts between ourselves and the ancient world.

Carol Osiek and Kevin Madigan in *Ordained Women in the Early Church, 30–600: A Documentary History* (Baltimore, MD: Johns Hopkins University Press, 2005) present convincing evidence for a much larger role of women in the history of the church than has previously been recognized.

Joerg Rieger's *Christ and Empire: From Paul to Postcolonial Times* (Minneapolis, MN: Fortress, 2008) documents how theological assumptions have been tainted by imperial thinking for centuries. Rieger is the coeditor with Pui-Lan Kwok and Don M. Compier of *Empire and the Christian Tradition: New Readings of Classical Theologians* (Minneapolis, MN: Fortress, 2007).

Lamin O. Sanneh's *Disciples of All Nations: Pillars of World Christianity* (Oxford and New York: Oxford University Press, 2008) ties the previous history of Christianity to its phenomenal growth in the global South today. This book is part of the invaluable Oxford Studies in World Christianity, of which Sanneh is the editor.

Charles Taylor's massive but thorough *A Secular Age* (Cambridge, MA: Harvard University Press, Belknap Press, 2007) traces the history of the emergence and acceptance of nonreligious and antireligious thinking, locating its sources well before our contemporary era.

For nonspecialists who want to keep abreast of the recurrent discoveries in early Christian archaeology and textual analysis, the monthly *Biblical Archeology Review* is an indispensable source.

Index

African churches
    cultural blending in, 51, 116–117, 177
    embracing interfaith dialogue, 136
    resembling early church, 56, 175
    support for ordination of women/
        gays, 178, 223
Age of Belief (Constantinian era)
    creation of "lost gospels," 88–89
    faith of the laity, 7–8
    "heretical" nonconformists in, 10–11,
        103–184
    intellectualization of faith, 46, 221
    learning lessons from, 184–185
    passing of, 15, 178–179
    revisionism in, 58
    tension between faith and belief in,
        5–8
    two-tiered belief system, 219–221
    See also devolution of early church;
        imperial church
Age of Faith (early church)
    Christianity as anti-imperial
        movement, 57–58, 62–64, 70–72,
        81–82
    creeds/hierarchies absent in, 57, 58,
        60, 77, 86, 174, 221
    diversity of, 57–60, 85–86, 173–174, 184
    emperor cult and pagan pantheons,
        70, 81–83, 174
    geographic spread of early church,
        78, 83, 85
    "heresy" unknown to, 57, 58
    lessons for contemporary
        Christianity, 55–57, 82, 172
    liberation theology reflecting, 72,
        194–196

    myriad of new religions in, 79–80
    people of "the Way," 77–78, 174
    persecution by Romans, 69, 70, 82, 91–92
    role of women in, 179–181
    vibrancy of, 5, 53–54
    See also devolution of early
        church; recent research on early
        Christianity; similarities between
        Age of Faith/Spirit
Age of the Spirit (contemporary)
    awe and wonder in, 22–23
    Catholic Church's changing views,
        46, 53, 84
    Christian fundamentalism in, 135–
        138, 151–152
    as Christianity's second chance, 55–56
    conservative Christianity in, 138
    current phenomenon of, 9–14, 85,
        213–218
    emerging-church movement, 218–219
    Holy Spirit in, 9–10, 94
    Joachim's vision of, 8–9
    new models for social engagement,
        171–173
    passing from Age of Belief into, 15,
        184–185, 220–221
    Pentecostalism in, 200, 202, 211
    See also global South; liberation
        theology; similarities between Age
        of Faith/Spirit
American consumerism, 208–211
Anglicanism, 176, 178, 223
apocryphal books, 156–157
Apostles' Creed, 110–111
apostolic succession
    in contemporary Catholic Church,
        56, 57, 117

apostolic succession —*continued*
   as fiction, 58, 60–61, 65–67, 87, 88
   Irenaeus's support of, 93
   robbing laity of power, 95
   role of First Clement in, 89–91
   See also hierarchies
Aquinas, Thomas, 46
Arius/Arianism, 103–106
Armageddon, 62, 138, 147
Asad, Talal, 214–215
Asian churches
   blending of cultural practices into,
      51, 177
   embracing interfaith dialogue, 136–137
   integrating into other religions, 222
   Pentecostal, 200, 202
   rapid growth of, 173, 191
   resembling early church, 20, 56, 175
Asian spiritual practices, 13, 218, 221
Assumption of the Virgin Mary, 74,
   119–120
Athanasius, 104–105, 177
atheism, 38, 183
awe and wonder, 2, 13–14, 22–25.
   See also mystery

Balasuriya, Tissa, 222
al-Banna, Hasan, 215
Baptists, 39, 50, 56
base communities, 172–173, 191,
   195–196, 223
belief
   belief/nonbelief axis, 16–18, 28, 183,
      219–220
   vs. faith, 3–4, 26–27, 213, 219, 223
   importance to Christian
      fundamentalists, 74, 141
   practice and, 16–18
   public beliefs rationale, 220–221
   See also creeds; doctrine
Bellah, Robert, 219
Benedict XVI, Pope, 67, 113–114,
   116–119, 121
Bible
   Cain and Able story, 31, 34, 135
   cultural influences on, 165–166
   in early church, 59

   Good as News, 161–163
   the Hexapla, 158–159
   historical development of, 156–157,
      167
   King James version, 157, 160–162
   message of hope, 42
   modern-day reading of, 168–170
   New Testament canonization, 90–92
   Old Testament cycle, 39–42, 53
   primacy to Christian
      fundamentalists, 148–151, 200
   recognizing various versions, 155–
      157, 163
   in religiously pluralistic world,
      166–167
   Revised Standard Version, 157–158,
      161
   Revolve, 162–163
   Woman's Bible, The, 165
Bible-believing Christians
   facing various translations, 157–160
   lack of original manuscripts,
      160–161, 166
   reclaiming the Bible from, 167–168,
      170
   in religiously pluralistic world,
      166–167
   replacing faith with the Bible, 165,
      166
   warfare with science, 182–183
bishops, 92, 93, 95–97, 107, 108, 179–181
Boff, Leonardo, 114, 116
Brazil, 199–200, 203, 204, 206, 209
Buddhism, 37–39, 48, 129, 167, 216–217,
   221

Cain and Abel story, 31, 34, 135
Calvinists, 145–146, 176
Campenhausen, Hans von, 90–91
Catholic Church
   Assumption of the Virgin Mary, 74,
      119–120
   Bible of, 156, 163
   challenges of modern cultural
      diversity, 116–117, 174–175, 222
   changing views of contemporary, 46,
      53, 84

Congregation for the Doctrine of the
Faith, 114–115
current charismatic movement in, 94
as extension of Europe, 118
First Vatican Council, 119, 120
Inquisition, 7, 109, 116, 182, 183
modern-day "heresy," 114, 116–117
public lay associations, 173
revisionist views of heresy, 108–109,
111
Second Vatican Council, 97, 114,
125, 219
Secretariat for Nonbelievers,
125–126, 219
"spirituality" in, 10, 13
traditionalists, 152, 189
view on early church degeneration, 74
See also Age of Belief; apostolic
succession; clerical caste;
devolution of early church;
imperial church
CEBs (ecclesial base communities),
172–173, 195–196, 223
charismatics, 6, 13, 93–94. *See also*
Pentecostals
China, 175, 191, 200, 208
Christian Conference of Asia, 136
Christian fundamentalism
adherence to beliefs/creeds, 74,
75–76, 144, 201
Bible to as divinely inspired/inerrant,
148–151, 166, 168, 200
concern with social issues/politics,
131–132, 223
cultural influences on, 148–150, 158
differences with Pentecostals,
145–146, 199–202
dispensationalism, 147
effort required to maintain, 152–153
emergence and core beliefs, 141,
147–151
"end times" beliefs, 62, 138, 146–147,
151
including in interfaith dialogue,
131–135
lack of concern for social justice, 143
lacking reference to Jesus, 141, 148

legacy of aggressive
argumentativeness, 150–151
as "modernists," 87
opposing "modernists," 144, 148, 149
part in Age of the Spirit, 135–138,
151–152
replacing faith with doctrine/belief,
141, 159–160, 166
separation in, 151
similarity to Catholic outlook, 6,
74, 119
stereotypes of, 139, 143
violence in, 132
waning of, 2
Christian history
colonial missionary expansion,
173–174
historical development of the Bible,
156–157, 167
overview of, 4–8, 14
papacy's impact on, 122–123
"people's history," 67–70, 221–222
post-Western Christianity, 173–177,
222
See also Age of Belief; Age of Faith;
Age of the Spirit; imperial
church; recent research on early
Christianity
Christian Right. See Christian
fundamentalism
Christianity
Christians as Body of Christ, 52
intrafaith disputes, 132, 135, 137–138
literalization of the symbolic, 24–28
practice and belief, 16–18
proposed minimization of belief, 28
Protestantism, 86, 108–109, 125, 156
tradition of church-state separation,
68–70
transformation of, 2–3, 19–20
See also Bible; Catholic Church;
Christian fundamentalism;
Christian history; creeds; faith;
global South; Jesus; Judeo-
Christian tradition; laity
Christmas cycle, 42–49, 53
"church," 97

Church of St. Praxedis, 180–181
church-state separation, 68–70
citizen diplomats, 172
clerical caste
　as the "church," 97
　corruption of imperial bishops,
　　107, 108
　devolution of church into, 55, 73,
　　179, 221
　dismissive of women, 179–181
　establishing imperial church power,
　　5–6, 88–91, 93, 95–97, 103
　heresy/orthodoxy dichotomy in,
　　86–88, 108
　influence of Ignatius and Irenaeus on,
　　92–93
　the papacy, 116–120, 122–126
　waning of, 196
　See also apostolic succession
Community of Sant'Egidio, 171–173, 183
comparative religion, 37, 38–39, 221
Congregation for the Doctrine of the
　Faith, 114–115
Constantine, Emperor
　Christianity immediately following,
　　107–108
　Christians as soldiers under, 73, 79, 84
　concern for church unity, 101,
　　103–104
　conversion of, 100
　early years of, 99–100
　establishment of imperial
　　Christianity, 5–6, 98, 101–103,
　　174, 221
　role in Council of Nicaea, 104–107
consumerism, 208–211
contemporary Christianity. See Age of
　the Spirit
Council of Nicaea, 47, 104–107
creation myths, 26–28, 31
creeds
　absent from early church, 57, 58, 60,
　　77, 86, 174, 221
　as apart from faith, 4, 18, 19–20, 54
　bishops and heretics, 108, 179
　Christian fundamentalism's
　　adherence to, 74, 75–76, 144, 201

codified/enforced by imperial
　church, 6, 7, 221
filioque and the Apostles' Creed,
　110–111
near triumph over faith, 119–121, 224
as poetry, 75
proto-creeds, 93
role in devolution of early church,
　74–76, 83–84, 107
unique to Christianity, 18
See also doctrine
crente (believer), 199
cross symbology, 100, 101–102
crucifixion, 50, 52, 53, 58, 79
cult of the emperor, 81, 174
cultural influences, 148–150, 158, 177,
　208–211, 219–221
cultural worldview, 37–38, 116–117, 119,
　174, 222
Cyprian, 97

Darby, John Nelson, 147
Das Heilige (Otto), 23
da'wa (Muslim duty), 214
de-Westernization of Christianity,
　173–177, 222
democracy, 205–206, 209
devolution of early church
　in claims of apostolic authority, 88
　in heresy/orthodoxy dichotomy,
　　86–88
　linked to power, 83, 88
　multiculturalism contributing to,
　　78–79, 83
　presence of other religions/cults,
　　79–83
devolution of early church
　recent scholarship on, 55
　role of hierarchies and creeds, 75–76,
　　83–84, 89–91
　various explanations for, 73–75
Didascalia Apostolorum, 95
direct revelation, 93–95
dislocation, 176–177
dispensationalism, 147
diversity
　challenges of, 178

in contemporary church, 85, 128
in early church, 57–60, 85–86,
173–174, 184
as unavoidable, 130–131
doctrinal fundamentalists, 145–146
doctrine
Assumption of the Virgin Mary, 74,
119–120
devolution of early church into, 55
doctrinal fundamentalists, 145–146
experiential elements more attractive
than, 13
formulated by elite clerical caste, 5, 6
papal infallibility, 119–120
See also belief, creeds
Dominicans, 114, 116

early church. See Age of Faith
Easter cycle, 50–53
Eastern Orthodox Church, 74, 80, 109,
110–111
ecclesial base communities (CEBs),
172–173, 195–196, 223
Eckhart, Meister, 10–11
Einstein, Albert, 21–26, 29, 33
Eliot, Charles, 147
emerging-church movement, 218–219
emperor cult, 81, 174
empires, 71–72
"end-times" beliefs, 9, 62, 138, 146–147, 151
Enlightenment, 181–182
episcopa (bishop), 180
eschatology, 9, 62, 138, 146–147, 151
Europe, 7, 118, 173–174, 196
Eusebius, 88, 96, 105–106
evangelicals, 136–138, 199, 201
Ezekiel, 44, 92

faith
during Age of Belief, 5, 7–8
awe and mystery, 22, 23, 35, 194
vs. belief, 3–4, 26–27, 213, 219, 223
Catholic hierarchy and creed over,
98, 119–121
Christian fundamentalism's belief
over, 141, 159–160, 166, 168
common need for, 128, 129

creeds as apart from, 4, 19–20, 74
as focus of Christian life, 18
intellectualization of, 46
of Jesus, 45–47, 49
from perspective of poverty, 172,
177, 194
regaining original meaning of, 179,
181–183, 223–224
resurrected in liberation theology,
194–195
Falwell, Jerry, 133–135, 137, 146, 155
filioque (and the Son), 110–111
First Epistle of Clement, 89–91, 156
First Vatican Council, 119, 120
Franciscans, 11, 109
Frye, Northrup, 169
fundamentalism, 1–2, 14–15, 131–133,
152, 183, 220. *See also* Christian
fundamentalism
Fundamentals, The (pamphlet series),
148, 149

Galileo, 182
geographic dislocation, 176–177
global South
explosive growth of Christianity in,
173, 176–177, 184, 222
impact of recent research on, 68, 136
inspired by Spirit, 9
Kingdom of God emerging in,
136–137, 187–188, 194–196
reclaiming the Bible, 167
similarity to early church, 175, 195
spread of liberation theology in, 191
See also Latin America churches
Gnosticism, 65
God
direct experience of, 8, 10
existence of, 3–4, 17, 21–22, 194
promises of, 40–42
relationship to Jesus, 46, 47, 103–105
Good as News (Henson), 161–163
Gospel of Matthew, 19
gospel of prosperity, 209–210
Gospel of Thomas, 64–65, 87–88,
164–165
Grande, Rutulio, 189–190

grassroots laity groups, 172–173, 191, 195–196
Greek Biblical translation, 78–79, 157–159
Greek religion/philosophy, 82–83, 219, 221
Gutiérrez, Gustavo, 192–195

Hamlet (play; Shakespeare), 30
Hebrew Biblical translation, 157–159
Hebrew cycle, 39–41, 53
Henson, John, 161
heresy
    Arianism, 103–107
    from within the church, 10–11
    church's violent suppression of, 6–7
    heresy/orthodoxy dichotomy, 60, 64–65, 86–88, 178
    heretics as innovators, 87, 197
    idea unknown to early church, 57–60, 78, 86
    Joachim's Age of the Spirit, 8–9
    modern-day handling of, 114, 116–117
    Protestantism as, 108–109
    revisionist view of, 108–109, 111
    as treason, 6
    Waldensians, 109–110
Herod, King, 42, 43
Hexapla, 158–159
hierarchies
    in contemporary Catholic Church, 116–118
    deterioration of early church into, 55, 73–76, 179
    direct revelation as challenge to, 93–95
    early/contemporary Christianity flourishing without, 8, 19, 61, 174
    emergence of, 57, 58, 89–93
    empires use of, 71–72
    near triumph over faith, 119–121, 224
    See also apostolic succession; clerical caste
Hilary of Poitiers, 107
Hinduism
    differing with Judeo-Christian worldview, 37–39

    fundamentalists within, 223
    lack of "beliefs" in, 221
    reach of, 128
    roots of, 56
    sacred texts in, 166, 167
    understanding of Jesus, 48
    violence in, 130, 132
Holy Communion, 76–77, 82
Holy Spirit
    Catholic retraction of exclusivity over, 53
    and charismatics, 6, 13, 93–94
    current resurgence of belief in, 9–10
    guiding the early church, 61, 77, 86
    at Pentecost, 52–53
    in Pentecostalism, 9, 145–146, 200–201
    speaking in tongues, 52–53, 56, 200
homoousios (same substance), 105, 108
Huxley, Aldous, 213

Ignatius of Antioch, Bishop, 91–95
Ikeda, Daisaku, 214
Illich, Ivan, 191, 193
imperial church
    amalgamation with Roman empire, 68, 72, 90
    birth of, 178, 5–6
    blurring essence of Christianity, 63–64, 98, 224
    challenge of mystics to, 93–94
    Constantine's role in, 98, 101–102, 174, 221
    domination of European culture and politics, 7
    immediately following Constantine, 107–108
    marginalization of women, 55
    representing one form of early Christianity, 60
    subverting faith, 98
    See also Age of Belief
Indian churches, 222
Inquisition, 7, 109, 116, 182, 183
intellectualization of faith, 46
interfaith dialogue
    beyond history of violence, 129–132

colored by diverse worldviews, 128–129
current crisis in, 128
hope for intrafaith dialogue, 135–139
including fundamentalists in, 131–135, 138–139
Vatican's Secretariat for Nonbelievers, 125–126
InterVarsity Christian Fellowship, 143–146
intrafaith relations, 132, 135–139
Irenaeus of Lyons, 92–95
Isaiah, 44, 47
Islam
basic posture of, 39
divisions in, 215–216
duty of concern, 214–215
potential causes of resurgence, 213–214
Qur'an, 166
radical, 2, 16, 152, 223
reach of, 80, 128
single affirmation of, 18
two-tiered belief system, 220–221
understanding of Jesus, 48
violence in, 130, 132

James, Letter of, 156
Jefferson, Thomas, 165, 205
Jesus
belief in Second Coming of, 146–149, 151
as Christ, 51–52
Christian fundamentalism lacking reference to, 141, 148
crucifixion of, 50, 52, 53, 58, 79
early church relationship to, 77, 78
faith of, 45–47, 49
in Gospel of Thomas, 164
on Kingdom of God, 19, 42–45, 47, 49
in liberation theology, 194–195
relationship to God, 46–47, 103–105
relevance in other faiths, 47–48
resurrection of, 52, 160
threat to the Romans, 42–43, 48–50, 63, 69–70
Jews. See Judaism
Joachim of Fiore, 8–10

Job, Book of, 159
John F. Kennedy School of Government, 134
John of Patmos, 62
John Paul II, Pope, 46, 84, 109, 110, 116, 121, 182
John XXIII, Pope, 121, 123–124
Judaism
currents in contemporary, 80, 217–218
expectation of messiah, 42
fundamentalists within, 152, 223
God of, 40
Jews blamed for crucifixion, 58
land fundamentalists, 152
religion as way of life, 19
Tanakh, 156
understanding of Jesus in, 10
violence associated with, 130, 132
Judeo-Christian tradition
Christmas cycle, 42–49, 53
in the early church, 53–54
Easter cycle, 50–53
Hebrew cycle, 39–41, 53
shaping worldview, 128–129, 169
Julian, Emperor, 107–108

Kennedy, Robert, 191
Keswick, 144, 145
Kierkegaard, Søren, 37
King, Karen, 65
King, Martin Luther, Jr., 191
King James Bible, 157, 160–162
Kingdom of God
emerging in the global South, 136–137, 187–188, 194–196
hope sustaining medieval laity, 7–8
human longing for the, 48, 224
inspiring early church, 60, 73, 78
interfaith dialogue and, 130
Jesus on, 19, 42–45, 47, 49
in Judeo-Christian tradition, 42–45, 47, 49
living beyond the crucifixion, 53
as "Reigning of God," 45
surviving papal infallibility, 120–121
undercut by Christian fundamentalism, 149

knowledge, beyond objective, 33–34
Koester, Helmut, 86
Küng, Hans, 114, 116

laity
    contemporary grassroots groups,
        171–173, 191, 195–196
    emergence of Muslim organizations,
        214
    faith of medieval church, 7–8
    new voice of the, 174–175, 222, 223
    power of church hierarchy over,
        55, 95, 97
    See also liberation theology
language, 78–79, 157, 158
"last-days" beliefs, 9, 62, 138, 146–147, 151
Latin America churches
    CEBs (ecclesial base communities),
        172–173, 195–196, 223
    contributions to democracy, , 138,
        204–207
    crentes as religious majority,
        199–200
    organization of peasant leagues,
        203–204
    threats to, 208–209
    See also liberation theology
Left Behind series, 62, 138, 147
Lent, 50, 51
Levinas, Emmanuel, 32–34
liberation theology
    connection to early church,
        72, 194–196
    faith-as-trust in, 194–195
    focus and development of, 190–191,
        194
    Gutiérrez's contribution to, 192–194
    possible fusion with progressive
        Pentecostalism, 203
    Romero as champion of, 183–184,
        187–190
    roots in poverty, 41, 177
Life of Constantine (Eusebius), 105–106
literalization of the symbolic, 24–28
lost gospels, 88–89
Luke-Acts, 168
Luther, Martin, 73, 156, 181, 182

Machen, J. Gresham, 150
Maier, Charles S., 71–72
Mark, Gospel of, 69–70, 160
Mary, mother of Jesus, 74, 119–120,
    157, 159
Maxentius, 99–100
medieval church, 7–8, 10–11, 74. *See
    also* Age of Belief
Middle East conflict, 130, 132, 147
Miles, Sara, 76–77
Miller, Donald, 202, 203, 211
missionaries, 175
Mithraism, 79–81, 174
modernists, 28, 86, 87, 144, 148–151, 201
Mother Teresa, 17
Muslim Brotherhood, 215, 216, 223
Muslims. See Islam
mystery
    common to all worldviews, 37, 38
    faith and, 35, 194
    and the "other," 31–35
    of the self, 29–31, 49
    of the universe, 24–28
mysticism, 13, 87, 93–94, 164, 218
myths, 26–28

Nag Hammadi codices, 64–66, 89, 164
Narcissus, 31, 34
National Association of Evangelicals
    (NAE), 137, 201
nature, 13–14, 22–23
Nature and the Destiny of Man,
    The (Niebuhr), 29
New Age groups. See spirituality
New Testament, 42, 90–92, 156,
    160–161, 168
Nichiren Shoshu, 216
Niebuhr, Reinhold, 29
nonbelievers, 16–18, 28, 125, 183
noncanonical gospels, 163–165
objectivity, 33, 34
Old Testament, 39–42, 53, 59
Origen of Alexandria, 95–97, 103,
    158, 177
orthodoxy, 60, 64–65, 86–88, 178, 181,
    218. *See also* Age of Belief

"other," 31–35, 130–131
Otto, Rudolf, 23

paganism, 51
papacy, 73, 116–120, 122–126
Paul, Apostle, 30, 42, 52, 60–61, 63, 76,
    77, 86, 93–94, 97, 177
Paul and His World (Koester), 86
Paul VI, Pope, 121, 125, 189, 219
Penn Christian Fellowship,
    142, 143, 146
Pentecost, 52–53
Pentecostals
    contribution to democracy, 204–207
    differences with fundamentalists,
        145–146, 199–202
    distinctions between North
        American/Latin American, 178,
        202, 206–207
    emergence of progressive, 202–204
    future outlook for, 210–211
    Holy Spirit in, 9, 145–146, 200–201
    main purpose of, 207
    pitfalls of leadership style, 207–208
    prosperity gospel, 209–210
    rejecting creeds, 201
    role in Age of the Spirit, 200, 202, 211
    speaking in tongues, 52–53, 56,
        93, 200
    threats to, 205, 208–210
    worrisome to orthodoxy, 93–94
people's history, 67–70, 221–222
Pius IX, Pope, 115, 118
Pius XI, Pope, 121–122
Plato, 4, 219–222
politics, 68–72, 131–132, 204–207, 223.
    See also Roman empire
polytheism, 81
post-Western Christianity, 173–177
poverty
    believers working to combat, 138, 164
    faith from perspective of, 172, 177,
        194, 210
    Jesus' concern for, 42, 47, 77
    liberation theology roots in, 41, 177,
        190, 194

lure of gospel of prosperity, 209
Muslim's concern for the poor, 214
prayer, 3–4, 13
priestly elite. See clerical caste
Prisicllian of Avila, 6–7
progressive Pentecostals, 202–204
prosperity gospel, 209–210
Protestant Reformation, 74, 156
Protestantism, 86, 108–109, 125, 156.
    See also Christian fundamentalism

Ratzinger, Joseph (Pope Benedict XVI),
    67, 113–114, 116–119, 121
reason, 182
recent research on early Christianity
    Christianity as anti-imperial
        movement, 57–58, 62–64, 70–72
    fiction of apostolic authority,
        58, 60–61, 65–67
    Gospel of Thomas, 64–65, 87–88,
        164–165
    inspiring intrafaith dialogue,
        135–136
    the people's history, 67–70
    producing radical shifts, 64, 178–179
    summary of three alterations,
        57–58, 72
    unity in diversity, 57–60
Reformation, 74, 156
religion
    changing nature of, 2, 14, 128, 222–223
    diversity in, 130–131, 166–167
    experiential elements of, 7–8, 13
    resurgence of, 1–2, 80, 128
    shaped by worldviews, 128–129
    spirituality as distinct from, 23, 10,
        11, 22
    violence associated with, 129–130,
        132, 170
    See also interfaith dialogue
"Religion and Belief" (paper; Bellah),
    219
religious worldview, 37–39. *See also*
    Judeo-Christian tradition
resurrection, 52, 160
Revelation, 62, 69
Revised Standard Version, 157–158, 160

revisionism, 58
Revolve (magazine), 162–163
Riccardi, Andrea, 171
rituals, 39–40, 50, 51
Robertson, Pat, 135
Robinson, James, 87
Roman empire
    Christianity as anti-imperial
        movement, 43, 57–58, 62–64,
        70–72, 81–82
    Christianity as official religion, 5–6
    emperor cult/pagan pantheons in,
        70, 81–83
    Jesus a threat to, 42–43, 48–50, 63,
        69–70
    persecution of Christians, 69, 70, 82,
        91–92
    rise of church in fall of, 68
    See also Constantine, Emperor;
        imperial church
Romero, Oscar Arnulfo, 183–184,
    187–191, 193
Rowan, Stephen C., 75

Saddleback church, 12, 76
"Saint Manuel Bueno, Martyr,"
    (short story; Unamuno), 3–4,
    27–28
salvation, 148, 149
Sartre, Jean-Paul, 31–33, 53
science, 22–23, 25–26, 33, 34, 182–183
Second Coming, 146–149, 151
Second Vatican Council, 97, 114,
    125, 219
Secretariat for Nonbelievers,
    125–126, 219
Seek That Which Is Above (Ratzinger),
    117–118
self, 29–31, 34–35, 49
Septuagint, 157
Shakespeare, William, 30
shalom. See Kingdom of God
Sharma, Arvind, 129
Shintoism, 80, 223
similarities between Age of Faith/Spirit
    content/practice of the faith, 76–77,
        175, 222

experiencing internal conflict, 14–15,
    177–178
geographic spread and diversity,
    173–174
similarities between Age of Faith/Spirit —
lack of hierarchy, 8, 19, 61, 174
    learning from the past, 55–57, 82, 172
    summary of, 19–20, 71
social engagement
    Christian fundamentalist's lack of,
        143, 147–149
    contemporary models for, 171–173
    as Muslim religious duty, 214–215
    by Pentecostals, 138, 202–203, 205
    spirituality leading to deeper,
        2, 11–12
    See also liberation theology
Soka Gakkai movement, 216–217, 223
speaking in tongues, 52–53, 56, 93, 200
Spirit. See Holy Spirit
spirituality, 10–14, 22, 23, 56
St. Francis of Assisi, 171–173, 183
Stanton, Elizabeth Cady, 165
Star Trek (TV series), 31
symbolism, 24–28, 75–76, 100–102
syncretism, 116–117

Tauler, Eckhart, 11
Tertullian, 87
texts, false, 88–91
Theodora, 180–181
Tocqueville, Alexis de, 206

Unamuno, Miguel, 3, 27
unbelievers/unbelief, 16–18, 28, 125,
    183, 219
unity, 57–60, 97, 101–104
Universal Church of the Kingdom of
    God (UCKG), 209
universe, mystery of the, 24–28
utopia, 44–45, 48

Vatican City, 115
Vatican Secretariat for Nonbelievers,
    125–126, 219
violence, religious, 6–7, 129–132, 170

Virgin Birth of Christ, 148, 149
Virgin Mary, 74, 119–120, 157, 159

Waldensians, 109–110
Waldo, Peter, 109
Wax, Seth, 11–12
"the Way," 77–78, 174
Weil, Simone, 4
Wenzl, Robert, 137
Wesley, John, 145
Wesleyans, 145–146
Williams, Rowan, 162
Woman's Bible, The, 165
women, 55, 85, 179–181, 223

World Council of Churches, 85
worldviews
   cultural, 37–38, 116–117, 119, 174, 222
   differences in religious and cultural,
      37–38, 128–129
   internalization of, 38–39
   mystery common to all, 37, 38
   religious, 37–39
   See also Judeo-Christian tradition
Wuthnow, Robert, 12–13

Yamamori, Tetsunao, 202, 203, 211

Zizola, Giancarlo, 125–126